ONLY YOU, DICK DARING!

ONLY YOU,, DICK DARING!!

or how to write one television script and make $50,000,000

a true-life adventure

by Merle Miller and Evan Rhodes

William Sloane Associates · New York · 1964

This book is for James T. Aubrey, Jr., Jackie Cooper, Dick Dorso, and Stuart Rosenberg
and
for Robert Alan Aurthur

". . . I must define what I mean by cannibalism. I mean the use of something alive, especially of our own species, and particularly any member of our own culture group, solely for our own supposed advantage, with no regard for their private interest and the common good of us all."

BERNARD BERENSON
in *Sketch for a Self Portrait*

Contents

8

9

Tease

The adventures that follow are wholly improbable, but they all happened; I know because I was there at the time and even made some of them happen.

The astute reader has already noticed that although this book is signed with two names, there is more than an occasional use of the first person singular.

The book was written in this way for the best possible literary reason; it was easier.

The *I* refers to Merle Miller and appears as sparingly as possible for someone suffering from an acute and galloping sense of megalomania.

Evan Rhodes, a writer and friend, gleefully abandoned an academic career to take up with a project we both were sure would make history.

It did make history though not exactly in the way we had in mind.

At the end, which was accompanied by both bangs and whimpers, it was Evan who insisted that an account of what took place had something fundamental to say about the way we live now, all of us. Everything is television.

Only You, Dick Daring! or How to Write One Television Script and Make $50 Million Dollars is a genuine collaborative effort; every word and punctuation mark is the result of an arduous and often acrimonious partnership.

Did Addison always agree with Steele? Fletcher with Beaumont? Hardy with Laurel? Evan, although he cannot spell, was right an unspeakable number of times. Nevertheless, my reputation for saintliness remains unmarred.

We have invented everything in this affluent country and have, God bless us, finally discovered the solution to a problem that sent a number of medieval alchemists to an early rack—a formula for making gold out of dross.

The three major television networks, the American Broadcasting Company, the National Broadcasting Company, and the Columbia Broadcasting System, are on the air 22,932.4 hours every year except leap year, which gives it 29.

In recent years more than 4064.2 of those hours have been devoted to an odd phenomenon called a *series*. A series is a program—they usually come in twenty-six- and fifty-two-minute lengths—in which most of the characters appear week after week after week after week.

Why so many series?

The possibilities for profit are nearly limitless, that's why. A network can make a profit of a million dollars—that's net, after taxes—out of a single series every year. Say the network has twenty series on the air. Say ten of the twenty series go on for five, maybe ten years. All clear?

No wonder more truck drivers, make-up men, janitors, and other creative people are leaving their chosen professions to go into the series business.

To get a start in the series business it is necessary to film something called a *pilot*. A pilot is a sample of what the series is all about—two interns who like to cut things off of people, two cowboys who like to shoot things off of people, two detectives who like to tear things off of people, etc.

In each of the last five years more than fifty pilots have been made.

Only You, Dick Daring! largely deals with the intrigue, insanity, and black magic involved in the production of *one* pilot for one fifty-two-minute television series called *Calhoun*.

No statistics were kept on the number of ulcers that started bleeding during the making of *Calhoun*, how many lives were shortened by how many decades, how many life-long friendships were ended, little things like that, but we do have a fair notion of the money spent. Every minute of the filmed pilot cost about $7000. Repeat, $7000 a minute.

However, as one of the many vice-presidents in this narrative remarks, "When a country goes to war it doesn't start balancing its budget."

The script for *Calhoun* was totally rewritten at least nineteen times by me; it was partially rewritten by me and Evan 782,946.17 times. It was tampered with unnumbered times by people I have never seen and by people I have seen.

As anyone who has the good sense to buy this book will discover, at one point it was reported that the president of a television network (Princeton, 1941, *cum laude*, English literature) was said to have thought *he* had written the script.

In all fairness—and if this book is anything it is *fair*—it should be admitted that while the mob writing of Calhoun took five months and eight days (a total of 3792.8 hours), longer than Shakespeare took to turn out *Macbeth, Hamlet,* and *Titus Andronicus*, it was never even as good as *Titus*. Although there were many times when I sympathized with, even envied the heroine of *Titus*. All that happened to her was they raped her, lopped off her limbs, and tore out her tongue to keep her from telling the truth.

She couldn't type or anything.

In a few sticky instances the principals involved have not been named. For the most part, however, any reader in partial control of his faculties will recognize most of them.

But all of them, the famous and the anonymous, are, being human, heroes; and all of the heroes, being human, are picaresque—lovable rogues and vagabonds.

There are sorties into strange lands where stars dwell, explorations into the lunar landscape of New Mexico, expeditions into bright bypaths where dragons are aroused but never slain, windmills tilted but never stilled, and the Holy Grail sought but never found. How could it be? The metal has long since been melted down to make Emmys and Oscars and other such objets d'art.

M.M.

E.R.

P.S. The reader who can afford one book or so every decade should be aware that despite its seeming casualness this is a *How To* book in the fine tradition of *Moby Dick* and *The Scarlet Letter.*

Only you, Dick Daring! tells you how to do both.

1

Only you, Dick Daring!

"Mr. Sutton [Willie] was asked why he robbed banks.
" 'Because that's where the money is,' he replied."

NEW YORK *Herald Tribune*

"A Mr. Aurthur called," said the switchboard operator. "He said he's a friend of yours and that it's important and please call him right back. . . . Are you still out?"

"Even more so," I said. "Any other calls?"

"Just the usual, although the man from the Diner's Club was very, very insistent. . . . Do you want me to ring Mr. Aurthur?"

"I want you to add him to the list," I said.

I looked at the bulletin board I had tacked on the wall facing my typewriter. Across the top in large Gothic letters was a warning to myself, "Don't Get Hit Today. Don't Hit Anybody. Don't Go Out."

A carbon of a memorandum was just below. "1) If the First National Bank of Brewster calls, I am out. 2) If the People's Savings Bank of Yonkers calls, I am out. 3) If anybody from the Director of Internal Revenue calls, I am dead."

I had given the original of the memorandum to the switchboard operator, along with a cherished ten-dollar bill.

I had at the time been holed up in the Gorham, a semi-residential hotel on West Fifty-fifth Street in New York, for the four months since, suffering from despair, distemper, and diarrhea, I stepped off a Varig jet from Rio.

What I was doing in Brazil is a subject not unrelated to this narrative, and we will come to it.

I had returned to the States because although at the time an enormous number of American embezzlers, thieves, and rapists were living in ease and splendor in apartments over-looking Copacabana Beach in Rio, I was broke—except for a non-transferable Varig ticket to New York.

I walked to the window of the fifteenth-floor hotel room.

It was a beautiful day, the kind in which the city and its people are at their best. The sun was bright; there was a com-forting June breeze, a slight haze, and the azure sky was without a cloud.

A group of angels screamed their way out of the St. Thomas Choir School down the block; a beautiful girl and a handsome Negro boy in ballet rehearsal clothes were stand-ing in front of City Center across the street, and Maximino, the gentle Puerto Rican delivery boy from the liquor store, was walking slowly down the street.

I looked east to Madison Avenue and the glazed brick tow-ers of the Winslow Hotel, where I had stayed when I first came to New York. I was then not quite seventeen and determined to remake New York City and the world in my own image and to write more and better novels than Balzac.

I was positive that within my lifetime Madison Avenue would be renamed Miller Boulevard and that Rodin would sculpt my poet's features.

I turned from the view of the Winslow and walked to the mirror that had been smuggled out of George C. Tilyou's Fun House at Coney Island.

"Let's face it, Honoré," I said. "You are in what at best might be called mid-career, and you have got a few money problems, among other problems we won't get into here. You have spent the last of the generous advance from your foolish publishers, and in four days your hotel bill will be due.

"You are living in an ivory tower, and it is a well-known fact that the only people who can get away with that are those whose golden locks are long enough to be braided into a ladder that will reach down to Fifty-fifth Street, and while you could certainly use a haircut . . ."

I turned away from the accusing mirror and hummed a few spirited bars of the aria, "Darling, I Am Growing Old, Silver Threads Among the Gold."

"Suppose you are broke, Fyodor," I said. "Suppose the creditors are competing for the pleasure of sending you to debtor's prison. Live like an artist, be overdrawn a little. Your good writer is your impoverished writer.

"You are in a sunny hotel room; the doors are double-locked, and you can now finish your new novel, and *this* one is a sure-fire candidate for the Reader's Digest Book Club. At least they are going to want to do a lengthy excerpt on that sweet schnook Alexey because if there is anything the *Digest* folks like it is sweet schnooks. . . . Remember your old mother's advice; do not be deterred by those in trade. Cultivate your garden, and do not forget that, as Cyril Connolly wisely pointed out, the business of the artist is to create masterpieces."

I started typing, "Alexey Fyodorovitch Karamazov was the third son . . ."

The phone rang again, destroying an immortal sentence that may never be re-created.

"There's a bearded man here," the operator said, *sotto voce,* "and he's carrying something that looks like a thumbscrew, and he says he's going to wait in the lobby until . . ."

"Thanks," I said. "I'll go down the fire escape again. And get me Bob Aurthur."

Robert Alan Aurthur is a friend of long standing, and we had been involved in several television projects together, some successful, some, to be conservative, disastrous.

Since I got back from Brazil he had been at United Artists Television; his job was developing and producing new television projects.

I knew that one of them was called *The Patty Duke Show,* which was all that I wanted to know about it.

"How are you, Merle?" asked Bob.

His voice, as always, sounded warm and interested.

"I am not in as good health as I was when a producer whose name I cannot recall abandoned me in the jungles of Brazil."

"You finish the novel?"

"I have."

I had dedicated the novel, "For my father and for my friend Robert Alan Aurthur, who believe, and for John Willey [my editor], who can identify."

"How did you like the dedication?" I asked.

"A little cluttered. Any book club sales yet?"

"No, but the Book of the Month Club was heartsick, and it was only because they were forced into selecting the latest Edgar Rice Burroughs that . . ."

"How about the magazines?"

"*The Saturday Evening Post* thought it wasn't literary enough, and the editors of *McCall's* thought it was too literary."

"In other words, you're broke."

"Not at all. I've written a piece for *Harper's,* for which they are paying their *top* price, and in August the editors of *Show* feel that . . ."

"In other words, you're broke. Come on over and see me."

"What about?" I asked, suspiciously.

"Jackie Cooper, you know, the actor, and Jim Aubrey, who's the big wheel at C.B.S., have come up with a wonderful idea for a television series, and we all agree that there is only one writer in America qualified . . ."

"Never. I would rather sleep under a bridge than write even one episode of a *series.* . . ."

"Around one," said Bob.

The offices of United Artists Television are at 555 Madison Avenue in a building the color and shape of a used cube of sugar.

It was then not quite completed but looked as if they expected to tear it down at any moment. The crypt of a lobby was coal-dust gray, although there was a dainty forest of bile-green trees, *genus plastica.*

The elevators, five with a menacing hole where a sixth was no doubt expected, were self-service. Muzak, naturally, and some nervous mosaics intended to be rainbows.

The United Artists offices were on the sixteenth floor. The black leather chairs in the reception room were brand new—and shabby. One oval table with a marble top had an enormous vase filled with gladioli, real. There were two smaller marble-topped tables on each of which was a white princess telephone.

The receptionist and telephone operator, a pretty girl with hair the color of artificial moonbeams, smiled as I stepped over a glut of beautiful young actors and actresses as well as a gaggle of exquisite boys of six or so. Each of the latter was accompanied by a Mother.

The receptionist announced me.

Bob Aurthur's office was at the end of a narrow corridor with a low ceiling. On the left were numerous filing cabinets and secretaries, both built along the same general lines. The secretaries glared at me and went on with their work, filing their nails, drinking Irish coffee, placing personal calls to Istanbul, and crocheting.

To the right were the offices of the executives, instantly identifiable because *they* didn't look up from their nailfiling, Irish coffee, personal calls to Istanbul, and crocheting.

Bob's office was in a corner looking out over Madison Avenue and the accusing face of a gigantic electric clock. There was a handsome jeweler's bench, mid-nineteenth century, several large antique toy fire engines—Bob collects antiques—scripts in various stages of preparation, and three leather chairs.

On one wall was a photograph from one of Bob's movies, *Edge of the City,* which he adapted from his television play, *A Man Is Ten Feet Tall.* Sidney Poitier was in both.

Most of the wall space was taken up with paintings by Bob's elder son, Jonathan—abstracts, portraits, and recognizable landscapes of East Hampton and the sea. The Aurthurs spend their summers in East Hampton.

Bob was on the phone, leaning back in a black leather chair that looked versatile and a little obscene.

He waved me in and continued on the phone, "Tell Dick Nash that just before I threw myself out the window I asked when I was going to get the rewrite."

N. Richard Nash and Bob were two of the writers who created live television plays in the late 1940s and early 1950s, an era widely referred to as the Golden Age of Television.

"I *can't* wait," said Bob. "I am going to kill myself, and I place the blame squarely on the shoulders of my oldest and best friend, N. Richard Nash."

Bob is a short, pugnacious man built like a padded goalie on a hockey team; his eyes are large and warm, and his smile expects the best of people.

That day he was conservatively dressed—olive slacks, a persimmon shirt, and sneakers the color of secondhand snow.

He said, "It is impossible for me to *read* a script that is all worked out in a writer's head but isn't on paper."

He put down the phone, rose, shook hands, and said, "You look thin."

"I was *heavy* when I went to Brazil."

The phone rang again, and he said, "Just one more, and then we'll talk."

He started shouting into the phone, "Goddamn it, I should get the Schmuck of the Year award for hiring him. I said he couldn't be *that* paranoid, but, goddamn it, he is. He's even worse. Give him a message for me; tell him I shall personally see to it that he is sent to jail for the rest of his life—in solitary—and not only that . . ."

The telephone vibrated; then Bob slammed it down and told his secretary to hold all further calls. He leaned forward in the leather chair.

"What kind of a chair do you call that?" I asked.

"If I tell you, you'll never speak to me again. It's called a Tycoon's Chair, and it comes from Norman Dine's Sleep Center."

"Bob," I said. "I have forgiven you many things, beginning with the time you sent me alone and unarmed to visit a hostile tribe of Pima Indians near Phoenix, Arizona."

"Now when the lawsuits begin," said Bob, "and you have to make out a deposition for the lawyers you are going to say, 'Bob Aurthur leaned forward in the Tycoon's Chair he bought from Norman Dine's Sleep Center and with a puckish grin said . . .'"

"There will be no lawsuits. I am not going to write a series."

"In a little less than two years," said Bob, "Reggie Rose has made an equity of two million dollars—two million dollars keeping money—on *The Defenders*, and commercially that isn't even one of the big ones."

"You said that I could retire after writing *The Truman Series*."

"This isn't just *any* series. This is the biggest thing planned for next year, one of the biggest series ever with two big stars, Jackie Cooper and maybe Barbara Stanwyck, and C.B.S. is going all out . . ."

"The trip to Brazil wasn't just *any* trip," I said. "As I recall, you and David Susskind said that it was my patriotic duty to go. You said the President of the United States needed me and that the First Lady had turned aside from all those other writers she keeps inviting to the White House and that if I did this . . . and David Susskind said that if I *didn't*, I would *never* be invited to the White House and my passport would be revoked."

"You are talking about the past," said Bob, "and I admit . . ."

I said, "A little more than four months ago I was alone in a leaky rowboat on the São Francisco River. The waters beneath were overflowing with man-eating piranhas and alligators; the jungles on either side were bursting with natives looking for Yankee heads to shrink, and the skies overhead were crowded with omnivorous buzzards. Where, then, was the President? Where was the First Lady? Where was David Susskind? Where was Robert Alan Aurthur?"

"I don't know about the others," said Bob, "but *I* was writing the pilot for a television series called *East Side, West Side*. I wrote it in three days; I had them over a barrel, of course, but in three days. Now every time they film an episode I get a check for $1000. Sometimes I have them send the check directly to my bank while I lounge in my Tycoon's Chair."

"I'm not a fast writer," I said.

"You could turn out this pilot in a very few weeks, and since this is going to be one of the biggest projects ever, every time the series goes on the air you as the writer of *one* script, the pilot, collect a royalty of at least a $1000. Every week. That could go on for five years, maybe ten, and I'm speaking only of the first run. When the series goes into syndication, you would get a royalty of at least $250 a week, and that could go on for the rest of your life, and I am not even speaking of the fringe benefits. . . . I don't want you to say no or yes this afternoon. I want you to go back to your hotel and think it over.

"Jackie Cooper is one of the hottest properties around. I know how you feel about actors, but he isn't like other actors. He is a *person,* and you and he will dig each other, and you'll love Barbara Stanwyck, and, Merle, this is going to be an honest series."

"Like *Beverly Hillbillies,*" I said, "and *December Bride* and . . ."

"Of course," said Bob, "when I mentioned your name to Jim Aubrey over at C.B.S. he wasn't at all enthusiastic."

"Oh?"

"Not at *all.*"

"Not that it matters; I never heard the name of Jim Aubrey until you mentioned it a few hours ago," I lied. "But would you mind telling me *why?*"

"I guess he'd read one of your books."

"And he didn't like it. Well, I don't think highly of his network, and if the subject ever comes up . . ."

"No, it wasn't that. He just said, 'But Merle Miller writes very sophisticated novels.' Do you know what I said back? I said, 'Nonsense. He never left Iowa. He's still a farmer.'"

"But what's that got to do with a series?"

"I told you; this series is about *real* people, farmers, and in particular it's about—the part Cooper plays—a county agent. Do you know what a county agent is?"

"Everything there is to know. I grew up on a farm and for the last ten years I've been a partner in a plant nursery."

Bob smiled menacingly.

"But I will not write even one script for a series!" I said, rising.

"Your house in Brewster," said Bob, "that's a nice house, but I'll tell you one thing wrong with it. No swimming pool. Now one of the reasons writers pop off at such an early age is that in addition to their being booze hounds they don't get enough exercise. If you had a swimming pool, maybe two swimming pools, which you could have after spending a few days writing a pilot for this series, which despite the doubts of Jim Aubrey I know you can do . . ."

After leaving Bob's office I walked over to Park Avenue, not hurrying, then over to Fifty-third Street. I seated myself in the plaza in front of the Seagram Building.

Carlos Roberto Moreira de Souza, my interpreter and friend in Rio, had said, "To the Latin architect the plaza is for people, and the beauty of the plaza is more important than the real estate. In New York it is the opposite."

The Seagram Building is an exception to that sound observation. It is startlingly serene against the imprudent ugliness on every side.

It was still a benevolent day, and nobody seemed to be in a hurry. No one was shouting, and even the sound of the traffic was soothing. As if somebody had turned down the volume.

All right, I thought, Bob Aurthur has done it again; he has dangled fame, fortune, and uncut diamonds the size of bowling balls in front of your eyes, but you do not have to agree to his devious enticements. Now that you are a man you can put aside childish things like money.

The worst that can happen is that your creditors will hurl you into a dungeon, in which case you can not only finish *The Brothers K.*, you will also have a moment to write the *magnum opus* you have too long postponed, *Don Q.*

And remember, "Fortune may yet have a better success in reserve for you, and those who lose today may win tomorrow."

And then I thought, It would be nice to have a swimming pool.

And then I thought, Four Eyes, you think you're in trouble now, consider, if you will, the last three times you made the mistake of saying yes to Aurthur's blandishments.

How about the first time—July 1959, wasn't it?—when he lured you into the Absinthe House and spoke glowingly of a live dramatic series he was producing? He said he didn't know *what* your contribution would be. Whatever it was you would win several Emmys and your reputation would, as it should, surpass those of Euripides and Zane Grey.

What happened?

When your play, *The American*, had finally been taped, the City Council of Phoenix, Arizona, offered a reward of $10,000 for your capture, provided you were dead; and a newspaper printed a front-page cartoon showing you and the director, John Frankenheimer, tearing down the American flag and stomping on it.

Next Bob Aurthur got you involved with David Susskind and former President Truman, which sounded like an interesting, profitable, and harmless enterprise. Result? Since your final visit to the President's domicile in Independence, Missouri, the state legislature has at last refused to compromise, and if you ever again cross the borders, it's the gas chamber.

I looked once more at the calm comfort of the Seagram Building. The sun was still warm, but I discovered I was shivering.

I thought of Rio de Janeiro and of the beauties of the beaches and the mountains that surround the city. I thought of Carlos who, shortly after we met, said, "Merle, you are the most nervous writer I never saw."

"Who was responsible for making you nervous?" I asked, aloud. "Robert Alan Aurthur is who."

Before July 5, 1962, I hadn't seen David Susskind for several months, not since it had become clear that the two episodes of *The Truman Series* on which Bob Aurthur and I had worked were going to add up to one of the most expensive disasters in David's career.

I had been certain he'd never want to see me again, although I was, as usual, totally blameless.

Nevertheless, on the morning of July 5, Bob, then a junior partner in Talent Associates-Paramount Ltd., of which David is president, called to say that David wanted to have lunch with us.

When David wants to be seen and to talk about his plans to be a U.S. senator by the age of fifty, lunch is at Sardi's East on Fifty-fourth Street. When he has business to discuss, Nedick's would do. I don't think David tastes food anyway, doesn't have time.

Lunch on this particular day was at one of those excessively decorated places not far from his office, 444 Madison Avenue.

The waiter asked about a drink and David said, "I don't want one, too early in the day." He looked at Bob and me and said, "Either of you chaps want a drink?"

Bob, who rarely drinks, said no; I, who often do, and a vodka-tonic would have been nice, said no. Somehow, the way David puts the question the most confirmed alcoholic wouldn't admit wanting a drink at lunch.

David said, "This sounds crazy. A man named Bud Dale from the White House called me on Tuesday. It seems the President is very upset that the Peace Corps is getting all the publicity, and he wants to plug Alliance for Progress, which in a way is his Marshall Plan, especially Food for Peace, and they want us to do a new kind of documentary—well, not a documentary really, a new kind of television show in *Brazil*."

President Kennedy was then planning to go to Brazil on a good-will tour in August.

David said, "I guess that sounds pretty crazy, doesn't it?"

It did, but I said, "It sounds very exciting."

David looked pleased with himself. "I thought I was in bad odor at the White House," he said. "I almost voted for Nixon, you know."

I smiled. Bob looked thoughtful.

David, reflecting no doubt on his close association with Presidents, said, "I figure the three of us that did *The Truman Series* ought to get together on this one."

The Truman Series—Bob Aurthur had lured me into it by promising that I would become the Boswell of television and, as I've said, get rich—had got off to a promising start, on the first day that I went to the Truman Memorial Library in Independence, Missouri.

After a few minutes of conversation with Mr. Truman I said, "Mr. President, could I ask you a question that you might consider impertinent?"

"Go right ahead," said Mr. Truman. "If I want to stop you I'll stop you."

"Well, sir, I've been wearing glasses since I was three years old, and I know you had to wear glasses when you were a boy. I wonder, sir, did they ever call you Four Eyes?"

The President smiled, and then he said, "I've worn glasses

since I was six years old, and, of course, they called me Four Eyes, and a lot of other things, too."

All of the networks looked at the two hour-long films we made, one dealing with the President's life in Independence before, during, and after the time he was in the White House, the other concerned with the weekend the President decided that the United States and the United Nations must try to stop the North Korean invasion of South Korea.

None of the networks wanted any part of the series. The reasons were numerous and had nothing to do with the quality of the two films—eventually, David sold the film and the rights to the series to Screen Gems.

He has said that his personal loss in the transaction was about $200,000.

My loss was that the President became, understandably, disenchanted with Susskind, Bob Aurthur, and me. It is a loss because I feel Mr. Truman was a great President and, just as important, a great human being.

"Bud Dale is coming up to my office after lunch," David was saying.

"Exactly who is Bud Dale?" I asked.

"I'm not sure what his title is, but he's very close to Kennedy."

Dale had told Susskind and later repeated to me that the facilities of the entire federal government would be at our disposal and that financing the show would be no problem—a simple telephone call from the White House to practically any member of the power elite, the Fords, Henry Kaiser, Gardner Cowles.

"Nobody can say no to a thing like this," said David. "The President wants it."

"Merle would have to go to Washington to do the preliminary research," said Bob.

"Could you?" asked David.

I said, "Nobody can say no to a thing like this."

Shortly after we got back to David's office Bud Dale arrived. I had expected him to be one of those elegant young men of the New Frontier. Not at all. His hairline was receding even more rapidly than mine and his clothes fit him loosely. His voice had more the sound of the Midway than the Harvard Yard.

I at once felt at ease with Dale, which was a mistake.

"The President wants a new kind of television," said Dale, which immediately gave Kennedy something in common with the rest of us.

"The President wants something people will look at," said Dale. "He wants to bring the message home."

There was no doubt of Dale's close association with President Kennedy. He kept saying, "The President wants . . . the President thinks . . . the President feels . . . the President says . . ."

At one point David said, "We'd want Mrs. Kennedy to narrate the show, of course."

Now one of the main differences between people like David Susskind and people like the rest of us is that we would have said, "Wouldn't it be wonderful if Mrs. . . ." or, "I don't suppose there's the remotest possibility that Mrs. K . . . ." But then we haven't presided over *Open End* for all these years; or told Nikita Khrushchev how to run the Soviet Union.

Anyway, Dale didn't blink; he just said, "Of course."

"Elizabeth Taylor and Jackie Kennedy are right now the biggest box-office draws in the world," David continued.

"All I have to do is say the word to Pierre," said Dale. Pierre Salinger was the President's press secretary.

"This show isn't going to be easy," said Bob, who up to then had been studying Dale in silence.

"You tell me what you need, and I'll get it," said Dale, "the Army, the Air Force, Mrs. Kennedy . . ."

When Dale left his parting words were, "The President is going to be very pleased."

"I don't believe a word of it," said Bob.

"I almost voted for Nixon, you know," said David.

The next morning Bob called me in Brewster.

"Everything looks okay," he said.

He had just talked to John Wood, publicity director for Food for Peace, who had offices in the White House.

Bob said, "Wood backed up Dale on everything . . . including Jackie to do the narration."

I flew to Washington the following Monday and spent most of the week there. I talked with a great many officials at the Brazilian desk of the Agency for International Development (A.I.D.), Food for Peace, and the Alliance for Progress. All of them were extremely helpful, with only one minor drawback. None of them had ever been to Brazil.

Up to then nobody had made a single specific suggestion about the kind of program we ought to do—except that it ought to be "different," ought to be "something people are going to want to look at," and "not your average run-of-the-mill documentary."

There had already been several documentaries filmed in Northeast Brazil, where poverty and unrest are greatest; nevertheless, that seemed to me the most appropriate area to do the program, and that first night in my hotel room I came across a press release from A.I.D. describing an agricultural cooperative called Pindorama.

I am fond of cooperatives, partly because my father has spent thirty years of his life in the cooperative movement and partly because cooperatives seem to me the best and maybe the only answer to the economic problems of the world.

The mimeographed press release said that Food for Peace was being widely distributed in Pindorama, and since that organization was in a sense the sponsor of the program, that clinched it—in my mind anyway.

Not only that, the President and Mrs. Kennedy were planning to spend several hours in Recife, the principal city in the

Northeast, and that afternoon at the White House Annex John Wood had told me, ". . . Mrs. Kennedy will be available for as many hours as you need her."

I had had lunch that day at the new State Department building with Bud Dale, and there had already been a couple of things that puzzled me. First, although he said I could reach him at the State Department, when I called him there the switchboard operators didn't know his extension.

"That's because everything's very new around here," Dale explained. "Everybody's just settling in."

What's more, at the State Department every time he made a phone call he made it from a public phone booth in the lobby.

"This is the *new* State Department Building," Dale explained, "and already it's overcrowded."

I nodded at both logical explanations, and at lunch that day I said to Dale, ". . . As I see it the purpose of this program is to show the American farmer exactly what happens to all the billions of pounds of surplus food we give away abroad."

Dale said, "The purpose of this program is to get Kennedy re-elected in 1964."

Bob Aurthur came to Washington the next day, and I gave him my story outline for the show. It was about one family moving from a feudal sugar plantation where the land was barren to the agricultural cooperative at Pindorama, where its members would learn to use tractors and scientific farming, get Food for Peace, and become landowners.

"In other words," the outline said, "in an hour we show this family moving from the fifteenth century to the twentieth. . . . It's really sort of biblical, a kind of exodus . . . in time."

"That's a good idea," said Bob, one of two men I have worked with in television who don't have to have a Nielsen rating to tell them what they think.

"This kind of show will have to be done on tape," said Bob.

I agreed. Film is fine for photographing actual happenings, but—some people disagree and are wrong—only on tape could we adequately do this kind of intimate personal story. Besides, nobody had ever done a taped show on actual location in a foreign country. Certainly not in the jungles of Northeast Brazil.

The following day—Friday—Bud Dale approved the story line, and so did John Wood. . . . As will be seen in the pages ahead all sorts of odd individuals have to approve story lines.

Anyway, after the Dale-Wood approval, we were all set— for almost five hours.

That afternoon's edition of the Washington *Star* announced that President Kennedy's trip to Brazil had been postponed—"at least until after the Brazilian elections."

Pierre Salinger had made that announcement from Brazil after a quick look at the unrest. I was told, unofficially, that the Secret Service had told Salinger that security for the President would be impossible in Brazil.

So far as Bob and I were concerned Salinger's announcement meant that the Brazilian project was over.

I flew back to New York, returned to Brewster, and resumed work on a novel, *A Day in Late September.*

Then in mid-August Bob called and said that the President's trip to Brazil was on again. So was the project, and we would be flying to Rio courtesy of Varig Airlines on September 19. Bud Dale had made the arrangements.

In the next ten days I wrote a six-page outline of *Exodus in Time* and everybody liked it, including Pierre Salinger and, I gathered, the First Lady.

I decided that as soon as I got back from Brazil I'd better get fitted for the tailored dinner jacket I'd wear to the White House.

Bob Aurthur, who was to produce and direct the show; Jane Wetherell, associate producer; and Claude Traverse, production manager, and I were met at the airport in Rio by various American officials.

They all said that it would be impossible to transport to Pindorama the electronic equipment we would need to tape the show. There were no landing strips in the area long enough for cargo planes, and the roads from Recife to Pindorama—a distance of about seven hundred kilometers—were impassable.

I didn't know until much later that none of these officials had ever been on the roads from Recife to Pindorama.

It was suggested that instead we do the show at a Brazilian government resettlement colony called Vitoria, only a few kilometers from Recife on a paved road. We were told that at Vitoria the Alliance for Progress and Food for Peace were in full operation.

Late Saturday we flew from Rio to Recife, and on Sunday morning we were warmly greeted by an A.I.D. official whose first words were, "Why is it you people always come on weekends? I haven't had a game of golf for almost two months."

I asked another official, Claude Villareal of the United States Information Agency, if it would be all right if I wore walking shorts to the Vitoria colony.

"That, I fear, would be counterproductive," said Villareal.

Since I *never* want to be counterproductive I wore long pants.

The Vitoria project was beautiful; the houses in which the colonists lived were all pink and blue, and everything was almost as neatly manicured as Darien, Connecticut.

None of us really were satisfied with the suburban look of the project, but it *was* only forty minutes from Recife and, although the paved roads were in need of repair, Vitoria would be convenient for the First Lady.

Bob Aurthur, Jane Wetherell, and Claude Traverse returned to New York on Monday, and I stayed on in Recife for three weeks. I went to Vitoria every morning and stayed all day, talking to colonists and administrators.

The more I learned the more dissatisfied I became. It was obvious that Vitoria was no more than an expensive show place for visiting Americans, particularly government officials who, after seeing the colony, might recommend more and larger U.S. grants to the Brazilian government.

Only fifty families had been moved into Vitoria, and the cost of resettling them had been so prohibitive it would clearly be impossible on a large scale.

Fifty families in a section of Brazil where the average life expectancy is twenty-nine, where half the babies die before they are one year old, and where ninety-five families out of every hundred are always on the verge of starvation.

The program we were planning to do would be seen by maybe twenty million Americans; to say that Vitoria represented a solution to the terrifying problems of Brazil would, I felt, be perpetrating a deception.

I decided I had to see Pindorama. Maybe it was another fraud.

And so two days before I left Brazil, using David Susskind's money, I chartered a *one*-engine plane, a fourteen-year-old Bonanza flown by an elderly Brazilian who reminded me a little of Spencer Tracy.

I normally wouldn't fly in a one-engine plane over Newark, New Jersey, but we flew over five hundred kilometers of unoccupied, uncharted jungle. I knew, however, that Spencer Tracy never crashes. After buzzing the village of Penedo three times—"The buzzing is to summon a taxi," said Spence —we landed at Penedo and were driven to Pindorama.

Pindorama was not pink and blue. It was an immense oblong clearing in the jungle, and the land looked arid and inhospitable. The houses were built of everything from palm fronds to mud to unaged wood.

Even the administration building was inelegant, but seated at a desk inside was René Bertholet, a Swiss in his mid-fifties and president of the cooperative. Bertholet has the face of a worldly saint who hasn't regretted a moment of his worldly experiences.

Early in our conversation he said, "I am a born trouble-maker."

I am fond of troublemakers.

Pindorama had no government support, and, although Alliance for Progress aid and Food for Peace had been promised, none had yet arrived. That was no doubt one of the reasons American officials had wanted us to do the program in Vitoria.

Nevertheless, the cooperative was real, and there were five hundred members, most of whom already owned their own houses and plots of land. I attended a meeting of the General Assembly—very much like a New England town meeting—and listened while everybody spoke his mind about the business of the cooperative and anything else that came to mind.

I decided then and there that if we couldn't do the program at Pindorama I didn't want to do it at all, and that evening after dinner I asked Bertholet the hard question. Would it be possible to transport twenty tons of the most delicate electronic equipment by road from Recife to Pindorama? The major part of the taping equipment was available at a television station in Recife.

He replied with a sentence he repeated many times later, "It can be done."

He said he would let us use the cooperative's truck drivers, who made the trip several times a month anyway.

"I don't know what my colleagues in New York will say," I told Bertholet, "but I'd like to do the program here."

When I got back to New York and told Bob Aurthur he said, "Of course that's where we have to do it."

David Susskind agreed, and so did Bud Dale, John Wood, and, we were told, Pierre Salinger.

Mrs. Kennedy could not come all the way to Pindorama, but John Wood assured us that we could tape her part of the show at a Food for Peace project in Recife; there were several. Not only that, Food for Peace officials in Washington promised that by the time we were ready to tape the program Pindorama would have the food that had been so long in arriving.

Until then Talent Associates had been putting up all the money for the expenses, which were already considerable. The telephone calls to the power elite that had been promised by Dale just never seemed to happen. In fact, most of the time it was difficult even to reach Dale.

Finally, David and Bob Aurthur managed to sell the idea of financing the project to the National Educational Television (N.E.T.) although we were still counting on Dale for U. S. Air Force planes to fly some of the equipment to Brazil.

About that time another slight hitch developed. N.E.T. without consulting David Susskind announced that the show was under way and that Mrs. Kennedy would be the narrator.

When the First Lady read the news in the *Herald Tribune* —a newspaper that it had been announced was no longer allowed in the White House—she was furious.

Nobody had taken the trouble to tell her about the plan.

She, I am told, said to Pierre Salinger, "*That* is the last show in the world that I'll *ever* narrate."

But I knew nothing of these worldly goings-on because I was in Brewster writing the script. It went beautifully, and I finished it in less than six weeks. That sometimes happens—like once every twenty years or so.

I made use of an actual family I had met at Pindorama, the family of Manuel Ferreira da Silva. The theme was the same as it had been in the beginning, an exodus in time.

I was pleased with the play, and so was Bob.

There were plans for a campaign to try to persuade every member of Congress to look at the play, N.E.T. had impressive ideas for promoting it, and Salinger had told Bob Aurthur that if the show was everything Bob said it was going to be, the First Lady would, after all, do the narration.

"You see," Bob kept saying, "justice sometimes triumphs."

Then, two days before we left New York, David Susskind panicked. In addition to our show, to which he had given a minimum of attention, he was also preparing a full-length motion picture, *All the Way Home*, the title of Tad Mosel's stage adaptation of James Agee's novel, *A Death in the Family*, which had won the Pulitzer prize but been a commercial failure. It had largely to do with a funeral, and as philosopher-poet Dore Schary has said, "America is an upbeat nation."

David was understandably nervous, a condition aggravated by a technical man, who, although he had never been to Pindorama, said our equipment would never withstand the journey.

He suggested that we do the play on film, and David agreed.

Bob Aurthur said, fine, but in that case David would have to find a new producer and director.

I said, fine, but in that case David would have to find a new writer and a new script.

David, who bleeds a lot on such occasions, bled a lot, screamed a lot, ". . . betrayal . . . $36,000 out of my pocket . . . project finished," and capitulated.

On October 27, 1962 a day when it looked as if the United States might invade Cuba—Bob, Jane Wetherell, Claude Traverse, John Wood of the White House, and I once more flew to Rio and a few hours later to Recife.

The rest of the crew was to arrive the following Wednesday; shooting was to begin on Saturday, November 3.

Everybody liked the cooperative and René Bertholet as much as I had.

Bertholet again assured us that the roads were perfectly passable, and we were introduced to the hearty truck drivers who were going to make the journey.

We met members of the cooperative we felt might be in

the play, a man who might play Manuel, a boy who could be his son Pedro, and an exquisite little girl we all instantly decided should be Manuel's daughter. All the members of the cast were to be amateurs.

It looked as if everything was all set for an historic production that would not only be moving and beautiful; it might even cause people in the United States to realize the importance of cooperatives like Pindorama and face the problems of Brazil, in fact of all Latin America.

The next morning a cablegram arrived from David, who was on location near Knoxville; he and the technical man had once more decided that the play had to be done on film.

Not only that, David had hired a film crew, which would arrive in Recife on Friday.

Bob cabled back that unless David wanted to send another producer and writer the show was off.

Other lively and costly messages were exchanged, but this time David was adamant; so was Bob; so was the writer.

"Okay," said Bob. "Let's go home."

I went as far as Rio, feeling done in.

On Sunday, on an awesome stretch of Copacabana Beach in front of the Excelsior Hotel, Bob said, "Why the hell are you coming back to the States? Stick around here for a while; travel around, have a good time, relax, and in six weeks, a couple of months at most, we'll be back and do this show. I've never wanted to do anything more in my life."

I was easily convinced, and after the others left I hired Carlos Roberto Moreira de Souza as interpreter, driver, and tape-recorder operator, and we returned to Pindorama. I had a vague idea I might do a book about the colony, a notion my publishers greeted with the sound of one hand applauding.

Carlos and I did record a few interviews with colonists and endless tapes of the folk music of the Northeast which is sly, irreverent and, it goes without saying, subversive.

I learned enough Portuguese to order a vodka-tonic, met

some charming Brazilians, and a number of dedicated Americans, most of them in the Peace Corps.

In addition, between November and late January I lined up a cast for the show, chose most of the locations, and had half of the village of Penedo ready to be extras, singers, and musicians.

I rewrote and, I think, improved the script.

Manuel Ferreira da Silva's story begins on a sugar plantation, the kind of place—I'd visited dozens of them—of which Bertholet said, "It is worse than the Middle Ages; then the landowners had to take care of their serfs; nowadays, the number of *arms*—sugar-cane workers—is limitless."

In the first act of the play the youngest of Manuel's sons dies of hookworm; four of the real Manuel's sons had died of similar diseases, but sometimes, very often really, realism . . .

Manuel decides that existence on the plantation is unbearable, and with one of his surviving sons, Pedro, he leaves the plantation to look for a job.

The father and son go first to São Paolo, then to Rio, and, finally, to Recife. The situation is the same everywhere. There are thousands of peasants in every large city in Brazil, almost all of them jobless and living in slums—*favelas*—where the conditions are as bad as or worse than on the plantations.

Finally, Manuel and Pedro hear about Pindorama, and they go there most of the way on foot. It is a distance of nearly a thousand miles. Several such journeys are made to Pindorama every week. To own a horse in Northeast Brazil is to own independence.

At Pindorama Manuel and Pedro are interviewed by Bertholet, who finds that they have all the qualifications to be successful colonists, but there is a list of several thousand peasants waiting to get into the cooperative, and all of them have priority over Manuel and his family.

In the final scene of the play Manuel and Pedro stand on the crest of a hill overlooking the cooperative; houses are being built, electricity is being installed, and tractors are working the land.

After a moment the man and boy start back to the sugar plantation, back to the Middle Ages.

At the end of the play Bertholet says, "Manuel Ferreira da Silva is a patient man. He will wait for a while because he has hope, but how long *can* he wait? . . . And what of the ten million other *matutos* [peasants] in Northeast Brazil?

"We do not live in a time when the hungry and dispossessed are patient. There are 500 families at Pindorama. I wish there could be 50,000. But even 500,000 would not be enough.

"We at Pindorama are grateful for American Food for Peace. But we need more. The more help we get the shorter our waiting list will be. And for me a waiting list of one is too long. The children of Manuel Ferreira da Silva are hungry *now*. His babies are dying *now*. . . . 'Cast thy bread upon the waters: for thou shalt find it after many days.'"

The propaganda was not subtle, and the quote from *Ecclesiastes* was a little Lloyd C. Dougles, but I believed it, and René Bertholet was delighted.

I had received a number of encouraging cables and letters from Bob Aurthur, which always made it possible to get through the day. The new starting date for taping *Exodus in Time* was the first week in February.

Then on the evening of January 30 while I was having dinner with Carlos and a group of Peace Corps volunteers the *maître d'* at the São Francisco Hotel in Penedo handed me a cable.

DONE FINISHED ALL OVER STOP LETTER FOLLOWS STOP BOB

Word that the show had been canceled was all over town in an hour, and if the Brazilians were not such amiable people, I believe they would have thrown me into the São Francisco River, which, as I have indicated, is filled with bloodthirsty piranhas.

All of the extras and musicians had expected that as a result of their appearance on the show they would become Hollywood stars.

The next morning before dawn I showed René Bertholet the cable, and he said, under the circumstances quite gently, I thought, "I believe Americans are better at promises than they are at fulfillment."

It wasn't until I got back to New York that I found out what had happened.

To tell even the more cursory details would make an account of the Brazilian experience longer than what I now refer to as the Jackie Cooper Experience, but these are the highlights: Varig had decided against providing any more free transportation; Bud Dale had failed to live up to a single one of his promises, *and* he didn't have an office in the White House or in the new State Department Building.

But, more important, the President's and Mrs. Kennedy's trip to Brazil had been canceled, this time permanently, and National Educational Television decided that without Mrs. Kennedy it wasn't interested in the show. They wanted a star.

"In other words," said Bob, who had put his life on the line and considerable of his own money into an attempt to save the project, "new dimensions in television but the same old results."

Eight months later, by the way, Pindorama had not yet been able to cut through the red tape, that of our government and the Brazilian but mostly ours, and could not yet distribute Food for Peace.

By the time I rose from the plaza of the Seagram Building it was dusk, and I walked back to the Gorham Hotel.

It was a peaceful evening, and I was going to keep my evenings peaceful. I was going to have no part of the Cooper television series.

That night I spent several hours on the journal I sporadically keep:

June 3 . . . Talked to Bob Aurthur about a television series; he wants me to write a pilot and said that if I did so I might become richer than William Paley, Chairman of the Board of C.B.S., Frank Stanton, President of C.B.S., and James T. Aubrey, Jr., President of C.B.S. Television.

Naturally, I said no.

He has asked me to have breakfast with him in the morning and for the sake of old friendship I shall do so.

Anyway, I don't even know what a pilot is, although I did see one once.

In the winter of 1950 I was the dinner guest—second sitting—at a house on Gramercy Park that once belonged to Mrs. Stuyvesant Fish. When I was there it belonged to Benjamin Sonnenberg, who wears Edwardian clothes and makes six million dollars a minute being a non-Edwardian Public Relations Counselor.

Anyway, at the Sonnenberg-Fish house I sat in a red leather chair in a projection room and saw the *pilot* film for a new comedy series.

When it was over, the P.R.C. asked what I thought of it.

I said, "Well, it certainly didn't make me laugh. It will never run."

I Love Lucy, for indeed it was she, was on the network of

James Aubrey, who doesn't like my novels, every week for six years.

Even now—thirteen years later—*I.L.L.* reruns can be seen practically every morning.

Not only that, something called *Lucy*, a spin-off of *I.L.L.*, is still on prime evening time on the Aubrey network once a week.

And Bob Aurthur wants me to write a pilot. No, Aurthur, I am sitting this one out. Let me know how you make out with Sitting Bull, Custer.

I had a couple vodka-tonics and continued:

Dear Diary . . . I wonder what an income tax collector looks like? I bet they all have mouths the size and shape of the top of a drawstring purse.

And how long would it take to write one script? Bob Aurthur did the pilot for *East Side, West Side* in three days.

And this series *is* about something important. And I *do* know about county agents, and the ones I've known I've liked, and how many people can I say that of?

There was a county agent named Ed Sentener who was a big help to my father when I was a kid. Help, my ass; he practically saved Monte's life. When we had to give up and the farm was sold at a sheriff's sale Sentener—a large blond man, I remember, with, I think, a mustache—helped Monte get a job delivering oil in Marshalltown and, dear diary, although you and I are too young to remember, during the depression jobs were few and far between.

This *could* be a good series. Couldn't it?

Come on, Merle. You are doing it again. You are lying to yourself, which is the worst sin of all.

My final entry on June 3 was:

Remember the advice of the wisest of men, Rochefoucauld, 'It is not enough to have achieved personal success. One's best friend must also have failed.'

Besides, Horatio, you cannot beat the system. Stay after school and write on the blackboard one hundred times, "You cannot beat the system, cannot beat the system, cannot beat the system. . . ."

On the other hand, Fyodor would never have written *The Idiot* if it hadn't been for his unpaid taxes and his gambling debts. This could be *The Idiot* of television series. . . .

I put away the journal, had three or four more invigorating vt's, and ordered a hot pastrami on rye from the Carnegie Delicatessen—my 187th h.p.r. since returning from the jungles.

Before going to bed I consulted my horoscope. I know most people look at their horoscope in the morning, but if I did that, most days I wouldn't get out of bed.

For you, Taurus . . . June 3, 1963. CRITICAL. This is not a favorable day to travel or deal with relatives. Protect your valuables from fire and theft. Difficult influences may make people easily angered and resentful. Avoid physical strain and worry. Use your imagination. Get finances in order.

The Schrafft's at 464 Madison Avenue is not at its best at a few minutes after eight in the morning, and neither am I.

But Bob Aurthur is not only energetic at that hour, I've even known him to be cheerful.

He did have the decency to keep his thoughts, if any, to himself until after I had had two large orange juices, two eggs and bacon, and twelve pots of coffee.

Then he put aside the *Times* and said, "Merle, have I ever lied to you?"

"Not about anything important."

"All right. Let me start out by saying that this is an opportunity that comes to very few writers, an opportunity to be independent, to buy some time, and that's what all writers want. I think. I know I do."

"Bob, I don't know the first thing about writing a pilot."

"But I do, and we'll be working together. The whole way. . . . Now I won't tell you that this thing won't be demanding, nerve-racking, and time-consuming. It will be."

"How long will it honestly take?"

"A couple months. At most, and as I say you'll not only get the royalty—$1000 or more a week every time the show goes on the air—your contract will give you the 'most favored nations clause,' meaning they'll want you to write all the scripts you want to write at the *top price*. You can write your own ticket, and these scripts will be about characters you've invented and believe in."

I started to speak, but Bob, who was wearing a blue jacket with buttons the size of doubloons, said, "You could do a good job on this, and you could say something important, and to a mass audience. And from here on in you'd have enough money to spend all your time on novels. . . ."

A few weeks earlier, Bob went on, Cooper, who had already been in two successful series, *The People's Choice* and *Hennesey,* had come to New York with an idea for a new one.

He wanted to play a volunteer in the domestic Peace Corps.

He brought the idea to United Artists Television to ask for help in selling it to a network, preferably C.B.S., on which *Hennesey* had appeared.

Bob said there are usually three ways to get a series on television. One is for a network to develop and finance the necessary pilot. It can also be done by an independent company like Four Star Television, the Hollywood organization once headed by Dick Powell. Talent Associates-Paramount Ltd. is the same kind of company.

A third way to get a pilot made is to have it accepted, developed, and financed by a major distributor of theatrical motion pictures—Warner Brothers, Twentieth Century Fox, Screen Gems, now associated with Columbia Pictures, or United Artists Television, part of the United Artists Corporation, which in recent years has had enormous success in the motion picture field.

A network is usually reluctant to put up all the cash necessary for a pilot or, for that matter, to spend the time and creative energy involved.

Usually, Bob said, if the network is interested in the basic idea for a series it may share the expenses with an independent company or a distributor.

The latter was to be the case with the county agent project.

"Cooper came to U.A. mostly because the William Morris Agency handles both him and U.A.," said Bob.

"Dick Dorso [Executive Vice-President in Charge of Programming at U.A. TV], Cooper, and I took the Peace Corps idea to Jim Aubrey. Aubrey's the most important man in television, in the history of television, maybe in the history of entertainment. He out-Mayers Louis B. Mayer ten times over. . . . At A.B.C. and N.B.C. they work by the committee system when they program, not at C.B.S. There Aubrey makes all the decisions, and he makes them by himself. He's one of this century's phenomena, and, as a novelist, Merle, you should be fascinated by him. . . ."

"How did he get all that power?"

"There was a vacuum and Aubrey stepped into it. Anyway, he didn't like the Peace Corps idea. He said, 'I don't like snoopers,' whatever that means. Besides, he said the domestic Peace Corps hasn't been approved by Congress yet and a series like that would be premature.

"Then he leaned back in his chair and said, 'I see a man in a dusty pickup in the Southwest. The man is wearing a Stetson and khaki pants. I don't know exactly what he is, but he's not a cop; he doesn't carry a gun. I don't want him to be a policeman or a law enforcement officer.' "

"That's all he said?"

"About all."

"Well, if the bottom falls out of the television racket, he could always make a nifty living with a crystal ball or tea leaves."

"He doesn't have to," said Bob. "C.B.S. now makes more money than the other two networks put together. Besides, what he was doing was describing sort of a present-day Western, you know, different, but not too different."

"For one thing, no guns."

"Aubrey knows Cooper could never play a gun toter; Cooper's biggest asset as an actor is that he's terribly sincere, terribly earnest, and he likes to play do-gooders. . . . The kind of people you write best about, Merle. You and St. Paul are always running hell-bent down the road to Damascus.

"After the conference with Aubrey, Cooper went to Washington to find out what kind of a guy wore a Stetson, khaki pants, and drove a dusty pickup. Somebody told him about county agents. He hurried back to New York, and Dorso, Cooper, and I went to Aubrey with the county agent idea, and that's how your name came into it. . . .

"Merle," said Bob, "you and I are going to have a great time on this one. . . . Writing a pilot is no different than any other kind of good dramatic writing.

"Here are some things you might want to consider about the county agent. You can accept any or none of them. It's strictly up to you; you're the writer. . . .

"Cooper thinks he's got Barbara Stanwyck lined up for this series. Which would be great. They ought to be great together."

"As—sweethearts?"

"No, as enemies, friendly enemies. Maybe she owns a ranch next to the county agent's, and she's sort of a man-killer, but he likes her. He talks over a lot of his problems with her.

"Then there's an uncle. The agent's father and mother are dead. Less complicated. The uncle brought him up, maybe the uncle's been done in by the depression."

The uncle and Cooper would be—if I agreed—the two characters who appeared in every or almost every show; Stanwyck would appear less often.

Bob said, "Sure the pilot will suffer some from the disease of the committee system—every vice-president will want to get his two cents in—but just keep one thing in mind, you'll be writing about a man you understand, a dedicated man. . . . At three o'clock Dick Dorso wants to talk to you. When I told him you were going to do the pilot, he was delighted."

"Would you mind telling me when that happened?"

"I told him after you left the office yesterday afternoon."

"Of course. By the way, what's Dorso like?"

"You wouldn't believe it if I told you," said Bob. "Another phenomenon. And he's a friend of Jim Aubrey."

As I walked away I decided that in addition to the swimming pool, which would look nice to the right of the front of the glass house, I would have a few tastefully arranged cabañas the color of money.

After I left Bob I recalled the sensible remark of a marginal merchant, a grocer in Cincinnati who once said to the father of my oldest friend, Tommy Stix, "Mr. Stix, for a millionaire, your fly is open."

For a writer who was about to be rich, I needed a haircut. So I went to the Plaza, the only hotel in New York where I am recognized as a prince traveling incognito, had a haircut, a manicure, and enough of the sun lamp to remind people, including the Executive Vice-President in Charge of Programming at United Artists Television, that I had not long before been lolling on Copacabana Beach.

I considered having my temples touched with gray; successful writers always seem to have gray temples. I decided against it—too obvious, too expensive.

Six months later, I had a gray streak on each side of my head and it was free.

From the Plaza I went to Tripler's where I have a charge account and bought a new shirt. I changed in the dressing room.

"What shall we do with the old one?" asked the clerk, holding my old shirt at arm's length in a pair of tongs.

It was then about noon and I called Hope Taylor, a friend who had worked in the industry in various capacities includ-

ing that of an agent. I knew that she had been Dorso's secretary briefly when he was vice-president of ZIV, which later
became part of United Artists Television.

Hope and I had lunch at Louis and Armand's, the only
restaurant in New York where I am recognized as a prince
traveling incognito and where I also have a charge account.

Over the second Gibson Hope said, "Well, I wasn't there
long, you know, but at that time Mr. Dorso entered—and I
mean entered—the office every morning at nine, on the nose,
and he always wanted a container of hot tea, *really* hot, waiting for him. With lemon on the side.

"Also, I had to have waiting for him an order of toast, as he
said, 'not black toast, burnt toast.'

"The minute I saw him open the front door I had to race
to the water cooler and put two teaspoons of *cold* water in the
hot tea, no more and no less. The cold water made the hot tea
lukewarm, but mine not to reason why.

"Another thing. He always used the royal *we*. Like Queen
Victoria. 'We are not amused." In Dorso's case every morning
as I trotted in with his tea he would say, 'My, don't we look
pretty today.'

"For reasons I won't go into there wasn't a single day there
that I looked pretty, and I think that was one of the reasons
that I quit and started collecting unemployment insurance . . . and if you want my advice, Merle . . ."

"I'm not eligible for unemployment," I said, "and when
Dorso sees me I am practically certain that despite my new
haircut and shirt he will not say, 'Don't we look pretty today.'
What else?"

"He's always dressed correctly. As my mother would say,
he's 'well turned out.' He's really quite good-looking. The
girl who was a secretary or two before me had a thing for
him.

"He's a good tennis player; I'm told that if he kept up with
it, I mean practiced every day, he might make the National
Open Tournament. Mrs. Dorso plays tennis, too. And people

say—I wouldn't know—that he goes to bed every night about nine-thirty and gets up every morning at six and he doesn't smoke or drink."

I immediately ordered another round and lit two cigarettes, one for each nostril.

"What time is your appointment?" Hope asked.

"Three o'clock."

"Well, you can count on him being fifteen minutes late," she said. "He always is, even if he could be on time. It's a matter of principle. And he'll have just come from someplace very important or seen someone very important.

"Whenever he went to lunch with a client he'd tell me the restaurant where he'd be and I'd have to page him there. Whether there were any messages or not I'd have to page him. I think that was one of the reasons I quit."

The waiter served lunch. Hope picked delicately at her *ortolan avec les pommes frites.*

"If you want to know about Dorso, ask David Susskind," she said.

"David and I only speak to each other through Presidents," I said.

"David used to work for Dorso, or the company that Dorso was a partner in with Al Levy and Marty Melcher, who at that time was married to one of their clients, Patti Andrews of the Andrews Sisters, and who at last report is still married to Doris Day, who was another of Marty's clients.

"Marty and Dorso went to Hollywood and formed their own company, and Al Levy and David stayed in New York and went into partnership in Talent Associates, Ltd."

"How do you know all this?" I asked.

"Oh, it's that kind of business. Everybody knows everybody else, or they know somebody who knows somebody. They're all friends or partners or related. One day they're all going to die of hemophilia.

"But Dorso really made his mark in Hollywood. He wrote and directed a slew of low-budget films for television."

"Which ones?" I asked.

"None that you would recognize," Hope said. "But he was successful and important and he went to ZIV as a vice-president and that's when I worked for him.

"I remember at that time the whole office was very excited about a new ZIV series that Aubrey at C.B.S. had just bought from us and was backing on prime time to the tune of a couple of million dollars.

"It was called *World of Giants*, WOG, around the office, and it was about an American spy who was six inches tall. Besides all the dangers of being a spy he had a *terrible* time with alley cats and vacuum cleaners.

"We walked around the office all day saying WOG, WOG. I think *that* was the reason I finally quit."

"How long did you work for him?"

"Four days."

"WOG, WOG," I said. "I'll have a double Gibson on the rocks but go easy on the rocks."

"Dorso never drinks," said Hope," "and he and Jim Aubrey are very good friends and are always working out at gymnasiums and can do push-ups and chin themselves up the next rung of the ladder any day. *They* never befuddle their brains with alcohol. . . . I'll have just a single but go easy on the onion."

Dick Dorso's secretary was a pleasant, sensible-looking girl wearing glasses and an air of harassment.

She smiled and said, "Mr. Dorso called; he's over at C.B.S., and he'll be a few minutes late."

"I could have told you that," I replied in a voice audible only to my inner ear.

"He asked if you'd mind waiting."

I said that I wouldn't, and she indicated a handsome period chair covered with light green leather.

"You like a cup of tea or coffee?" she asked.

"No, thanks."

She excused herself, leaving the door open.

Dorso's office was about twice the size of Bob Aurthur's. It had a utilitarian gray carpet, wall to wall, two chintz-covered sofas, a black leather chair, and two non-objective paintings —a black blob on a white background and a white blob on a black background. On a ledge below the window facing directly on Madison Avenue were photographs of two pretty, dark-haired girls.

One wall was taken up with a stylized Chinese panel, and there were half a dozen Chinese vases. Several were used as the bases of lamps, and at least one contained plastic yellow flowers.

A dictating machine stood on a ledge under a window looking north on Madison Avenue, and there was a telephone with the expected row of buttons. Dorso's desk was in no way extraordinary except that there wasn't a paper of any kind on it, not even an appointment book.

An expressionless Buddha was placed near the black leather chair.

The total effect of the office and its furnishings was Byzantine, and I was reminded of something my agent and friend Harold Franklin once said. He was being interviewed for a job, but his prospective employers seemed to be embarrassed every time Harold mentioned the subject of money; finally, Harold said, "Look, all of us in this business are Armenian rug merchants in Byzantium; so let's get down to business."

"See?" said one of the prospective employers, a man I dare not identify beyond saying he is one of the most important talent agents in the business. "I told you he was intelligent."

As I waited in Dorso's office I thought, Although I am a little more than six inches tall, I have yet to meet a harmless alley cat that in my presence doesn't become a raging twelve-foot tiger, and as for lethal vacuum cleaners . . . WOG. WOG.

I continued practicing my WOGS during what I expected to be a long wait for Dorso.

Actually, he was only ten minutes late; but he did make an entrance, and while he paused at the door as if to wait for the applause of recognition that greets the star; his secretary, looking more harassed than before, handed him a great many messages. A great many people apparently wanted to get in touch with Dorso *immediately.*

He was wearing an Ivy League-type suit of summer weight, gray; the jacket was thrown over his shoulders, and he had on a red, white, and blue belt.

Dorso is a man of medium build with light brown hair combed flat on his head; he is wiry and thin, has dark brown eyes, what appears to be a perfect set of good-sized teeth, and the expressive hands of a performer.

He asked his secretary to ask Bob Aurthur if he'd mind sitting in on the meeting, and then he turned to me and smiled, using all of his teeth.

"I'm delighted that a writer of your caliber is interested in the Jackie Cooper Project," he said, "though I'm not surprised. We are all very, very excited about it."

He shook my hand, still smiling.

"I just saw Larry White, at C.B.S.," he said, "and I told him about you. He was delighted. He wanted to know how we were able to get *Merle Miller* to write for television."

"If the subject comes up again," I said, "you might tell Larry White that perhaps the major factor is malnutrition."

"I'll tell him that," said Dorso, laughing. "Sit down, sit down," he said. "Make yourself comfortable."

"This is a very beautiful chair," I said.

"Chippendale, circa 1770. Of course it needs recovering, but it's a *chair*."

Bob Aurthur came in, looking tired. He sat on one of the sofas, and Dorso seated himself in the black leather chair next to the Buddha. Dorso sits very straight, much the way the plebes sit in classrooms at West Point.

"I guess Bob has told you," he said, "this is what I call our cultural hour. In a minute I'll get into my lecture on the nature of a pilot. Bob, of course, has heard it before."

Bob indicated that that was true.

Dorso asked Bob if he knew a novelist who had also written for the movies and television. Bob did.

"Does he drink a lot?" asked Dorso.

"He lives every day as if there was never going to be a tomorrow," said Bob.

Dorso nodded, clearly pleased.

"How old is he?"

"He'll be fifty-one," said Bob.

Dorso smiled again; he was fifty-four.

"I played tennis with him on Sunday, and he was out of

breath, puffing away, even before the first set was over, and he had dark circles under his eyes. I thought he probably drank a lot."

Dorso's eyes are always clear and without circles, and only once in our acquaintance was out of breath.

We talked of several other matters of no importance, and then, without warning, Dorso said, "I've given the matter a great deal of thought, and I believe that The Bomb has made another war impossible."

I nodded, thinking what an impressive way to begin a lecture on the nature of a pilot.

"That's all to the good, of course," Dorso went on, his left hand caressing the head of the Buddha; Bob Aurthur was, as nearly as I could make out, doing his Canadian Air Force Exercises.

"On the other hand, man is made up of love-hate, the one warring against the other," Dorso said.

I had read that head doctors were going to be very big on television the next season and wondered if the county agent would be moonlighting, doing a little therapy on the side.

"If there are no more wars, what happens to these hostilities?" asked Dorso.

I said, "I gather you're not married."

Dorso smiled. Bob started phase two of his exercises.

"These are perfectly natural hostilities," said Dorso. "They explain the little brush-fire wars breaking out all over Africa and in the Far East. They explain, at least in part, the violence associated with the Negro struggle for civil rights."

Dorso straightened his jacket and pushed his sheer white shirt deeper into the patriotic belt.

"That last is a good thing, of course," he said, "a necessary thing! We cannot live in a society in which there are basic inequalities."

Bob muttered something; I couldn't tell what, though I thought I caught the words, "Four score and seven years ago . . ."

"I'm a writer, too," said Dorso. "I won't say I was as good

a writer as you, but I *understand* writers. You'll find that out. Not that you're always going to love me."

He paused, and while he adjusted a crease in one gray trouser leg, Bob started the next day's exercises.

"Actors, writers, most creative people have to be loved," said Dorso, "but I don't. You won't hear anybody say, 'I love Dick Dorso,' except maybe my daughters"—he pointed to the photographs of the two dark-haired girls—"and maybe my wife. But as I say, I don't have to be loved. That's one of the things I learned during my analysis.

"As a writer I was miserable," he went on. "The tension, always waiting, will they or won't they buy my script. But my analysis taught me to make do with myself and I'm much happier in this job than I could *ever* have been as a writer."

The telephone rang.

Dorso looked at it with friendly surprise, and so, I thought, did Bob.

"It must be an emergency," said Dorso. "I told them I didn't want any calls unless it was an emergency."

He picked up the phone, listened for a tense moment, then said, "Tell Hunt I'll call him in about fifteen minutes."

He put down the phone and smiled again.

"That was the Coast, and it was an emergency. It's *always* an emergency in this business. It's an impossible business. When we get through with this pilot—"

His expansive gesture included Bob, himself, and me. "It will be like—well, a writer and I made a pilot in Hollywood, and when we finally finished cutting it, the writer said to me, 'Dick, you and I have been through a war together, Pearl Harbor to V-J Day.' And it's true. There's no other experience comparable. You never really find out about people until you've been down in the crucible with them."

I nodded, although I had at that time never been down in a crucible, even alone.

"Why do we do it?" asked Dorso. "What is the appeal? I'll tell you what the appeal is. It's what I call the razor's edge. It's the element of danger. What else has the same kind of challenge? Politics, I suppose. There you have to get out and sell *yourself*. . . . But a man like me—I have a limited education, and in businesses, like General Motors, for instance, I just wouldn't have the technical knowledge. This is the only business for somebody like me. The rewards are great; you operate by instinct, and it's the belly decisions that count, and you can't always win.

"Only one out of every four pilots made goes on the air, and of those, fifty per cent fail. If you win one out of five you're doing great. It's like Willie Mays at the beginning of every season. He's nervous, tense. He knows he can't win them all."

Bob examined the design on a Chinese plate.

"Well," said Dorso, "I promised you my lecture on the nature of a pilot."

He rested his elbows on the arms of the leather chair, his hands making a temple in front of his face.

"In the first place a pilot is not entertainment."

I reached in my pocket, took out the goose quill I am never without, and enough papyrus to record the Sermon on the Mount and Pericles' Funeral Oration.

"And a pilot is not for the public," Dorso went on. "It is definitely not for the public. Its success or failure depends solely on five *very* bored men in a projection room."

I wrote, "P. not E. not for P.*Very*. Bored. 5."

"These five men have seen hundreds of pilots, maybe thousands, and they would much rather say *no* than yes. If they say yes, they're committed. They're in trouble. They've made a decision. Their ulcers start acting up."

The goose quill wrote, "Decisions. Ulcers. Up."

"If they say *no*, they can go out and get drunk, play golf, anything. No problems."

I wanted to ask who the five men were—network executives, possible sponsors? I didn't though. That was the first of many times in the months to follow when, if I didn't know, I didn't ask.

"You can't give them time to *think*," said Dorso, making

think sound like a pretty unpleasant thing to do under any circumstances.

"The minute I hear a cough I know we're in trouble. . . . Now I may sound as if I'm not being serious, but I'm deadly serious. These five guys. I know them; I respect them, and they know and respect me."

"Cough. Deadly."

"I've had experience with pilots, and I've got a gut instinct where they're concerned. I believe you could say I've had some success in this field. . . . Now you've got to capture them in the first thirty seconds, *and* they've got to stay captured. No time for introspection, no time for soul searching, and the hero has got to win. You can't tell these five men, 'Well, sure he loses in this one, but most of the time he comes out a hero.'"

I made note of the fact that Willie Mays would never do as the hero of a pilot.

"In the first thirty seconds the pilot should go like this, 'Fifty thousand murderous Berbers are headed toward Cairo, and only you, Dick Daring, can stop them.' Dick Daring, that's our hero, in this case Jackie Cooper, county agent. 'Only *you*, Dick Daring, can stop them.'"

I pictured Jackie Cooper, unarmed, wearing a Stetson and khaki pants, driving a dusty pickup straight through a howling, murderous mob of Berbers.

"Are you with me so far?" asked Dorso.

I said that I was with him; Bob Aurthur had his eyes closed.

"Of course there's an antagonist," said Dorso. "*He* wants to let the Berbers into Cairo; he wants to stop Dick Daring, but he's not a stupid antagonist. He's not a jerk. I don't like a stupid antagonist."

I wrote, "Stop Dick Daring. No stupidity."

"Now by the end of the first act, *everything* is in jeopardy. Dick Daring's job, Dick Daring's integrity, Dick Daring's everything. But by the end of the third act he has won, and in the fourth act you wind up the loose ends. . . . In a pilot, of course, you also have to introduce all of the continuing characters, show who they are, what they do, what their relationship is to Daring, and you have to keep everything moving at all times, moving, moving. Fast, fast. Action. No studying of the navel, no introspection."

"Intro., No. Navel, No. *Fast*."

"These five men in the projection room, they must feel when it's over that they can't believe it's over. That's why we shoot some of our pilots just a little bit short and cheat just a little. Are you with me, Merle?"

I nodded; Bob lighted several cigarettes.

"Any questions?" asked Dorso.

"Couldn't be clearer," I said.

Dorso smiled and stood up, and so did Bob and I.

"Television is a mass medium," said Dorso, "and we all tend to forget that. If you write a book and it sells thirty thousand copies you've got a best seller on your hands. If you make a movie and it is seen by fifteen million people, it's a hit. But *we* are talking about something that is seen by maybe twenty-five million people every week, maybe forty million. Each and every week. . . ."

As Bob and I walked down the hall away from Dorso's office I heard him saying, "Hello, Hunt; no, Hunt. This is *not* going to be a West Coast project. I've talked to Jim, Hunt."

"I wish Mr. Dorso had had more time," I said to Bob. "Now that he's told me how to write a pilot I would like him to fill me in on how to write *Remembrance of Things Past* and *Tristram Shandy,* because those are novels I have always wanted to know how to write."

"Forget all that," said Bob, "you'll be working with me."

"Roberto, there are a number of writers who can handle this assignment admirably, Ouida, for one; I believe that she has never stirred out of Surrey or Wuthering Heights or wherever it is, but she is an expert on Berbers. Remember *Under Two Flags?* Or P. C. Wren? *Beau Geste* was up to its ass in Berbers."

"I think you ought to get on the phone to the Department

of Agriculture and find out all you can about county agents, especially in the Southwest. Cooper's coming to town on Monday, and by then maybe we can come up with a story line."

I looked at the notes I had taken.

"P. not E. not for P. *Very*. Bored. 5. Decisions. Ulcers. Up. Cough. Deadly. Stop Dick Daring. No stupidity. Intro., No. Navel, No. *Fast*."

"I do have one question," I said. "Do you by any chance know the name of Dorso's analyst?"

I spent the rest of that day and all of the next two on the phone and ran up a bill that will keep A.T.&T. solvent for years. Most of the time I spoke with people in the U. S. Department of Agriculture (U.S.D.A.), in Washington and in the field.

I learned a good deal about county agents, the kind of jobs they do, the kind of people they work with, the kind of men they are.

There is an agent in almost every county in the United States, and he has three bosses, the land grant college of his state, the Department of Agriculture, and the commissioners of his county.

He never makes much money; the top salary in most states is $12,500.

The agent is a college graduate, usually in one of the agricultural sciences—agronomy, animal husbandry, plant pathology. After five or six years on the job he is encouraged to come back to the university for a Master's degree, and after ten years for a doctorate.

Ed Roche, who is in the Extension Service of the U.S.D.A., said, "The agent is a teacher, actually a member of the faculty of the land grant college, but he takes the university to the farm. He spends a lot of time working with kids, the ones in 4-H Clubs. Do you know about the 4-H Clubs?"

I said that I did, not adding that except for dishonesty, poor eyesight, and stupidity on the part of the judges my baby beef would have won best of show at the Marshall County Fair. As it was, Eulalie—my calf—got a third prize, and there were five entries.

Many people said of county agents what Dean Philip J. Leyendecker of New Mexico State University later repeated, "Basically the job attracts the same kind of people as the Peace Corps."

Duane Nelson, also of the Extension Division and a former agent in New Mexico, said, "I suppose you'd get to be an agent because you want to do some good in the world."

I gave everybody I talked to a shortened and, I thought, realistic version of what a good pilot ought to be. I did not mention Dick Daring.

I said, "The story has to be a single dramatic incident—a man, the county agent, has to be in conflict against some one person or some one thing."

"How about the agent against nature?" asked Ed Roche. "The agent against drought, against insects, wind, winterkill of crops, fire, erosion, animal diseases, crop diseases, floods?"

"Man against insects," I said. "Tell me about that. I'm reading Carson's book, *Silent Spring.*"

"We call it the *Uncle Tom's Cabin* of our time," said Ed. "The use of chemicals is a hot issue with the public right now. There could be a lot of controversy with the agent right square in the middle. He could make the point that chemicals are essential and safe—but only if used properly. Come on down to Washington and we'll line up the experts in the field."

"I like that idea," I said. "Who could I call in the Southwest, Arizona or New Mexico . . . ?"

Ed gave me the name of a man in Arizona, and then he said, "And you *must* talk to John White at New Mexico State

University. He knows more about what's going on in agriculture in the Southwest than anybody else."

I called the man in Arizona first; he was not very cooperative, but when I talked to John White, I liked him at once; he seemed interested, knowledgeable, and anxious to help.

I gave him my capsule version of my pilot speech.

When I finished, John said, "This isn't going to be another of those shoot-em-ups, is it?"

I assured him that it was not.

"In the first place," I said, "Jackie Cooper wouldn't stand for it, and *I* wouldn't write that kind of thing. This is going to be about real people involved in real situations. . . . The basic rule for the series is this—not everything has to have happened, but there will be nothing that *couldn't* happen, and everything has to be scientifically accurate so that every agent in the country and every farm family will look at it and say, 'That's *exactly* right. *That* is true."

"Is this for American television?" asked John.

Later I said, "Mr. White, is it possible that a drift wind could pick up an insecticide that's just been sprayed on a crop—cotton, let's say—and carry it to another area where it might do harm?"

"Oh yes. That has happened. These drift winds start in California, and they increase in velocity, and by the time they get here they can do a lot of damage. . . . In the case of a wind picking up an insecticide and spreading it, the insecticide could contaminate neighboring streams, killing the fish; it could contaminate nearby forests, killing a number of small animals. But why don't you and Jackie Cooper come on down and see us? We'll *show* you what it's like."

"We'll try to come," I said.

I didn't go to bed at all that night—the first of many in the months ahead—but by morning had what I thought was a fair four-page outline for a pilot script. No murderous Berbers, but the basic idea demonstrated what the series was all about—the public good versus the private interest.

That idea is fairly basic to our society, and it has concerned more than a few philosophers.

The outline went like this:

A heavy drift wind is predicted for the county, and the agent, the protagonist, knowing what the wind might do, gets on the radio to warn people.

The antagonist, a wealthy rancher and farmer, has arranged to spray his crop the day before the drift wind is scheduled to arrive, and he is going to do it no matter what. Try and stop him.

The county agent does try.

"Do you realize the harm that might be done?" he asks the antagonist.

"Sure, it *might*," he says, "but I'm gambling that it won't. I'm taking that gamble because if I don't spray tomorrow my entire cotton crop *might* be wiped out."

"It's the future of your cotton crop against the future of this county," says the agent.

"Maybe."

"In that case," says the agent, "I'm on the side of the county. . . . I'm going to court to try to get an injunction to stop you."

The wealthy rancher-farmer also happens to be one of the county commissioners, so that the agent's job is at stake.

There was more, but that will do.

It was dawn when I finished typing, and as I shaved and showered, I felt a little like Harriet Beecher Stowe.

I was waiting in Bob's office when he got there a few minutes after nine. I gave him the outline; he read it and made a few suggestions for changes, and at around eleven he and I met with Dorso, who was wearing either the same or an identical red, white, and blue belt.

"I understand you've come up with a wonderful idea," he said, seating himself in the black leather chair.

"Pretty good," I said, nervously backing into the Chippendale.

"Merle," said Bob, "in the language of television, you say, 'Dickie, old buddy, this idea is going to send you. It will absolutely rock you off your bonanza.' "

Bob looked at me, and I nodded. We had already agreed that Bob was to *tell* the story.

First, because people in television are like people in Iowa. Iowans are ninety-nine per cent literate. Can read but don't.

Second, I am struck mute when faced with presenting an idea I have had anything to do with.

Third, Robert Alan Aurthur happens to be one of the great actors of our time.

When Bob had finished his performance, Dorso sat quietly for a time, his hands once more making a temple in front of his face.

"It might work," he said. "We'll see what Jack says, and if he likes it we'll have to see what Larry White at C.B.S. says. . . ."

Bob walked me to the elevator.

"I have witnessed more than a few memorable performances in my time," I said. "Richard Burbage on the opening night of *Hamlet*, Julian Eltinge in *Mother Courage* . . ."

The elevator arrived on a lilt of song.

"I hope Jackie Cooper likes the idea," I said.

"He'll be in my office at nine o'clock on Monday," said Bob.

Cooper had spent the weekend making public appearances at the naval air base in Pensacola, Florida.

He was in the Navy for twenty-six months during the Second World War, part of the time in an officers' training program at Notre Dame, where he washed out after flunking calculus. After that, he was the drummer in a Navy band in the Central and South Pacific.

Cooper had originally planned to fly to New York on Sunday for our Monday meeting but because of weather didn't get in until late Monday evening. He sent a long telegram of apology suggesting that we meet in Bob Aurthur's office on Tuesday morning at nine-thirty.

I was a few minutes late, having walked around the block four times.

Cooper was already in Bob's office; he is always, I found, a punctual man.

He rose, smiled shyly, and we shook hands.

"I'm sorry we couldn't make it yesterday," he said.

Then he said that he was delighted that Bob had succeeded in interesting me in the project and that Bob had told him some of the things I had found out from the Department of Agriculture.

"It's wonderful," he said, "just wonderful. This is going to be a great series; the talk in Hollywood already is that it's going to be next year's *Defenders*. I can't wait to hear the story line."

I said, "I'd rather Bob told you."

Bob did, acting it out in much the same way as he had for Dorso on the previous Friday. This time, however, instead of saying, "And then the county agent hears about the storm," Bob said, "*You* hear about the storm that's headed *your* way; *you* have a daily broadcast anyway, you know; Merle's found out that most county agents do, and some of them have weekly television programs, too; *you'll* probably have both. Anyway, *you* hear about the storm, and *you* call the radio station and say *you* have to get on the radio and warn people and because *you're* a scientist and know all about insecticides *you* realize . . ."

Cooper listened intently, but every once in a while he turned to me and smiled.

He is a man of medium height with an overlong torso, a bit short in the leg. His light brown hair is wavy, and he has a pronounced widow's peak. His brown eyes are dark and didn't seem to be happy. He has a straight nose, his mouth is wide with a thin upper and a protruding lower lip.

It is an unactorish face. Frank Sinatra and Lee Marvin, two actors with whom I have worked, have faces that are by no means handsome, but there is something in their appearance and manner that demands that they be noticed.

Cooper, on the other hand, seems to plead with you to like him, which is appealing, whether on the television screen or in real life.

That first day he was dressed in a gray, single-breasted summer suit cut in a conservative Hollywood manner; he had on a sheer white shirt and a thin black silk tie, and on a chair beside him was a handsome letter case made of soft brown leather, with the initials *J.C.* stamped in gold on one side.

He listened with close attention to what Bob was saying, and when Bob finished, he smiled and said, "That's wonderful, just wonderful."

He turned to me and said, "It's just beautiful, Merle; you've certainly done a lot of work. . . . I'm very excited. This is really going to make them sit up and take notice."

Bob said, "Merle thinks the two of you ought to go to New Mexico and talk to some of the people at the State University and maybe some county agents. Besides, the more you two get to know each other, the better."

"I couldn't agree more," said Cooper. "I'm always for taking a look at the real thing. The real thing is always better than *any*thing you can make up. Don McGuire [who originated and wrote many of the scripts for *Hennesey*] and I used to argue about that. Merle and I certainly ought to fly down to New Mexico and take a look. When could you leave, Merle?"

"Tomorrow."

"Wonderful, just wonderful. I was hoping you'd say that."

That afternoon Bob, Dorso, Cooper, and I sat around a rectangular table in the conference room at United Artists while Bob acted out the story for Larry White, Director of Program Development at C.B.S. Larry White first achieved fame as the producer of a very successful series, *Captain Video*.

White, a pale, uncertain-looking man, placed the palms of his hands flat on the table, resting his chin where the tips of his fingers met.

He neither reacted nor moved during Bob's performance. I was sure he had fallen asleep.

After Bob finished, nobody said anything, although Mr. White raised his head and hands, pressed his left elbow against the table top and placed his chin on the back of the cradle he had made of the back of his left hand.

Dorso adjusted the red, white, and blue belt and then rested his nose on the dome of the temple he had made of his hands.

Finally, Cooper said, "This is the second time I've heard it, and I've read Merle's outline, and I think it's just wonderful."

Bob said, "It's very timely; everybody's talking about the Rachel Carson book, and nobody seems to know for sure about these insecticides, but everybody's scared. All over the country. There've even been letters in the Long Island papers about the spray they use on potatoes, whether it contaminates the air and how far it drifts."

White moved his head, and Dorso said, "Of course this is very rough yet; Bob and Merle just came up with the idea over the weekend."

"Would the network have any objection to the subject matter?" asked Bob.

"I don't see that there'd be any trouble on that score," said White. "Last spring we had Rachel Carson on a program, discussing her book. There were a lot of protests but the network went right ahead and did it."

"I think Merle's done a wonderful job," said Cooper.

"It's rough, of course," said Dorso, "and anyway, Jack's going to fly down to New Mexico tomorrow. He and Merle are going to take a look around. Maybe they'll come up with something better."

Cooper said, "I think it's wonderful, a very exciting story, but, of course, maybe Merle will come up with something even *better* when we're right there on the spot."

Bob had telephone calls to make, and Cooper invited me to have a drink with him in the bar of the Pierre, where he was staying.

We walked from 555 Madison, between fifty-fifth and fifty-sixth, to the hotel, at fifty-ninth and Fifth Avenue.

"Larry White never did say whether he liked it or not," I said.

"The important thing is I like it," said Cooper.

I said, "I hate meetings like that."

"You'll have a minimum of crap like that, I'll see to it."

It was then a few minutes after five, and the streets were crowded. Not many people noticed Cooper. But then not many people noticed me either.

An elderly messenger passed him, then turned around, passed him a second time, and shouted, "Hi, Hennesey."

Cooper smiled vaguely, and we walked on.

A girl in her early teens stopped him in front of the Pierre and asked him to sign her autograph book.

"You bet, honey," said Cooper.

The bar at the Pierre is dark and at that hour of the afternoon noisy.

A waiter bowed and smiled. "Good evening, Mr. Cooper. I gave my boy the autograph, and he said, 'Thank Hennesey for me, Dad.'"

Cooper smiled back and we sat down at a small corner table and ordered drinks.

"This is a fine hotel," said Cooper. "I usually have the same suite, either on the thirty-fourth or the thirty-sixth floor, and they know me. They don't give out the number of my suite or anything like that. . . . Of course, when I first came to New York nobody cared what my room number was."

After he was discharged from the Navy, Cooper said, nobody in Hollywood would hire him, not even for a Z-picture.

"I was floundering, really floundering, who was I, was I anybody. . . . So I got in the car and started driving across the country. Fast. . . . One night I was high-tailing it through Kansas, and I ran into a wind storm and the wind blew the top off the Jag. It was early, five in the morning, around there, when I got to Kansas City, and it took a long time to find somebody to fix the top, but I finally did. It was the oddest thing. When the repair man finished he said to me, 'Mr. Cooper, I live in the same apartment house as your father, and I know nothing would give him greater pleasure than seeing you.'

"I hesitated. I hadn't seen my father since I was two years old when he walked out of the house one day and didn't come back. Although later we heard from him. Or rather we heard from his lawyers. The minute it got in the papers that I was making a lot of money—when I was in *Skippy,* about that time—there was a letter from his lawyers wanting money. And from that day on, every month the check. But I never saw him.

"That morning in Kansas City I didn't say anything for a while. Then I turned to the man that fixed the top of my car and I said to him, 'You tell my father I think it would be best for him if he kept his memory of me—whatever it is—and I kept my memory of him—whatever it is.' "

Cooper was silent for a time, sipping his drink.

Then he said, "If we finish up in New Mexico in time, I'd like to get home for the weekend. I'll have been away since last week. I'm a family man. My family is important to me."

Cooper has four children, John Anthony, eighteen, by his first wife and three by his present wife—Russell, eight, Julia, six, and Christina, five.

"I call home every day," he said, "sometimes two or three times a day. If I'm away fifteen minutes my wife Barbara thinks something has happened."

I asked Cooper if his present wife is a Californian.

"She's from New York," he said. "She's a native-born New Yorker, one of the few. She was twenty-seven years old when we met and had a job in an advertising agency. Very successful. She used to say, 'I'm not going to get married just because everybody else is. When I feel it, I'll say yes, and when I feel it, he'll feel it.' . . . We've been married nine and a half years. It took a long time, but now I've got some continuity in my life."

After a second drink I excused myself.

"I thought maybe we could have a little dinner," said Cooper.

I said that I would like to but that I had a dinner engagement of long standing.

He seemed disappointed.

"Well," he said, "I'm pretty bushed. Like last night. I got in, had a couple slugs and some dinner, called home, looked at the tube for a while, and went to bed. That's what I'll do tonight, I guess."

"I'll see you tomorrow afternoon."

"We've got bags of time to have dinner together," said Cooper, "bags of it. . . . You're going to get some continuity in your life out of this. That's what everybody needs, continuity."

When I got to the door of the bar I looked back.

Cooper was signing the check and smiling. The smile was like the one I remembered from *The Champ*, an indefinite smile, a smile that didn't seem quite sure whether its wearer should expect a kick or an embrace.

Two middle-aged men were staring at Cooper glassily.

"Jackie Coogan," said one. "Remember him in *The Kid?*"

That evening I had dinner with Evan Rhodes, who during the untenable times that followed was a patient—sometimes —Sancho Panza to my always gallant Quixote.

We ate at the Derby, a village steak house where Evan has a charge account.

I told him about Cooper, about his father, the drunks at the Pierre, and the fact that for an actor I found Cooper unobjectionable.

Evan was not enthusiastic, but then that morning his novel had been rejected for the four hundred and thirty-second time.

"Cooper was the greatest child actor of his day, perhaps any day," I said after my third brandy. "As a matter of fact, when Jackie Cooper cried in the jail scene in *The Champ*, I cried my heart out."

"I did not shed a single tear," Evan said. "It couldn't compare with Louise Beaver's death scene in *Imitation of Life*. And when Ferdie Washington threw herself on the coffin— that's what *I* call crying."

"But now you're talking about the classics. Even Rochelle Hudson . . . Still, you must admit that Cooper was great in *Treasure Island*."

"Sure, but what has he done since *Treasure Island*?"

"What has Robert Louis Stevenson done since *Treasure Is-*

land? Cooper's a very respected man in television," I said. "And he is many times over a millionaire . . ."

"My television set has been broken for the last ten years or so," said Evan. "I wonder if you would mind filling me in on . . ."

"Well, in *The People's Choice* he was a town councilman who had a heart of pure gold and he lived in this trailer and had this talking dog, Cleo, and he used to discuss the political problems of the day with Cleo, and she . . ."

There was something unsympathetic in Evan's look; so I said, "In *Hennesey,* which has won all sorts of awards, Cooper played a Navy doctor who claims that he graduated at the foot of his class, but despite the fact that some people mistake him for Dr. Kronkite, he always comes out on top. . . ."

I could see that I was getting nowhere; so I said, "Look, suppose your father had run off when you were two years old . . ."

Evan said, "There's a scene in the movie *Moulin Rouge* in which Toulouse-Lautrec and Zsa Zsa Gabor are driving in a carriage on the banks of the Seine. Suddenly they come upon a drunken harridan lying, face down, in the gutter, an empty gin bottle clutched in one grimy claw. Lautrec stops the carriage, climbs down, and goes to where the hag is lying.

"He at once recognizes that the poor wreck is La Goulue, who only a few short years before had been the toast of all of Paris. Lautrec is shocked; he stoops beside the woman, which in his case takes very little effort.

"Zsa Zsa is anxious to get to P. J. Clarke's or wherever they're going. She leans out of the cab and shouts, 'How about shaking a leg, Tulley?'

"Lautrec turns to her in dismay, 'But, Zsa Zsa, have you no heart? This outcast is La Goulue, once the toast of all of Paris. We cannot blame her for what she has become. Her mother was a whore. Her two brothers suffered from unmentionable diseases. Her uncle was a rapist, her aunt an ax murderess, and her father was a drunk.'

" 'Whose father wasn't?' shouts Zsa Zsa. 'Let's get a move on.' "

"Besides," I said, "Jackie Cooper is awfully glad that they were lucky enough to get a writer of *my* caliber . . ."

"We will now listen to an interlude of gypsy violin music," said Evan.

The next morning I called John White in Las Cruces and told him that Cooper and I were flying to El Paso—the nearest major airport—and would be there early in the evening.

"Should I tell the newspapers?" asked John.

"I wouldn't. We're going to be very busy. Would you make the reservation for us at a motel?"

"I'll make the reservation in your name," said John.

Cooper and I were driven to the airport in a chauffeured Rolls-Royce limousine, a way of traveling that is quite easy to get used to.

Between June and mid-November I made seven jet flights from one coast to the other, five during a twenty-one-day period. Six times I was met at the airport by a chauffeur.

The seventh and last time I got back to Idlewild at two in the morning. No chauffeur, no limousine.

I turned to the porter who was managing my portable typewriter and the brand-new Mark Cross bag, dinosaur leather with gold and diamond fittings.

"*How* am I going to get to the St. Regis?" I asked. (You see, by this time I had abandoned the Gorham and had become the kind of man who mentions what hotel he is staying at.)

"You could take a taxi," said the porter.

"Do you mean *I* am supposed to go to New York at this hour of the morning in a *taxi?*" shouted a mountebank who sounded suspiciously like me.

"Well, you could walk," said the porter.

That first afternoon, however, I threw a few pennies and some crumbs of stale angel food to the bowing peasants on the sidewalks and to the wretches forced by circumstances to drive their own Cadillacs.

On the jet Cooper's seat was the first on the right as you enter the plane, next to the window; my seat was on the aisle.

As a result Cooper was served the first drink and the first dinner, and the stewardesses, matronly-looking women chosen, I presume, for their competence, treated Cooper with the deference that is reserved for those whose names are Household Words.

Cooper spent most of the time reading the afternoon newspapers.

He did tell me one thing that I found fascinating. He said that in all the memories of his youth he saw himself through the eye of a camera.

"I guess that's one reason I'm a good film editor," he said.

"I remember one day in the little schoolroom at M.G.M. I can see the teacher, and I can see myself and the placement of the desks, everything, and I can hear the teacher's voice saying, 'Someday China is going to be a very rich and dangerous power.' That was long before China turned Communist or anything like that, and it's odd that I remember it. But I see it all just as clear as if it happened yesterday."

John White, who was waiting at the El Paso airport, drove us to Las Cruces.

John is a gentle, friendly man, and the three of us were on a first-name basis from the first few minutes on.

"Merle has told us about what you fellows have in mind," he said. "We're all excited. This could be very important, and there just isn't *anything* like it on television."

Cooper asked John if he were a native of New Mexico, and John said, "No, I was born in Cleveland. I came here in 1944 —just for a little bit—and I'm still here. I get back to Cleveland every once in a while, and when I see the pace people go through *there*—well, maybe we get a little lazy around here, but maybe we live longer."

It was dark by that time, and there were great stretches of unoccupied land on either side of the highway. In the distance was the black shadow of the Organ Mountains.

"Cotton's a big product around here," said John, "and pecans; we grow a lot of pecans; there's one fellow makes maybe a quarter of a million dollars a year just from his pecans alone. And chili peppers; we've got a lot of Spanish-Americans. They don't like to be called Mexicans. . . . Agriculture used to be the biggest industry before White Sands Missile Range came along."

On the outskirts of Las Cruces were huge billboards, "40,-000 Friendly People Welcome You to Las Cruces, the Home of New Mexico State University."

"We're growing fast," said John. "This county, Doña Ana County, they made a survey, the birth rate is the highest in the world outside of a few places in India, and we've got more Ph.D.s in New Mexico than in any other state in the Union. That's because of places like White Sands and Los Alamos."

The streets of Las Cruces were almost deserted.

"Not much goes on here in the evening during the week," said John. "You fellows like something to eat?"

We said we would, and John took us to a short-order place on the main street. A few cowboys sat at the counter, having coffee, and two Spanish-American boys were drinking Cokes and playing the juke box.

We ordered sandwiches and coffee, and John said, "We've got a lot of characters around here. You hear about that old man, John Prather?"

We hadn't, and John said, "He came here in 1884, I think

it was, just a kid, with his brother and his father, and they homesteaded it on a cattle ranch. Old John Prather's been here ever since, lives out on his ranch with his housekeeper. Independent as a hog on ice. . . . When they came along and started buying up land for White Sands, old John wouldn't sell. His place was right square where they were going to have the target area, and they did everything to get him off the place. Buzzed his house and sent the thing to the courts and all the way up to the high mucky-mucks in the Defense Department in Washington, but he wouldn't budge. He just sat there on his front porch with a gun in his lap and said he'd shoot the first man that tried to get him off his ranch, didn't care who it was. He said, 'This is my home, and I'm going to stay, and nobody's going to make me move.'

"There was a lot of hemming and hawing and all kinds of stories in the papers, but, finally, the government backed down, and people came down here all the way from Washington to shake his hand. He was right, and, eventually, everybody realized it. They're writing a book about him, maybe two books I hear, and there's a song. Even made up a song about him."

"Is he still there?" I asked.

"Still there," said John, "and my guess is he will be until they carry him out feet first."

John had made a reservation for Cooper and me at the Mission Inn Motel, which has large, pleasantly furnished rooms, a swimming pool, an excellent coffee shop and restaurant.

We checked in, and John said he'd pick us up the next morning at around nine.

"Everybody at the university is looking forward to meeting you," he said, "the president, the dean. Everybody. You just say the word, whatever you want, and you'll get it. A thing like this could be very important to us."

I asked Cooper in for a nightcap, but he was tired and said good night.

After he left I had several drinks and wrote in the journal for more than an hour.

I put down everything John White had said about Prather.

> This is *really* what the series is all about [I wrote]. You *can* fight city hall; in this case, not only city hall but the U. S. Government, and you can win because you're *right*. . . . In the story I'd like to write the old man would suddenly find the whole community against him. He'd be a pariah because the Army would threaten to move the base some place else unless the gave in. And the people in the county would be terrified. Look at all the money they'd lose. No new shopping center, no new housing development. The antagonist stands to lose a lot of money if the base isn't built. . . .
>
> The only person who understands the *issue* at stake is the county agent. He says, "No, by God, this man is protecting the most basic right of all. . . . A man's home is his castle. . . ." And he and the old man *win*. . . .
>
> I don't know how the Berbers would work in, but I'll let Bob Aurthur thrash that out with Dorso.
>
> I like this one much better than the drift wind idea.

I had left a call for seven-thirty, and shortly thereafter a cheerful Spanish-American waitress arrived with a good-sized pot of hot coffee.

After a cup of coffee, I went to the night table where I was sure I had left the two bridges that cover two large chasms in my front teeth.

The upper bridge was there, but the lower was not.

Could I have left it under the bed?

I rolled the bed into the middle of the room. No lower bridge. I looked under my pillow. Not even a nickel.

I looked on every table. No bridge. I crawled on my hands and knees from one corner of the bedroom to the other. No bridge. I ran my right hand over the window sills. No bridge.

There was no bridge in the bathroom.

By that time I was in a state of panic. I looked in the pockets of the shirt, the slacks, and the sports jacket I had worn the day before. Nope. I searched through the pockets of my trench coat. Huh-uh.

The telephone rang. I was to have met Cooper in the coffee shop at eight; it was then eight-fifteen.

I picked up the phone, praying I wouldn't lisp.

"You up, old buddy?" asked Cooper.

"Thort of."

"You all right?"

"I feel thwell."

"You sound funny."

"Oh no. I'm thimply great."

"John is picking us up at a quarter of nine."

"I'll be there in a few minuteth."

I shaved, cutting myself twice; I showered, trembling under the tepid water.

I dressed and then made one final, frantic search for the bridge. It was unsuccessful.

"Merle," I said to myself, "is this your death wish again?"

I hurried to the front desk. The cordial woman behind the desk smiled broadly. I didn't dare smile back.

I said, "How thoon doeth the maid get here?"

"Not until nine."

"I've got an emergenthy," I said. "I loth a bridge in my room."

The woman had the grace not to smile.

"Ith very embarrathing."

"The housekeeper will look for it. I'll help her. You go in and have some breakfast."

"You sure you're all right, pal?" asked Cooper. "You look pale."

I nodded vaguely.

Cooper read his copy of the El Paso paper and I pretended to read mine.

When the waitress came up to the table, I said, "Only coffee." . . . No *s*.

"That all?" she asked.

"Not hungry."

John White arrived a few minutes later.

"You look pale, Merle. You sleep well?"

"Like a log."

Cooper signed the check, and we went outside.

The housekeeper, a dignified Spanish-American woman, came up to me.

"Could I speak to you for a moment?" she asked.

She was smiling, and in her right hand was a tiny package wrapped in tissue paper.

Cooper and John White walked ahead, and the woman handed me the package.

"It was on the typewriting machine," she said.

I slipped the bridge into place and then with a fully bridged smile tried to give her a ten-dollar bill.

She shook her head.

"I am happy that I could help," she said.

Still smiling I walked up to Cooper and John White.

"You look a hundred per cent better," said Cooper.

The university campus was crowded with pretty girls who looked at if they had been 4-H Club beauty queens and ruddy-faced young men wearing levis, sport shirts, and Stetsons. The rowdy ones are called *stomps,* a name given to the often disorderly cowboy dances held, usually on Saturday nights, in the area.

We met the president of the university, Roger B. Corbett, who told us how to produce a television series and delivered part of a lecture on the incompetence of Russian farmers that, I felt sure, had been used at one or two fund-raising dinners. He also spoke of the insidious influence of the federal government and other familiar subjects.

We spent more than an hour with Dean Philip J. Leyendecker, head of argiculture and home economics and director of the Extension Service.

In the latter capacity Dean Leyendecker is responsible for placing most of the county agents in the state in their jobs.

The dean is a quiet, articulate man who talked with enthusiasm about the manner of men attracted to county agent work.

In New Mexico, he said, many of the agents are bilingual, and a number speak three languages, English, Spanish, and, say, Navaho.

The men who become county agents are likely to have the

highest I.Q.'s in their class, he said, and they are all disciplined workers.

All agents, he went on, seem to have three things in common—a love of people, a love of the soil, and a disinterest in time clocks.

Dean Leyendecker also talked about home agents.

"Their job," he said, "is to teach 4-H Club girls and very often their mothers how to garden, how to cook and what to cook, how to sew, keep house, and dress. How to be a woman. You might say—we have said—that the home agent is one third glamor girl, one third walking encyclopedia, and one third pack horse."

The series took a step forward right then.

In New York Bob had suggested that the Stanwyck role in the series, if we got Stanwyck, might be as a lady rancher.

"She's a man-killer," said Bob, "but Cooper likes her and goes to her for advice."

There was no question that Stanwyck was a competent actress, but she had played the role Bob described a few times before, and so has just about every other actress in Hollywood who got past her fortieth birthday, which is a difficult thing for an actress to do.

Stanwyck as a home agent; that was something else again.

A glamor girl? No problem. Who could forget her as the stripper in *Ball of Fire,* or in *Double Indemnity* when she wore a long blonde wig and a short bath towel?

A walking encyclopedia? I'd read in a publicity release, "Miss Stanwyck is interested in serious things . . . her record collection is one of the largest in Hollywood . . . rock 'n' roll to Bach. She reads constantly and rapidly. Thirty books a month is not unusual."

One third pack horse? The same publicity release said that in 1954 she had been adopted by the Blackfeet tribe, inducted as a member of their Brave Dog Society and given the tribe's most revered name, Princess Many Victories, III.

". . . She rides, she shoots . . . She has bathed in the

waters from our glaciers. . . . She has done very hard work
. . . rare for a white woman. To be a member of our Brave
Dog Society is to be known as one of our Brave People. Princess Many Victories, III is one of us."

It sounded as if Stanwyck would be a natural in the role
of the home agent.

The dean promised us complete cooperation, and as he
shook hands he said, "We are delighted with the whole idea;
all of us around here are. And it's not just that county agents
are something we know about. Well, of course, we don't
know your business, Jack—but much of what we see on television—and I don't mean *Hennesey*, just doesn't seem real to
us."

"The next time I come to Las Cruces I'll bring you a blueberry pie," I said.

The dean got his Ph.D. at Iowa State College, which is only
thirty miles from Marshalltown, and we had earlier talked
about a restaurant in Marshalltown, Stone's.

As my mother has said more than once, "People have been
known to drive all the way from Moline, Illinois, just for a
piece of Mrs. Stone's world-famous fried chicken and blueberry pie."

Mrs. Stone is dead, but the blueberry pie at Stone's is still
pretty fair, and blueberry pie is what we fought the Second
World War about.

"All we hope is that you present a true picture," said the
dean.

I thought of what Dean Leyendecker had said quite often
later.

That afternoon John drove us to Deming, about forty miles west of Las Cruces.

Although the yucca was in bloom, tens of thousands of white blossoms as far as the eye could see, the countryside looked bleak. There were occasional herds of cattle feeding on sparse outcroppings of grass or huddled near watering spots.

Deming itself is without much grace; it has the harsh air of the Texas panhandle, and the softening influence of those from below the border seems non-existent.

The office of the county agent, Leonard Appleton, is in the courthouse, a dark, unlovely building with the smell of disinfectant, urine, and stale air. The sign outside Appleton's door said, "County Extension Service. New Mexico State University and United States Department of Agriculture. Agriculture—Home Economics—4-H clubs."

The office was small and businesslike without an inch of unused space. Appleton—everybody calls him Ap—sat behind a scarred desk, and his secretary sat behind another. Luna County is not rich. Ap has no assistant, and there is no home agent.

I asked Ap a great many questions, and at the same time Cooper made notes on his dress—khaki pants, sport shirt, rubber-soled shoes, fishing hat. Ap drove a 1956 Ford pickup.

Ap had, he said, been a farmer before he became a county agent.

"I prefer farming, but I just couldn't seem to make it. I like this work, too. I like working with people, and I must say I never run out of things to do. We're expected to go to a lot of meetings, all the service clubs, Kiwanis, Rotary, Lions. And the Farm Bureau. All of those. I could go to a meeting, a different meeting, three times a night if I wanted to. . . . Officially, I work a forty-hour week, but it's likely to run up to around eighty most of the time. . . .

"In a sense I'm a scientist, but I don't spend much time in the laboratory. What I do is pass on to the farmer what the laboratory scientists have discovered, in the Department [U.S.D.A. in Beltsville, Maryland, where the U.S.D.A. Experimental Farmers are located], and down at the university. . . ."

Ap has a Bachelor of Science degree in farm management and a Master of Science in soils.

I asked if there was much resistance on the part of farmers to using new techniques.

"The younger the farmer is and the better educated the more anxious he is to learn. . . . But I try never to hurry things, and I'm not inclined to rub anybody the wrong way. It's our function to be helpful."

Ap spoke with great enthusiasm about the 4-H Clubs. At that time there were five clubs in the county with a combined membership of 133 members, aged ten to seventeen.

Early the next month Ap and several parents were taking thirty-five 4-H Club members from Luna County to a camp in the Sacramento Mountains not far off.

Because of President Kennedy's physical fitness program, which had been announced a little earlier, the emphasis at the camp was to be on physical fitness.

"Our main job is to keep the kids busy from five-thirty in the morning until ten-thirty at night, and that takes some doing," said Ap. ". . . There are never any juvenile delinquents in 4-H Clubs. If somebody wants to become a member, he comes to us; we never go to them, and that makes a difference. . . ."

I made a note that the 4-H Club camps had to be the basis for a future script.

Later the four of us—Ap, John White, Cooper, and I—went for a drive in and around the town.

Of the 1,800,000 acres of land in Luna County only 36,000 are irrigated, most of them around Deming. The irrigated land looked rich and fertile and was green with tender plants of cotton, the principal crop of the area.

We stopped at the farm of Grover Xavier McSherry. Xav is an enthusiastic, big-boned young man with a ruddy face, light blue eyes, and thinning blond hair.

His fondness for Ap was immediately apparent.

"We turn all our problems over to him," said Xav. "He's our brains."

As we walked around Xav's bountiful 400 acres of land and inspected his barns and other outbuildings I remembered something my grandfather, who had farmed 640 acres of land near Montour, Iowa, once said, "You don't have to look at a man's crops to know whether he's a good farmer. All you have to see is how well he takes care of his equipment."

My grandfather never had a tractor, but Xav had six, all polished and under lean-tos. All his machinery was in good shape; the barn was large and clean; there was a neat-looking shack in which Xav's workers—most of them from Mexico—were housed, and Xav's own house, which was not impressive.

That much hadn't changed. It was the same when I was a boy. The house was always the most modest building on the farm. No profit in it.

Xav had a $250,000 operation, which placed him economically among the upper five per cent of farmers in the county.

"I specialize in the three *c*'s," he said, "cotton, cattle, and children."

He had seven children, a herd of fifty cows, and more than 300 acres of cotton.

Xav seemed by nature to be a cheerful man, although that day he had discovered a blight of some kind in one field of cotton. Ap promised to return the next day and make tests to find out what it was.

In addition to the cotton blight three of Xav's Herefords had pneumonia, and, "All of a sudden dwarfism has stuck its sneaky old nose up with some of the new calves."

Ap thought the latter might be the result of too much inbreeding in the herd; he said he'd get in touch with some of the animal husbandry people at the university and try to find out what was known about dwarfism and what caused it.

I mentioned Xav's seeming cheerfulness in the face of these combined disasters.

"I leave the worrying to Ap," he said. "If *I* ever started worrying I'd sell this place and get a job in town. I don't have the time to worry, too busy with the three *c*'s."

On the way back to his office I asked Ap about the weather in the area.

"We have a hot, dry summer," he said, "a beautiful fall, a mild winter, and a boisterous spring."

I didn't know what it was going to be about, but someday I was going to write a script for the series called *A Boisterous Spring*. It would be a comedy.

That night Cooper and I had several drinks before dinner, and it was an enthusiastic evening.

We both liked the people we had met; we spoke of Ap's dedication, of Xav's optimism, of Dean Leyendecker's promise of cooperation, of John White's enthusiasm for the series, and of its assured success.

"This is going to make something like *The Defenders* look sick," said Cooper. "It'll run for five years at least."

I tried multiplying $1000 a week by thirty-nine weeks and thirty-nine weeks by five years but got lost somewhere around the twentieth week.

The next morning I woke up early, and after a Spanish-American boy brought my coffee, I sat by the window for a while.

It was an immaculate day with cool, freshly laundered air. The pale sky was crowded with great piles of cumulus clouds, and in the distance were beige and moss-green outcroppings of lunarlike rock formations.

In the courtyard two maids and the boy who had brought the coffee were laughing and speaking quiet Spanish. I was beginning to understand how the Conquistadores must have felt when four centuries ago they first looked on this beautiful valley.

Later in the morning John White drove Cooper and me to Mesilla, which is two miles from Las Cruces.

On the way he pointed to a drab graveyard and said, "That's where Pat Garrett's buried. He's the sheriff that finally shot down Billy the Kid."

"Boot Hill?" I asked.

"The Masonic Cemetery," said John.

Mesilla is a dusty relic of a village that was briefly the capital of a territory taking in all of lower New Mexico.

After a desultory border war between the United States and Mexico, Franklin Pierce, not the most memorable of our

Presidents, sent James Gadsden, a retired Indian fighter who had made himself a dubious fortune, to Mexico to negotiate the Gadsden Purchase. The cost was $10,000,000, and the village of Mesilla was included, although it had been built by Mexicans who had made it clear that they did not want to live in the United States.

The U.S. infantry arrived in the plaza of Mesilla on July 4, 1855 and according to Paul Horgan, an old friend who has written a beautiful and monumental history of the Rio Grande, the Army band played "Hail Columbia," "Yankee Doodle," and "The Star-Spangled Banner." No Mexican music was played, but the Anglo—North American—governor of the territory made a long speech, all of which was translated into Spanish.

Apparently most of the Mexicans were unhappy at what was going on, but since this is a free country, they were given a choice. Either they could sign a loyalty oath to the United States, which most of them did. Or, according to a young soldier who was on hand that historic day, "they were notified to leave and take refuge in Mexican dominions."

Horgan quotes the soldier as saying, "This was the best Fourth of July since I have been in the Army. . . ."

Mesilla claims that Billy was tried there—twice, that the Emperor Maximilian sought refuge there rather than face the firing squad, and that the Apache chief Geronimo hid out in a cave north of town to escape the pursuing U.S. cavalry.

There is little evidence to back up any of these claims; nevertheless, on the day in June when Cooper and I first went to Mesilla, it was pleasant enough. The plaza was framed with cottonwood and willow trees in full leaf; there was a small bandstand, and the benches were filled with men and women, most of them Spanish-American, who were in no hurry to go any place.

Most of the buildings facing the square are fake adobe. There is a fat little church, San Albino, neo-Spanish in design, and in the southeast corner the Billy the Kid bar and the La

Posta restaurant. The gift shops are self-conscious, but the Mesilla Design and Book Center is one of the best bookstores in the Southwest.

John took Cooper and me to meet the proprietor, Betty Bowen, an energetic woman of great charm who, although she has spent most of her life in the Middle West and New York, has a Southwestern openness and natural hospitality.

Her store and the living quarters in back are real adobe and very beautiful. Horgan calls the style "Rio Grande Palladian. . . . The line of inheritance was clear through centuries from Rome to Spain, to Mexico, and up to the Rio Grande. Spirit moved. It survived, as it always does survive materials."

I mentioned to Mrs. Bowen—under the circumstances quite casually, I thought—that my new novel, *A Day in Late September,* was to be published in the early fall, possibly about the same time we filmed—if we did film—the pilot in the area of Las Cruces and Mesilla.

Mrs. Bowen said that if the latter should happen she wanted to give an autographing party.

"Could I come?" asked Cooper.

Mrs. Bowen said he *must* come.

In a burst of uneconomic enthusiasm I then picked out $36.84 worth of books about the Southwest, "for research."

Cooper insisted on paying for the books.

"It'll go on the old expense account," he said. "Besides, not many writers I know can *read.*"

Don Chappell is a tall blond man in his early thirties, and his office is brighter and larger than Ap's. Doña Ana County, of which he is agent, is one of the most prosperous in the state. One 4000-acre farm has an annual gross income of $6,000,000, and of the 800 farmers in the county, 250 are college graduates. Six are Ph.D.s.

On one wall of his office Don had a framed quotation written by Thomas Jefferson; "I know of no safe repository of the ultimate powers of society but the people themselves, and if we think them not enlightened enough to exercise their control with a wholesome discretion, the remedy is not to take it from them but to inform their discretion by education."

I asked Don to send me a copy of that quotation, which he did, and later when I wrote eighty-three pages of notes about county agents, about the Southwest, and about the characters who were to be involved in the series, I included the quotation.

I feel sure *somebody* must have read it.

Don Chappell, Cooper, and I talked for hours about county agents and the kind of people they deal with.

We then had the $1.50 buffet at the Mission Inn, after which Don drove us to several ranches.

The last stop was at the ranch of Arthur Alvillar and his family.

Arthur had been born in the Chihuahua Province of Mexico, had come across the Rio Grande as a laborer, and now —"Thanks to Don here"—owned his own ranch. It wasn't as large or as prosperous-looking as Xav McSherry's, but the equipment was equally well taken care of; the livestock was healthy; the cotton crop and the pecan trees were flourishing, and Arthur made a good living for himself, his wife, and his three sons, Arthur, Jr., David, and Raul.

After we finished looking at the farm, Mrs. Alvillar insisted that we come in for coffee and cookies, which we did.

Arthur, Jr., talked about the trip that his father, Don Chappell, and he had made the year before to the National 4-H Club Congress in Cleveland.

"I had never flown before," said Arthur, Sr., "but Don went, and so I wasn't—upset."

At the congress Arthur, Jr., won second place in the national tractor-driving contest.

"He would have won first prize," said Don, "but there's a kid from Connecticut who keeps winning it. Third year in a row, I think. Raul is going to the congress next year."

"And I'll win first prize," said Raul, "naturally."

Raul is twelve; Arthur, Jr., is eighteen. David was not at home that afternoon.

Mrs. Alvillar went to the sideboard and took out all the ribbons, the plaques, and the cups that her two sons had won in various 4-H Club competitions.

"We owe much to Don here," said Mrs. Alvillar.

Late that afternoon Don drove Cooper and me to the El Paso airport in his Volkswagen station wagon. His wife, two sons, and a neighbor boy went along for the ride and to watch Hennesey.

"Why did you become a county agent?" I asked Don.

"Well, I'll tell you, when I got out of the Navy—I'd been overseas, the Pacific and the Atlantic, a long time—when I got out I figured there were only about two ways to make a million dollars quick. One was to be born with it, and the other was to be a county agent."

At the airport Cooper carried my excess baggage; by this time it had increased by a few hundred pounds—the books I had found in Mesilla, all of the pamphlets issued by the U.S.D.A. from 1896 on, an accumulation of genuine Navaho blankets cleverly stamped *Made in Japan,* Spanish chests dating back to the days of the Conquistadores and several cartons of pre-Mayan pottery that an antique dealer had kept hidden in a dusty back room until the right person came along.

As Cooper and I hurried toward the runway two elderly women whose faces were stamped with "mother love" and "grandmother love" confronted him.

One of them said, "I look at *Hennesey* every week. It's our favorite program and the whole family comes in to watch and I remember you in *Peck's Bad Boy.*" She asked for an autograph.

"I'm sorry, dear," said Cooper, "but my hands are full."

He walked on, and the woman shouted after him, "I'll never look at Dr. Hennesey again as long as I live."

On the plane to Los Angeles I said, "They think they own you, don't they?"

"In a way, I suppose," said Cooper. "But I think she was embarrassed to be turned down in front of her friend."

Just before the plane reached Los Angeles a man who had had more than American Airlines' two free drinks stooped in front of our seats, glared at Cooper and said, "I like Dr. Kildare."

I had gone to Los Angeles primarily to attend a meeting at
Television City the following Monday. James T. Aubrey, Jr.,
was, as I understood it, to play the double role of presiding
judge and executioner.

As the chauffeur drove us from the airport to Beverly Hills
I said to Cooper, "Just what is the purpose of this trial on
Monday?"

"Jim's going to want a sort of progress report on how everything's going," said Cooper.

"In other words he won't accept a plea of guilty of sorcery
in the first degree."

"You just write up all the wonderful things we found out
in New Mexico and all your wonderful ideas, and he'll love
it," said Cooper.

"From all I have heard he is not much of a judge of literature, which is easy enough to understand because I have
read that he wanted to be a writer himself once and didn't
make it, and so he has become a *critic*. And as Gautier so ac-
curately said of critics, 'They are like eunuchs in a harem.
They see the trick done every night and are *furious* that they
can't do it themselves.'"

"He just wants to know where we're going," said Cooper.
"It's nothing to worry about."

My room at the Beverly Hills Hotel was a little larger than the tennis court and almost as comfortable.

I had the blue-plate special in my room, tongue of larkspur with all the trimmings, a half bottle of burgundy willed by the last Pope Gregory to his successor, the late Louis B. Mayer, and a tot of brandy smuggled from the cellar of Louella XVI.

The phalanx of waiters treated me with a deference indicating that they recognized me as the Lost Dauphin and knew that Jackie Cooper Productions, Inc., was picking up the tab.

I swirled a little Courvoisier in the crystal snifter and said to my patient companion, the air-conditioning unit, "Discard those hostile thoughts about Southern California. Remember two hundred people arrive here every day to stay. Are they crazy or are you? . . .

"Remember what my Finnish neighbor Lydia Rahlson has said, 'The yoo-hoo you yoo-hoo into the forest is the yoo-hoo you get back.' Your trouble is you haven't been yoo-hooing nice; you haven't given sunny Southern California a chance. Put out of your mind the fact that Fred Allen said, 'California is a great place to live. If you're an orange.' Fred Allen has gone on to his reward, and you haven't got yours yet, and keep in mind what your old Mums, Dora, is always telling you, 'The Lord helps them that help themselves.' This is the world capital of themselves-helpers; start getting yours while the getting's good. You are no longer Louis Loser; you are Wellington Winner. . . . From here on in let the underdogs shift for themselves. What have the underdogs done for you lately? You are right square in the middle of Upperdogsville, and this time it is going to be different. This time they'll teach you the fraternity handshake."

It was then that, as has happened before during the brandy course, several Little Voices spoke to me.

"Surely you are joking," they said.

"I have never been more serious in my life," I said, plagiarizing a line from my most recent screen play. "All I have to do is stay here this one week, see, seven days and seven nights, and it will seem like no more than seven or eight years or thereabouts, and then I will be allowed to go back to New York, where I will write this one script, which will only take about thirty minutes, after which all I have to do is lean back in my Tycoon's Chair, which I am going to keep in my Finnish sauna, near my swimming pool, and I will yoo-hoo un-hostile words into the forest while they send the checks directly to the bank. . . ."

"Remember what La Rochefoucauld said," the Little Voices replied. " 'The true way to be deceived is to think oneself cleverer than others.' "

"Oh shut up," I said.

"You yourself said," said the Little Voices, 'Little Voices sometimes speak to you, and when they do, *always* listen because the Little Voices are *always* right.' "

"Nobody is *always* right," I said.

"James T. Aubrey is," said the Little Voices, and then they began humming to the tune of "The Volga Boatman," "James T. Au-brey, James T. Au-brey."

16 *You've got to tell them where the bathroom is*

The next morning I slipped on my smog mask, forced a mint-fresh century note into the contemptuous hand of the hotel doorman—and he finally managed to get me a cab driven by the late Ben Turpin.

Jackie Cooper Productions is on the lot where they used to make Republic Pictures, many of which starred Vera Hruba Ralston, who coincidentally was married to the head of Republic Pictures.

For some reason Republic is now out of business, and the lot has been taken over by C.B.S., Four Star Television, and numerous independent companies like Cooper's.

Rawhide is filmed there, along with other C.B.S. Westerns, and the place teems with individuals got up in cowboy costumes and with Jaguars equipped with tape-recording machines, telephones, hi-fi, and full-length mirrors.

Cooper's offices were not ostentatious, and neither were his two secretaries. One of them, Dorothy Fisher, spent the day taking dictation on my notes on the trip to New Mexico.

I did not finish, but Mrs. Fisher said that when I did, Cooper would want the notes mimeographed to give to various people.

"When we do mimeo them," she said, "what color do you want the cover to be?"

I said that I had no preference.

"You don't?" she said. "Well, you're the first writer I've ever worked for that didn't insist on a certain color. I guess they're superstitious."

The first *County Agent Notes,* twenty-nine pages of them, had a brown cover, and then there were *Further County Agent Notes,* gray, *Still Further County Agent Notes,* lilac, and *Final County Agent Notes,* puce; 83 pages altogether, outlining enough story ideas to keep the series running for a decade or so, enough about county agents to get me an M.S. in agriculture, enough about New Mexico to get a Good Citizenship award, and enough about the mythical town and county and the characters to please all the actors.

Eventually all these notes were mimeographed and put together in a tan folder.

Not only that, they turned out to be so much in demand that a second edition was mimeographed; the cover of that one was green.

After dictating the first ten pages of notes to Dorothy Fisher, I went back to the hotel, and slept straight through until noon Sunday. I relaxed—but not much—with some friends in a middle-class housing development called Bel Air, but my mind was on Judge Aubrey.

Court would open the next afternoon at three.

Monday morning I got up at five and by nine had finished the notes.

Dorothy Fisher came to the hotel a few minutes later, somewhat flustered because she had mislaid her contact lenses.

Nevertheless, she said she would have everything typed in a couple of hours, which she did.

Cooper and I had lunch at the hotel, and while we ate, he read the notes, looking up every once in a while to smile encouragingly.

When he finished he said, "They're just beautiful, Merle. You certainly have the knack of being able to think on the typewriter. Everyone is going to be excited by these."

He thought a moment, then said, "I'll tell you what let's

do. Let's read the notes to them. We'll just take these two copies, and I'll tell them if they've got any comments or suggestions they should hold off until we've finished. Otherwise, they'll be interrupting us every two minutes."

"I've heard Aubrey doesn't like people over forty," I said.

"He's going to love these beautiful notes you've written," said Cooper.

Dick Dorso had flown in from New York and was in the office of Hunt Stromberg, Jr., when Cooper and I got to Television City, a Los Angeles Provincial Modern kind of building.

"Jim is on his way," said Stromberg, somewhat uncertainly, as if he weren't sure whether he was announcing good news or bad.

Stromberg is a chubby, soft-spoken man whose father is a movie producer responsible for a series-type succession of feature films in the late 1920s and early '30s, *Our Modern Maidens, Our Dancing Daughters,* and *Our Blushing Brides.*

Cooper, Dorso, Stromberg, and I talked about this and that; Stromberg kept saying he was a great admirer of mine, but he never got around to saying why, possibly because we were all eying the door, pretending we weren't.

When the door did open, it was only a vice-president, Robert Lewine.

Those who indulge themselves in vice-president-watching —which can be as relaxing and edifying as birdwatching— will want to note that Lewine was at that time West Coast Vice-President of the network; Stromberg was then the West Coast Vice-President in Charge of Program Development, not to be confused with Larry White, who is Director of Program Development.

For reasons that surely wouldn't interest anybody but another vice-president or a vice-president-watcher Lewine's job was considered more important than Stromberg's.

"Jim ought to be here any minute," said Lewine, and Stromberg said, "Yes, Jim is on his way."

Dorso said, "Jack says he and Merle had a wonderful trip, and Jim is going to be very pleased."

Cooper said, "Jim is going to love Merle's beautiful notes, and it's too bad Jim and all of you couldn't have met all the wonderful people Merle and I met."

I said nothing, wishing I were back in the glass house, throwing stones or up, eating worms, or dead.

Aubrey stood just inside the door for a moment, his ice-blue eyes fixed on some distant object.

Cooper introduced us.

Aubrey has a hearty, disinterested handshake, and he carries himself with the air of a man used to authority and a lot of push-ups.

I was reminded then and throughout our brief encounter of the Muscular Clergymen who used to appear so prominently in so many late eighteenth- and early nineteenth-century novels.

It was easy to imagine Aubrey delivering one of those hell-fire and brimstone sermons that used to be so popular on Sunday mornings, before ministers turned therapists.

Dorso said, "Jack and Merle Miller here have been down in New Mexico, Jim, doing some research."

Aubrey received this information without comment or show of emotion.

"We had a wonderful, wonderful trip, Jim," said Cooper.

"We've been talking about their wonderful trip," said Stromberg.

"Everything is falling into place, Jim," said Dorso.

Aubrey lowered his muscular body into a regulation leather chair; he placed his highly polished black shoes on top of a low table.

Cooper said, "Merle has written some beautiful notes on our trip; we learned so much, and Merle has written it so beautifully. We're going to read it, and if anybody has any questions we think it would be best if you just jotted them down and we'll discuss them when we've finished reading."

Everybody except Aubrey nodded a lot at this enlightening information.

After a moment, Cooper started reading, " 'The county agent is actually a faculty member of the state university. . . . In many counties, particularly in the south of New Mexico, the word 'Mexican' is an epithet like 'nigger' in other parts of the South. In general, there is never any racial discrimination against Spanish-Americans except near the Texas border where in some towns there are signs saying, 'No Mexican in town after dark.' "

Cooper read well and with enthusiasm; Aubrey reacted not at all in the beginning, but after a while what might, I suppose, have been construed as a smile lingered briefly near his lips, and once or twice he even seemed pleased, as if he had known all along that in the beginning was the word, "I see a man in a dusty pickup."

Aubrey is a tall man, a little over six feet, I should guess, and he has a flat stomach.

I could picture Aubrey exercising with bar bells but never working up a sweat.

He is conventionally good-looking, no surprises—high cheekbones, a wide mouth, a straight, assembly-line nose, the unrevealing blue eyes, and imperial brows.

The day I met Aubrey he was wearing an unobtrusive striped tie and a white shirt with French cuffs and round cuff links on which were the initials *C.B.S.*

His dark summer-weight suit was well cut with narrow lapels and no padding in the shoulders.

There is the suggestion of a wave in Aubrey's neatly trimmed brown hair; it is graying at about the same rate as mine but he hasn't lost as much.

The trimming is done by Jerry, Hair Stylist for Men, on the second floor at 601 Madison Avenue.

Jerry also styles Dorso's hair, the hair of Dan Melnick, a former vice-president of the American Broadcasting Company, where Aubrey was once a vice-president. Melnick used to be head of the mail room at C.B.S. where Aubrey is now president. Melnick is now a partner of David Susskind, who, as has been noted, was once a partner of Dorso's in a talent agency. Susskind, now a producer and television conversationalist, is also a client of Jerry, and so is Ted Ashley, a small, energetic man who is head of the highly successful agency, Ashley-Steiner—Famous Artists.

Dorso, Melnick, Susskind, and Ashley are all best friends of Aubrey.

Cooper continued, " '. . . There are 250 college graduates farming in the Rio Grande Valley in Doña Ana County. Those are the easiest to reach with new ideas. There are six Ph.Ds either on farms or ranches . . .' "

Aubrey is a graduate of Princeton, *cum laude;* he is also a graduate of Phillips Exeter. I thought of him listening to and looking at *The Beverly Hillbillies,* the most popular program on the C.B.S. network for two straight years and a series for which he takes personal credit.

I thought of the six Ph.D.s; I thought of the 250 college graduates, of Dean Leyendecker, and the Alvillar family.

Then for a while I thought of nothing at all.

Aubrey placed his elbows on the arms of the leather chair, lacing his hands together just below his chin.

Dorso, Stromberg, and Lewine were listening to Cooper but kept glancing at Aubrey. He did not return their glances.

I read several pages of the notes, not well. " '. . . Another job of the county agent is to help farmers set up cooperatives. For example, Don Chappell arranged with the bank in Las Cruces to finance thirteen farmers who wanted to buy a cotton gin and market their cotton cooperatively. . . .' "

Cooper read some more, " '. . . There are more men with advanced degrees and I.Q.s of 180 and above in the county of Los Alamos than in any area of similar size in the world.

But only a few miles away the Apaches live in much the same way they lived five hundred years ago. And no one has ever taken the trouble to inquire into their I.Q.s.

" 'There will be both Ph.D.s and Indians in our stories, people who cannot wait to bomb and blast us into the twenty-first century, and those who insist on clinging to the fifteenth. Since life is filled with complexities and ironies the agent may discover that the Mescalero Indian boy in the 4-H Club is more eager to learn and, thus, more educable than the man at White Sands who spent ten years getting all the degrees M.I.T. had to offer. . . .' "

As I listened—and God knows the sound of my own prose is less likely to offend my ear than that of any other living writer under seventy—the more I started to think, You know something. It could be good. It could be exciting. It could be honest. It could be important. . . .

At the end of page 13, a little less than halfway through the notes, Cooper paused, lighted a cigarette, and said we would go on in a few minutes.

Aubrey nodded, waited a moment, and then rose and without a word left the room.

Stromberg scurried after him, and Cooper, Dorso, Lewine, and I talked of this and that, keeping our eyes on the door, pretending not to.

A few minutes later—maybe five, maybe less—Stromberg bustled back into the room, sat down behind his desk, and said, "Shall we go on?"

"Shouldn't we wait for Jim?" asked Cooper.

"Let's go on," said Stromberg.

The performance continued, but from then on it seemed to me deadly and pointless. The audience of three shuffled its feet, coughed, cleared its throat, and made meaningless doodles on pieces of note paper.

Cooper read, " 'The agent is not a displaced person. He is *not* always at war with his environment; to the contrary, he loves it.' "

I felt that Cooper was pushing too hard, hamming it up; he was perspiring.

" '. . . The agent does what he does because he enjoys it. What he does happens to be socially useful as well, but that is really incidental. The agent is very much a man of the twentieth century, but many of his values are those of the nineteenth.

" 'He believes in living up to his obligations; he believes that a man's word is his bond. He believes in fulfilling his duties. He doesn't talk about these things; he does them. . . .' "

The words sounded stilted, pretentious, out of place. Had I ever believed them?

"Merle, why don't you take over for a while?" asked Cooper.

I took over, posting a mental closing notice for the show.

" 'I was told many times the story of the old Indian who had an impeccable reputation as a weather prophet. Farmers in the area wouldn't have dreamed of planting a crop or making plans to harvest without consulting him.

" 'But one day a group of farmers arrived at his shack to ask for his prediction for the next day, and he said, "I'm sorry, but I don't know what the weather will be like tomorrow."

" 'The farmers were aghast. "But why?"

" ' "My radio has broke," said the Indian prophet.' "

Cooper read the final paragraphs, " 'He [the agent] is concerned not only with what is happening in the county today but with how what is done today will affect the county ten years from now. Or a hundred. . . .' "

When he finished, there was an indecisive silence.

Finally, Stromberg said, "Well, you fellows have certainly done your homework."

Dorso smiled. "I think it's wonderful," he said, "just wonderful. I had no idea you'd come up with so much."

Lewine said, "It's impressive."

"But Jim didn't come back," said Cooper.

"Jim didn't have to come back," said Stromberg, a man suddenly inspired.

We looked at him hopefully.

"He didn't come back because everything was in good shape," said Stromberg. "If there'd been *trouble* he would have stayed."

Of course, why of *course* that was it. How stupid can you be, Four Eyes? Aubrey didn't *hate* it; he *loved* it. If you weren't such a trouble trope, an injustice-collector, a . . .

"I *knew* he liked it," said Dorso, "because it's just fascinating material."

"It certainly is," said Stromberg, "and we're all very pleased to have a writer of Merle's stature interested."

"Jim smiled several times," said Cooper.

"There's a *lot* of room for humor in a series like this," said Dorso. "It's not a comedy, but we don't have to be serious all the time."

"Of course we don't," I commented wittily.

"Now, Merle," said Stromberg, "when you write the script, there's one thing about a pilot; the audience, you've got to tell them where the bathroom is."

Stromberg looked around, and since everybody else was agreeing, vehemently, too, I not only nodded; I took out the quill and wrote on the cuff of my shirt, "y.g.t.t.t.w. BATH-ROOM . . ."

I have, naturally, never had that shirt laundered, and it has turned a little green, but I have willed it, along with my other dirty shirts and manuscripts, to the State University of Iowa libraries.

And if I ever see Hunt Stromberg, Jr., again I mean to ask him what he meant, because, otherwise, whoever it is that has the misfortune of trying to write his Ph.D. on Milleriana is going to be awfully confused. . . . As am I.

-   "You've got to tell them where the bathroom is?"

"We've got a big star," said Dorso, looking with approval at

Cooper, "and we've got to surround him with a *strong* supporting cast."

"Pat Neal would be just wonderful as the home agent," said Stromberg.

The movie *Hud* with Paul Newman, Miss Neal, and Melvyn Douglas had opened a few weeks before to excellent notices, and, more important, was making money.

"Pat Neal would be wonderful," said Cooper, "but I've got Barbara all lined up for the part, and she'll be wonderful."

"But if you *can't* get Stanwyck," said Stromberg, "and Stanwyck would be wonderful, Pat could do it. Maybe she's ready to do a series. And she's so warm. Or maybe Claire Trevor. I think she's available."

Dick Dorso said he thought those were both wonderful suggestions.

"And you know somebody was saying maybe Jack would have an uncle in the series," said Stromberg, "an older man, you know, somebody he turns to for advice . . . and maybe we could get Melvyn Douglas to play that part. He's such a wonderful actor. He's so warm."

"That's a wonderful idea, Hunt," said Dorso.

Cooper, Dorso, and I walked to the parking lot of Television City.

"Fellows," said Dorso, "you were both just magnificent, an absolute triumph. That was one of the most successful meetings I've ever attended. I'm proud of both of you."

"I could tell Jim liked it," said Cooper. "He was very impressed; I could tell that."

"I'm going to call New York and tell Bob Aurthur that the meeting was a smash," said Dorso. "He'll be proud of both of you."

"The way Jim listened it was just like he knew all along that wonderful material was there waiting for us," said Cooper.

"God bless both of you," said Dorso.

On the way back to the hotel I mentioned to Cooper that ⅃ hadn't been able to forget the story of John Prather, the old rancher who singlehanded had made the entire U. S. Army back down.

"It's been on my mind, too," said Cooper, "and if you can come up with an idea about how the county agents fits in, it would make a wonderful pilot. We could get Charles Bickford to play the old man. Why don't you organize your thinking, and we'll have breakfast in the morning and then go see Dick. I think he'll like this idea."

We had an appointment to discuss the possible story outline with Dorso at ten. I said that I'd have the outline by nine, and we could have breakfast in my room and discuss it before seeing Dorso.

"God bless you, Merle," said Cooper.

The next morning for the second day in a row I got up at five and by nine had written a six-page outline incorporating most of the ideas I'd worked out in Las Cruces.

Cooper read it and made a few suggestions for changes, and at ten we knocked on the door of Dorso's suite. I was already exhausted.

"I still haven't got over what a wonderful meeting we had yesterday," Dorso said, looking clear-eyed and rested, "and

I'll bet you fellows have come up with a wonderful idea for a story line."

I started to say, "It will knock you on your bonanza," but didn't.

I said, "I think it's pretty good."

"It's a very beautiful idea," said Cooper, who was, after all, brought up in the Hollywood Hills and Culver City.

Cooper, pacing up and down the room, started acting.

He had read the outline only once, but he acted every part with great sincerity—the agent, the home agent, the office assistant, and the old man. ". . . If they come after me, they better bring a box. I am staying until hell freezes over."

When Cooper finished, Dorso smiled with his teeth.

"I love it," he said, "it's just wonderful."

"I knew you'd like it," said Cooper, "and it's the kind of story Jim is going to like, too."

"It's just wonderful," said Dorso, smiling some more.

I am a slow learner, but I was beginning to understand the language.

"Of course I'm a catalyst," said Dorso. "That's what I'm paid a lot of money for. I don't have to be loved."

Here come the Berbers, I thought, and started doing the multiplication tables backwards.

"As I said, it's a wonderful idea; it's got a *hero*. Now a *hero* has got to be a worth-while human being. Puzzled at times, confused on occasion, but in the end *resolute*. And this story has got those elements, *and* it's got a villain and a straight story line without any flashbacks. *And* you wouldn't have to use any montages. I never liked montages anyway. If there's one thing I *always* knew as a writer it's that a montage is simply a lazy writer's way of telling a story. And *nobody* would ever accuse Merle Miller of being a lazy writer. . . ."

. . . Twelve times twelve is or is it are . . . a hundred and twenty-one.

"The kind of writer Merle is, *he* could turn out a beautiful script on this subject."

Begin with the *but*.

"*But* could I be the devil's advocate for a minute? You won't mind, will you, Merle, because if we're going to work together we've got to be frank with each other at all times, don't we, and I don't have to be loved."

One times one are one.

"Now in the first place—and don't answer me now—just keep it in mind—is this story indigenous to the region? Could it happen any place besides the Southwest?"

I kept it in mind.

"And in the second place, while this is a wonderful, wonderful story, it is a very, very familiar story. It's been done ten thousand times. . . . Now it's true that a *good* writer like Merle could bring dimension and depth to this *familiar* story, but it is still a familiar story. Not that there are many original story ideas in the world. As a writer I learned that. Nothing is *really* original. Even Shakespeare. Especially Shakespeare. None of his plays were *original*."

Dorso tucked more of his shirt into his trousers, tightening the red, white, and blue belt.

"But I told you, Merle," he went on, "and I know Jack's heard my lecture on the nature of a pilot, these five men in the projection room, they *don't* know that. And the minute something is *familiar* to them, they get nervous."

I nodded; Cooper looked nervous.

"A story like *this* should be the seventh in the series, maybe the eighth," said Dorso, "but not the *pilot*."

"I still like it," said Cooper.

"I *love* it," said Dorso, "but we are talking about a pilot."

"Charles Bickford would be wonderful as the old man," said Cooper.

"Or Mel Douglas," said Dorso. "He'd be wonderful, if you can't get Bickford. But not for the *pilot*."

One times one are two.

Dorso went on, "But Merle is going back to New York this weekend, and he's going to spend a lot of time with Bob

Aurthur, and if they don't come up with something we can *all* get behind, we can always come back to this *familiar* idea. But with all the exciting ideas you fellows came back with after only two days in New Mexico I *know* we have only scratched the surface. . . ."

Somewhat later, largely to fill up an unexpected silence, I said, "One of the things I like about this project is that we are going to be able to show all kinds of people. For instance, some of the commissioners in our county will be Spanish-Americans, and the agent will speak Spanish and maybe an Ind—"

I saw Dorso go pale under his tan.

"Of course he will," he said, "and of course there will be Spanish-Americans in this series."

I nodded, thinking, *But . . .*

"But not in the pilot," said Dorso.

When I was able to, I said, "Of course not, but why?"

"Because of the Puerto Rican problem in New York," said Dorso. "We may not realize it, but we *all* feel guilty about that."

I adjusted my bifocals and said, "I'm not quite sure I follow you, Dick."

"What I mean is if you have Spanish-Americans in the *pilot* these men in the projection room, there will be something they don't like. *They* won't know what, but *I* know. It will be their guilt over the Puerto Rican Problem."

I nodded. Why hadn't I thought of that?

"We're all three liberals," said Dorso, "and we're all *guilty*. We all feel we ought to be down there in Birmingham at this very minute fighting for civil rights. Where are we? We are in an expensive suite in the Beverly Hills Hotel. That's what gets us down where we live."

"Dick," I said, "I don't feel as if I ought to be in Birmingham."

"Oh, you writers," said Dorso.

2

The friendly lynch scene

"Oh, pilot, 'tis a fearful night! There's danger on the deep."

THOMAS HAYNES BAYLY

After we left Dorso, Cooper suggested that we go to his house, about a half block from the hotel. His wife and children were at the house in Palm Springs.

The street is wide, and the huge houses on both sides are all expensive—$100,000 and up, way up—and of varying degrees of architecture.

Cooper's house, Beverly Hills Moorish, has a broad front lawn on which are a number of flamboyant plants.

His study is a large rectangular room, the predominant colors brown and near brown. On one wall is a collection of guns.

Cooper was at one time a pilot and a first-rate racing car driver; he was a staff driver for the Austin Company and in 1953 raced an Austin-Healy more than 142 m.p.h. He later told me he had given up both "because I no longer wanted to die." Now his hobbies are trout fishing, usually in Oregon, hunting in Mexico, swimming, and playing the drums.

"There's a book I want your opinion on," said Cooper. He went to the built-in shelves. Most of the books were fairly recent best sellers still in their dust jackets.

The book was *African Genesis* by Robert Ardrey, a playwright and former screen writer who has in recent years turned anthropologist.

Cooper couldn't find the book but eventually I did read it.

Ardrey's thesis is that man is not a fallen angel; he is, like other animals, predatory, carnivorous, warlike, hostile, aggressive, greedy, not to be trusted, and *mean.*

Cooper seated himself.

"I still like the Prather idea," he said. "Talk it over with Bob Aurthur and see what he has to say. . . . After all, Dick Dorso isn't a writer, but Bob is, and so are you, Merle. I'm not a writer, of course."

I nodded, not mentioning that I had read an interview with Cooper in which he had said, "I'll be a writer when I'm not good for anything much."

I forgave him for that; after all, he was only nine years old at the time. If he had been *ten* . . .

"But I do know a little something about television," said Cooper. "Back in the fifties, with Fred Coe, Del Mann, and Bob Aurthur, I like to think it's when I grew up as an actor. . . . Merle, let me tell you my ideas about a pilot."

I got out the old papyrus and the quill.

"You've got to grab them in the first thirty seconds."

I wrote "Grab" and waited, trembling, for more. . . . Berbers? . . . Bathrooms?

There was no more. Cooper seemed willing to leave the rest of the script to me.

We talked about a number of other things, and at one point Cooper said, "With *Hennesey*—toward the end—it was opposite *Ben Casey,* and Aubrey got nervous."

Hennesey had gone on the air in 1959 and during its three-year run had what the networks consider a solid rating, an over-all average of thirty-seven per cent of the viewing audience. Nevertheless, during the latter part of the '61-'62 season, General Foods, one of the sponsors, had dropped its half of the show. According to Cooper, Aubrey had suggested a change in format apparently to compete with the popularity of A.B.C.'s *Ben Casey* and N.B.C.'s *Dr. Kildare,* both with doctors who had become teen-age idols.

Each network has its own doctor.

"Aubrey wanted me to take Chick Hennesey out of the Navy and make him a country doctor. It may not seem like much, but that was a big decision for me. Night after night I used to pace up and down this room and sometimes I didn't fall asleep at all.

"In a sense I owe a debt to the Navy and always will, and the audience was used to Hennesey's being in the Navy. I didn't know what to do and I asked Barbara [Mrs. Cooper]. She said, 'It's not only you that's involved. It's your family and it's all the other people on the show. But you do what you think is right.' She's always saying that: 'You do what you think is right.'

"So in the end I decided I just couldn't do what Aubrey wanted and *Hennesey* went off the air."

That night I wrote in my journal:

> I will never understand why some people make such a fuss over Hollywood stars. Since I have been here I have seen Glenn Ford and Danny Kaye and Judy Garland and they look *exactly* the same as they do in *Photoplay* and *Movie Magazine* and *Silver Screen*. . . . Jackie Cooper seems to know what he is doing. And everybody I've talked to about him says he's a respected man in the industry.
>
> This is the first time I've been in Hollywood that I haven't hated it and I think it's because of him.
>
> Besides, you know me, dear diary; I am a sucker for people who do what they think is right. . . . One of the first things I liked about Harry Truman was that sign he used to have on his desk, the Mark Twain quotation, "Do what is right; it will please some people and astonish the rest."

The next afternoon Cooper arranged for me to see a movie in a projection room on the lot where his offices are located, C.B.S. Studio City in North Hollywood.

This was where a good deal of the indoor shots for the county agent series would be filmed.

There was a pass waiting for me at the small sentry box

at the front gate, and I walked past the extras waiting to get in, cowboys in frontier garb and girls with hoop skirts and bright sashes. The actors were young, healthy, and they all had Max Factor sun tans.

The lot occupies about a square city block and has clusters of sound stages, studio buildings, and outdoor sets. On the edge of an old Western town set a man was cleaning his Chevrolet convertible with a brilliant red feather duster.

He was big-boned and barefooted, wore a white T-shirt and bleached-out blue jeans. The feather duster threw me off a bit, but I finally placed him, Channel 2, Thursday, 8-9 P.M.: Eric Fleming, who plays Mr. Favor, trail boss of C.B.S.'s *Rawhide*.

One of the films I saw that afternoon was *The Rainmaker* by N. Richard Nash, which started its career as a television play produced by David Susskind during the Golden Age of Television.

There was an actor in it who Cooper thought might appear in the county agent series. The actor did not impress me.

I saw Cooper only briefly; he was on the back lot where they were filming the first of a Friday night historical series, *The Great Adventure*, a C.B.S. project for the '63-'64 season.

Cooper played the commander of a Confederate submarine, the *Henley*, which shortly before the end of the War Between the States sank a Union warship, the *Housatonic*.

An elaborate set had been constructed—including a wharf and a tank of water. The latter was to be the bay where the *Henley* was first tested, the harbor where it ran the Union blockade, and the ocean where the submarine sank the *Housatonic* and then itself sank. It was a square tank, not very large.

Cooper was wearing a shaggy blond wig under his Confederate cap.

We shook hands and he said, "I wish you didn't have to go back to New York. You could do the work here just as well, and I've got a secretarial staff that's twice as good as U.A.'s.

You know how good Dorothy Fisher is. She's one of the few people anywhere that understands writers, and she'd be at your personal disposal all day."

"I wish I could, Jack, but I can't."

"I know," he said. "I know. . . . Well, if anything comes up, call me. Anything. And write. We're going to have bags of time together, old buddy. Bags of it."

I was being driven to the hotel in a studio car, which was waiting near the main gate.

It was dusk, and Cooper started toward his office, very slowly. He turned once, waved, and smiled hopefully.

Underneath his make-up he looked tired, older than his years, and abandoned.

I walked on—because what else do you do, ever—remembering two things he had said to me, I believe on the plane to El Paso.

I had said that I was going to the twenty-eighth reunion of my high school class in August, in Marshalltown, Iowa, and he said, "I bet there were kids you went all through school with."

"Some," I said, "a lot maybe. Of course, I was never part of the gang—any gang."

"But at least they let you have a childhood," said Cooper.

I started to say—and I started to say—and I started to say —but what I did say was, "Yes, Jack, they let me have a childhood."

That same evening he was talking about his experience in the Navy.

"I felt I belonged," he said. "I mean I was part of something."

I shouted, "See you, Jack, and I'll call you."

"You do that. Any time. Call me any time. Call me collect."

The next morning I was driven to the airport by a chauffeur who, though he had an Italian accent, must have had Brazilian ancestors. He drove with elaborate disregard of life and limb, mine and his, in that order.

I have been told—and I see no reason to doubt it—that there is an ordinance that forbids walking in Beverly Hills. I decided that there must also be a bounty on all pedestrians caught on the run. As the pedestrians say in São Paolo, "He's seen us; start running."

"We get a lotsa the funeral trade," said the chauffeur. "People dies, family, first thing they do is they want a limousine. Lotsa the funerals. I bet you I been to hundra, maybe two hundres funerals."

He described in detail each of the funerals he had attended.

"You betcha," he said, "we get lotsa the funerals."

"I see no reason to doubt it," I said.

In the hotel room at the Gorham, this time I was on the thirteenth floor and on the side from which, if I'd had the stomach, I believe I could have caught a glimpse of the Americana Hotel.

I read the galleys of the novel.

Later that week I made various academic sounds on a

C.B.S. radio program, *Invitation to Learning,* for which I was promised an *honorarium* of a hundred dollars. When money is being discussed and they throw a Latin word at you, the sum involved is never of any *consequencium.*

That week I also developed several characters who, I thought, might appear in the series, including an office assistant, female:

> Lydia Willard has a desk in the main office, just outside those of the county agent and the home agent.
>
> She is a graduate of the state university were she majored in home economics. She has been married. Her husband was a local boy who became a Navy flier. She went with him to Pensacola, to the Hawaiian Islands, and to Hong Kong. He was stationed with the fleet off Formosa and was killed in a take-off from a carrier. [The Navy background was suggested by Cooper.]
>
> Lydia was meant to be married. She does not feel that being a housewife demeans and degrades her. She is one of a species that is rapidly becoming as extinct as the great auk, she is a *woman.*
>
> She was born on a ranch, and she can ride and round up cattle and, if necessary, work in the fields. But in doing these things she has lost none of her femininity.
>
> Lydia is not a magazine-cover beauty, and there is not an ounce of glamor in her, but she has other, more important qualities. She has warmth; she can understand and identify with problems of other people. She wears well and will age well. . . .

I described a few other characters, among them the county agent's uncle, suggested by Bob Aurthur but fashioned after an uncle of mine who was wiped out during the depression. He now farms 640 acres in Iowa, has sent four sons and two daughters through college, reads Marcus Aurelius *and* Winston Churchill, is fond of the music of Johann Sebastian Bach *and* Ella Fitzgerald, went to Russia with a group of farmers to discuss American agricultural methods, and when Nikita Khrushchev, the Czar of all the Russias, visited Coon Rapids,

Iowa, my uncle was one of those who had lunch with him at the Garst farm.

The uncle whom I created was also able to read and write without moving his lips. What's more, I made use of the fact that cows, by no means the most intelligent of God's creatures, gave more milk while listening to Muzak. Sweet milk, too.

The uncle and the agent were to share a house, and I wrote,

> . . . The barn is wired to pick up the sound of the hi-fi from the house. While Russ [the uncle] milks in the morning the music is often a Haydn symphony—as clear and bright as the coming day.

Remembering the era of Mabel Dodge Luhan and D. H. Lawrence in Taos, I created an art colony. There are as many painters, sculptors, and musicians in the Sante Fe area as there are Ph.D.s at Los Alamos.

I created an antagonist and the antagonist's wife.

Finally, I outlined a few new story ideas. I had a feeling old John Prather's *familiar* story was not going to survive, and as has happened once or twice before in my life, I was right.

On Thursday of that week I went to see Harold Franklin at the William Morris Agency, 1740 Broadway.

As a result of creeping socialism and unwarranted federal interference with free enterprise, M.C.A. (Music Corporation of America) was a few years back forced to choose between being a talent agency and a producer of television shows and motion pictures.

No less a voice than David Susskind's was raised against M.C.A. at the F.C.C. (Federal Communications Commission) hearings in Washington in June of 1961. . . . He said "M.C.A. . . . a giant monopoly in restraint of trade. . . ."

Susskind had worked for M.C.A. long before Talent Associates, Ltd.

The officers of M.C.A. voted to divest themselves of the

business of being agents and decided to concentrate on producing, I believe on the grounds that producing was more creative and soul-satisfying.

Since then, William Morris has been the largest agency in the business; Ashley-Steiner is the second largest.

Genealogists may wish to note that Ted Ashley, head of Ashley-Steiner-Famous Artists is also a nephew of Nat Lefkowitz, who is the head of the New York office of William Morris.

Ashley at one time was in the mail room at William Morris (not to be confused with Dan Melnick, David Susskind's partner, who was once in another mail room) and was later his uncle's secretary, although I do not believe he takes shorthand.

After a time, Ashley, in the new Horatio Alger tradition, left his uncle's agency, taking with him a few of his uncle's clients, with whom he set up his own agency.

He prospered. When M.C.A. disbanded as an agency, three hundred clients went to Ashley-Steiner.

Ashley, at forty-one, is one of the most successful television packagers in the business. During the '63-'64 season his agency represented twelve series, among them *The Defenders.*, C.B.S.; *The Nurses,* C.B.S.; *The Danny Kaye Show,* C.B.S.; *Twilight Zone,* C.B.S.; *Candid Camera,* C.B.S.; *Tell it to The Camera,* C.B.S.

No wonder Ashley can afford to get his hair dressed by Jerry, Hair Stylist for Men, and exercise at Nicholas Kounovsky's Gymnasium, where his best friend Jim Aubrey also exercises.

Those who are concerned with the future of the Republic will, I believe, be relieved to know that the mail room at William Morris teems with young men, all of whom were at birth registered with Jerry and Nicholas Kounovsky.

After they have graduated from the mail room they become secretaries to agents, and, since not all of them have uncles at William Morris, a few take shorthand.

Eventually, some of these young men become junior agents

and from then on . . . Well, the sky is hardly the limit. Any more.

Harold Franklin, who never worked in a mail room but who did once work in the U. S. Army Signal Corps, as did Hunt Stromberg, Jr., was at a meeting when his secretary let me into his office, a pleasant corner room twenty-one floors up.

From one window there is an agreeable view of Broadway with its theater and movie marquees. William Morris can almost see all the money it's making. The other window looks out over the Hudson, on which there are almost always ships on their way to and from someplace I want to be.

Harold's office is a restful room; he has a small, stylish table instead of a desk and the only comfortable leather chairs in the industry. He always has at least one good-sized modern painting on the wall.

I've known Harold and been his friend and client for almost ten years.

There was a fifteen-month divorce during which time my agent was Hope Taylor, who used to be Harold's secretary; that was before she was Dorso's secretary.

Harold is a man of great good taste and, as has been observed, considerable erudition.

Harold Stern, who is Bob Aurthur's lawyer and David Susskind's lawyer and Daniel Melnick's lawyer, once said of Harold Franklin, "He's the only agent in the business who knows how *Macbeth* comes out."

Neither Harold Franklin nor Harold Stern has enough hair to interest Jerry.

When Harold Franklin returned from his meeting, I said, "Does William Morris represent everybody involved with this project?"

"So far," said Harold, "and that's nice for you because we won't be taking any commission from you."

"It's also nice for the agency," I observed.

The total budget of the pilot was then estimated at $250,-
000, out of which, if the series was sold, William Morris would
get $25,000. We'll come to what it stood to make out of the
entire project.

"Harold," I said, "the way it works, it's like betting on every horse in the race with the horses putting up the money."

Harold laughed—though not, I felt, with his usual aban-
don.

We discussed the fact that Joe Jacobs, chancellor of the
exchequer at United Artists Television, had offered $5000 for
the writing of the pilot script. Harold had suggested $10,000
and they had settled on a fee of $7500, pending my ap-
proval.

I should note here that I was feeling affluent that day,
having just received the check for my Brazil piece from
Harper's magazine, $450, and having the prospect of my
$100 from Latin quarter of C.B.S. radio.

That would pay my overdue hotel bill and leave me
enough over for a few hot pastramis and a keg or two of
vodka.

Harold said, "Seventy-five hundred dollars is an awfully
good fee for writing a pilot these days."

"Harold, I'm terrible at fractions. Make it an even $10,-
000 and call it fair play."

Harold called Joe Jacobs.

"Joe," he said, "Merle is very, very unhappy at the figure
$7500. I *told* you he would be unhappy. I . . ."

Joe Jacobs is, I later discovered, a very soft-spoken man,
but that day Harold held the phone a few inches from his ear.

Finally Harold said, "Joe, Merle is here now, and he is getting on his high horse, and it is a well-known fact that Merle
has the highest horse in show business."

There was a long silence.

Harold said, "And, Joe, I think I ought to tell you; Merle
might just walk away and *leave.* I've seen him do it. And that
very successful meeting with Jim Aubrey in California last

week? You've heard, haven't you, that Aubrey *loved* Merle's notes?

"He doesn't *need* the money, you know, and if it weren't that he's so fond of Bob Aurthur and now Jack Cooper, but I simply will not allow . . . No, Joe, Merle doesn't *care*. . . . He's getting up . . ."

I was getting up; I said, "Harold, for God's sake, if it's going to queer the deal or . . . the credit department at the Diner's Club has threatened to tear out my tongue . . ."

"Joe," said Harold, "I tell you Merle says it's ten thousand or he's not interested, and frankly, I think he's a fool to settle for that. I think he ought to get . . ."

There was another long silence.

"Of course Merle Miller is not Tennessee Williams," said Harold. "You're perfectly right, Joe, and he's not Faith Baldwin, Taylor Caldwell, or Fannie Hurst . . . and I could name you a hundred other writers he's not. . . . Look, Joe, I think the time has come for an act of generosity on the part of United Artists."

I sank into one of the chairs; well, I thought, I can always take the assignment from that peachy magazine editor who wants me to write a series of short stories. ". . . literary. I mean we aren't afraid to publish John O'Hara and Carson McCullers. . . . Anything that appeals to you as long—well, our audience *is* the Young Adult Audience, late twenties, early thirties, and naturally, a love story . . . There's enough trouble in the world without people wanting to read about it. . . ."

I'd get $9.80 for writing one of those stories. Before taxes.

"I don't know now, Joe," said Harold. "Merle's left. I *told* you he would. I'm not sure that ten will be enough. Now he may want twelve-five or even fifteen. . . . I don't know where he's gone, maybe back to Brazil.

"Joe, I'll have to call him. I'll *try* to persuade him to take the ten thousand. Yes, it is, Joe. Very generous indeed, but that's only *my* opinion. Yes, I will, Joe. I'll do it for you."

Later that morning I went to Bob Aurthur's office.

The pilot for *The Patty Duke Show* was about to go into production and several dozen people were having hysterics in the hallways.

Bob was, as usual, unperturbed; he was in the midst of a telephone conversation.

"Goddamn it to hell, I'll see that he's drawn and quartered . . . . hot pokers . . . whipping posts . . ."

Jane Wetherell, a handsome girl who never has hysterics and always wears clothes that are going to be featured in next month's *Vogue,* was waiting to talk to Bob.

I hadn't seen her since she left Rio in November.

Bob was shouting, "I am firmly opposed to capital punishment, but in his case . . ."

"Trouble?" I asked Jane.

"Good heavens, no. This is the most relaxed day since I've been here."

Bob finished his telephone colloquy, and Jane asked him about casting a certain actor in *The Patty Duke Show.*

"No," said Bob. "He may have talent, but he's trouble. I don't mean your average run-of-the-mill trouble. I mean *trouble.*"

Jane nodded, sighed, and left.

"All actors have to be loved *all* the time," said Bob. "Judy

Garland's appearance at Carnegie Hall is a good example. That was like an orgasm with thousands of people. . . . Actors can't settle for being loved by just one person. . . ."

"Jack Cooper is an exception."

"Maybe. You know him better than I do, but most actors— unless you give them constant assurance and support . . . the way I do on the phone all day long . . . Look, they've made a study of actors and identity at the University of Chicago, and they've found out something very, very interesting. Actors don't have *any* identity. They are not people, and never forget it."

After Bob's secretary brought us lunch, he said, "How was the trip?"

I told him, ending with the story about John Prather and Dick Dorso's reaction to it.

"The Prather story's a good one," said Bob, "and it's the kind of thing you do very well. One man against the world. Prather, Ira Hayes, you.

"But I think you ought to know that Fred Coe's got a pilot that Dick is also trying to sell. That one—it's the series in which Arthur Hill plays a magazine writer—that one ends with an old man trying to stave off automation by standing at the shaft of a coal mine with a shotgun."

"But what's that got to do with . . . ?"

"Dick will fight the Prather idea the whole way for fear it might interfere with the sale of the Coe series."

"Then why didn't he say so?"

"I was perfectly right," said Bob. "You have never left Iowa. . . . Have you and Harold Franklin talked contract?"

I said that we had and said, "There's one thing that worries me. They're going to want to have an option on me to be script supervisor of this series."

"Of course. You're part of the package. When C.B.S. sells the pilot they're going to want to know how many more scripts you're going to write and if you're going to supervise the others that are written. They'll *insist* that you be script supervisor."

"No."

"Look, at this point in your life maybe it wouldn't be a bad idea for a while. You could get a little house at Palm Springs . . ."

"No."

. . . I should perhaps explain to the reader that my motives in this matter were unselfish. I didn't want to be script supervisor because I don't like other writers much and neither enjoy nor am very adept at telling them how to brush up their prose. That's one of the reasons I had to give up teaching creative writing—speaking of non sequiturs—after one furtive summer session. I was always encountering students like the woman in her sixties who had written nine novels, all unpublished because of a conspiracy among publishers. "They *know* I'm fifty years ahead of my time, and they just can't *stand* it." Or the blond boy who was an excellent tennis player. One night—I had thought up to then that he was sitting at my feet—he said, "Merle, do you just want to be prolific or do you want to be good, too?" . . . Nope. I have enough trouble getting my own nervous prose in shape. And, besides, as script supervisor I would have had to live in Looking-Glass Land.

Bob was saying, "This is June, and the subject won't come up until next April. Wait till they ask you."

". . . I don't think that's fair to Jack; he keeps talking about how we're going to be married together for years and years. . . ."

Bob gave me a smile usually reserved for the aged, the infirm, or those with fewer than the average number of marbles.

"Put it the other way around," he said. "Suppose next April *you* want more than anything in the world to *be* script supervisor. And suppose U.A., C.B.S., Cooper, whoever, want somebody else. Which has happened in this rat race a time or two that I can remember.

"You know what would happen? You'd call your old buddy Cooper, and he'd cry, and you'd cry—you're both big criers—and he'd do part of the jail scene from *The Champ*, and he'd say, 'Merle, *I* want you; *I* love you; *I* need you'— and he might even mean some of it—'but I'm helpless.' "

"And so I lie."

"Merlo, when next April comes and you decide you don't want to be story editor at $1000 a week or maybe $1500 to *start* with, get your lawyer to draw up a letter a few days before. All it has to say is, 'I quit; sue me.' Make several copies. Mail them to everybody involved, U.A., C.B.S., Cooper Productions, and then get on a plane and go to Mexico City, Rome, Paris, wherever you want to. Don't let anybody except your lawyer know where you are. Not even me. . . .

"Because if you do, all of us—if we do want you—will fly to where you are, and we'll offer you all the money in the world. And you'll do the old Merle Miller act. You'll say, 'Yes.' Not only because of the money but because you want to be loved. I guess that's it. Or maybe it's because you're a nice guy.

"You'll end up doing something you hate, and then you'll hate yourself, and then you'll hate me, and I don't want you to hate me."

"Okay, but what about the pilot? If it isn't going to be about Prather, what is it going to be about?"

"You're the writer," said Bob. "Talk to some of your buddies at the Department of Agriculture and John White and people like that. You'll come up with something."

"I already hate you."

From the hotel I called Harold.

I said that, though we hadn't talked about it, I imagined it would be written into the contract that U.A., C.B.S., and Jackie Cooper Productions had an option on my services as script supervisor.

Harold agreed.

"That's fine, but, if that's the case, then I want a clause in the contract saying that I don't have to let them exercise their option. In other words, if they can say no to me, I want to be able to say no to them."

"But that's impossible. It's never been done before," said Harold. "Those are big corporations."

"Harold, I'm a big person."

"Thank God I'm going to get away from all this for a while," said Harold, "and when I'm in Athens . . ."

By the end of June I had a pretty good idea what I wanted the story line to be—and none too soon. There was to be a Summit Meeting at C.B.S. on July 10, and at that time it would be decided whether or not to continue the project.

The glass house was available, and I decided to return, at least for the four-day July 4 weekend.

Cooper was flying in from California on Saturday, and I invited him to come to Brewster on Sunday.

I left the city with some reluctance, despite the fact that I regretted almost all of the old buildings that were being torn down and deplored all of the new ones. But I had not found the city a jungle. . . . That, however, is another book.

The thought of being in the country alone frightened me. But then what doesn't?

This particular chapter is being written in mid-March. The unblemished air is cold, and once in a while there is a gentle gust of snow, but the sun is shining, and the branches I cut from the wild apple tree—I think it's a wild apple or else it's a wild cherry or else it's a maple—are about to burst into bloom in the living room.

Well, to be realistic, one small bud has appeared on one twig. I am not known for my green thumb, but I have something of a reputation as an ornithologist and yesterday was able to identify the first two robins of the season.

They looked with dismay at the snow and the glass house, and *she* said, "I told you we should never have left The Beach."

I believe they were robins, although they could have been towhees which look a lot like robins, though smaller.

I *know* they were birds.

I am an insatiable reader of journals and the last few nights I've been tasting, a few delicious pages at a time, Bernard Berenson's *Sunset and Twilight*. On May 2 of his eighty-seventh year he wrote, ". . . A home grows out of one's tropisms, one's whims, one's caprices. . . . One should make one for oneself. That means staying put for a lifetime and to live in it leisurely. . . ."

I am a slow learner and a self-deceiver and constantly tell lies to myself.

I spent the spring and early summer a year ago assuring myself that *I* didn't care where I lived. Roots were an illusion. And all this nonsense about everybody needing a place to belong? A slogan made up by the real estate lobby.

Myself, I could be happy in a hotel room or a Brazilian jungle.

Then on Thursday, July 4, Independence Day, Evan and Hope Taylor drove me to Brewster. I sat in the back seat among my possessions, several thousand boxes of books, clothes, camera, Chemex, binoculars and bird seed, and some newly acquired doodads.

None of the doodads was of much importance, except possibly a fertility symbol I had picked up in Bahia, "the good place," the oldest city in Brazil. *There* it is a prison offense to even think about tearing down one of the moldering, exquisite baroque buildings that are often three and four hundred years old.

The glass house—I had not been in it for more than eight months—is a few miles north and east of Brewster. It seems to float in the air; two of the walls are glass, two are brick. The living and dining rooms overlook a series of endless hills, and the bedrooms and study look into a pine forest.

Progressive Architecture once called the house "A Prism in the Pines." At one time or another—never mind why—I had thought of it as a prison in the pines.

When I returned to it in July, I wasn't sure what I thought, but when we came up the drive, which is also lined with pines, I recognized that the house was something rare in contemporary life, a work of art, and that if I couldn't be happy in it, I probably couldn't be happy anywhere.

Evan, Hope, and I had lunch, and then they went off to an engagement in Connecticut. I spent the rest of Thursday and Friday morning working on the story line.

It went surprisingly well, and, as rarely happens, I knew

I'd be able to meet the deadline—the meeting on the following Wednesday at C.B.S.

Friday afternoon two friends came for the rest of the weekend, Ruth Knight, an airlines executive, and Arnold Ehrlich, a magazine editor I've known since we were both copy boys on the late Philadelphia *Record. I* made $15 a week, but then I was in a sense a college graduate.

Arnold is the second funniest man around, and the three of us drank some, laughed, and talked all night.

I explained about the series but added that even though I would be rich beyond the wildest dreams of avarice, I would remain the same simple soul I had always been.

They asked what I would do with my wealth, and I mentioned the cabañas, the sauna, and the pools.

"One of the pools will be in the shape of a tear," I said, "in memory of Jackie Cooper's prison scene in *The Champ.*"

"It's going to be like the time at Moss Hart's place in Bucks County when he started putting in forests and dredging rivers," said Arnold. "George Kaufman said, 'It just goes to show you what God could do if He had money.'"

Cooper came up from the city by train on Sunday afternoon.

At the time I had no car, and Kay Flanagan, wife of the owner of Flanagan Taxi in Brewster, drove him to the house. She was obviously awed by him and liked him, and he gave her an autograph for her son, Tommy.

In her line of work Mrs. Flanagan meets a lot of people, and since she is not a taciturn cab driver, word quickly got around that I had had as my guest a famous actor.

I found myself treated with far more respect in the village, and several injudicious merchants allowed me to open charge accounts.

Cooper brought an enormous wheel of fortune of cheeses as a house gift. He looked around, I thought admiringly.

"This is your weekend place," he said.

The house is forty feet wide and sixty feet long.

"No, I live here—well, I'm going to live here all the time."

He seemed surprised.

We sat on the terrace under a friendly spruce. Ruth served the cheeses Cooper had brought, and beer.

Cooper did most of the talking and told a number of amusing stories about the Hollywood of his youth.

He was not high on child stars and thought they were for the most part reflections of the talents of the director.

He talked about a screen test when he was six, a crying scene that changed his whole life. The director had tried everything to get Cooper to cry. First he pretended to have a policeman run in and arrest Cooper's mother. Then he pretended to fire an assistant director whom Cooper liked. Finally he made believe that he shot the *Our Gang* dog, and that made Cooper cry. The screen test got him the job in *Skippy*.

After that, year in and year out, he was forced to act the same kind of thing.

Arnold, who is not impressed with presidents, saints, or Nobel prize winners, decided to take a later train than he had originally planned.

Ruth asked about the child stars who'd been contemporaries of Cooper's.

"None of them ever made it," he said, running down the list. He described one as a screaming faggot, one as an alcoholic, one as a drug addict, one as an oversized *Hausfrau* in Europe, one bankrupt, and so on. . . . But then, I thought, we are all able to observe, without pain, the misfortunes of our contemporaries.

I asked *casually* about Elizabeth Taylor.

Among other things Cooper said, "She's a man-eater."

"In that case," said Arnold, "why Eddie Fisher? He's hardly even an appetizer."

"What about Lana Turner?" I had once written a picture, *The Rains of Ranchipur;* it was about a very heavy rain in Ranchipur, India—and that's about it. Richard Burton had played an Indian doctor, and Miss Turner was visible, though I had never met her.

Cooper said that he always liked Lana.

"She used to treat the rest of the kids at the studio school like infants," he said, "and she always seemed to me to be—confused—by older men. When we were doing *The Ziegfeld Girl,* I played Judy Garland's boy friend, Lana used to invite me to her dressing room for a slug of brandy. She still likes the brandy. But I tell you—if she stood at the top of those stairs"—he pointed to the wooden steps leading to the terrace—"you'd look up and even in the bright sunlight she'd look just great. Just magnificent. . . ."

Arnold returned to the city and Ruth made dinner.

Cooper and I moved inside and had a few drinks, and he showed me the entertainment section of the Sunday *Times.*

The lead news story on the television page quoted Michael Dann, the C.B.S. vice-president in charge of making public pronouncements, as saying that one of the network's major projects for the '64-'65 season was to star Cooper as a county agent in the Southwest. The writer was to be Merle Miller; Robert Alan Aurthur was to be creative consultant.

"Does that mean we're in?" I asked.

"No question about it," said Cooper. "They're talking in terms of a thirteen-week commitment. I've told Mort [Mort Rosenthal, one of Cooper's lawyers] that it's twenty-six weeks or nothing."

"Suppose they don't like the story line?"

"They'll love it. The way Jim Aubrey loved your notes. Shall we talk about it?"

"Let's wait till we get together with Bob Aurthur," I said, not feeling it incumbent on me to mention that I hadn't yet finished the story line.

Cooper called his family and talked at great length. After that he washed the lettuce, wrapped it in two towels, and put it in the freezer of the refrigerator.

"You can keep it there for an hour or two," he said, "and it won't freeze. You bring it out and it makes a crisp, delicious salad."

"You'd make somebody a good husband," said Ruth.

"I have," he said, "three different times."

The salad was crisp and delicious.

At dinner Cooper talked about Errol Flynn, one of the few people I ever heard him discuss with unqualified approval. Both he and Flynn were great horsemen.

". . . He was just like everything you ever read about him, you know, gallant and dashing and brave, and always successful with the ladies. . . . There was a friend of his, Freddie McEvoy, who was kind of a playboy. McEvoy was drowned trying to save his wife in a storm while sailing around West Africa. . . . I think that's the way Errol wanted to go, gallantly, trying to save a woman. That would have appealed to him."

Mrs. Flanagan arrived around eight-thirty to take Cooper and Ruth to the train.

He shook my hand, very hard, and said he had had a wonderful time and that it was a wonderful dinner and that when I came to California I must have dinner at his house, "often. We don't entertain much, just a few people we like once in a while. But you'll have to come a lot. . . ."

I cleaned up the remains of the dinner, packed the dishwasher, made myself a drink, and for a long time sat alone on the terrace.

A breeze ruffled the branches of the spruce trees, and on the distant road, minuscule cars were on their tedious, reluctant way back to the city.

I thought of the day with some satisfaction.

Cooper and I had talked of the odd world we live in; he had just read one of my novels and said he liked it.

"You're a cynic, I think," he said. "I'm not. I believe good things can happen and you can help make them happen. . . . I'm more of an optimist than you are. But there's nothing wrong with being cynical.

"We'll have a lot of arguments, not about work; I never argue about work, and I never interfere with my writers. You write it, and I'll play it. Because you're a good writer. Of course I've worked with a lot of bad writers, but I always respect them. If they're doing their best. . . ."

I felt I had gained a friend and, after a certain age, which I have reached and passed, that happens rarely enough.

He said something else I liked, too.

"This series—it's got to be written in a way people like John White and Don Chappell and the others we met in New Mexico are going to *respect*. Just the way the Navy respected *Hennesey*. Otherwise I'm not going to be in it. They can find themselves another star."

After a while I went inside the house.

Every light was turned on and I wandered through the rooms, touching things.

I looked at the bookshelves and remembered the woman who some time before had said, "Your books certainly all look well thumbed."

"That's because I have a thumber who comes in on Thursdays," I told her.

I remembered where each book was bought and why and what each had or had not meant to me.

I took down one, opening it, ". . . Miss Stein called me and said she wanted to have me meet Matisse. . . . Miss Stein and he seemed full of hidden meanings."

"We are all filled with hidden meanings, Miss Toklas," I said.

The Autobiography of Alice B. Toklas. "Gertrude Stein

in her work had always been possessed by the intellectual passion for exactitude in the description of inner and outer reality."

I thought of the spring Miss Stein and Miss Toklas came to Iowa City; I was—I believe—a sophomore at the university and among other things I did to earn eating money was interview on the university radio station (WSUI) all the celebrities who visited the campus.

When the two famous ladies from Paris arrived I naturally interviewed them, although I had never read Miss Stein, had only a vague knowledge that Matisse painted—but what? —and wasn't quite sure if Miss Toklas was a friend, a servant, or a paid companion.

I remember, however, that they were kind to each other, and even at seventeen I realized how rare that was.

After the war I once more saw Miss Stein and Miss Toklas, this time in Paris. I approached them with diffidence and embarrassment, prepared not to mention the interview. But when they asked where I had gone to school and I said the State University of Iowa . . .

"I was very ignorant," I said. "I'm afraid I asked ridiculous questions."

"You were young," said Miss Stein, "but that is a condition of life one unhappily outgrows."

I replaced Miss Stein's book; next to it was *The Red and the Black*, ". . . For Merle who will, I hope, write as well as Marie Henri Beyle—but have a larger audience. . . . David. . . ."

David. Whose last name I could no longer remember. He had been a bomber pilot, shot down over Tarawa. . . . I remembered the peace strike he and I had called; I remember our singing—hundreds of us, "I ain't gonna study war no more; oh, I ain't gonna study w-a-h n-a-w mo-ah . . ."

". . . *Moton Kalimar . . . Molka . . . Jenesis . . . 'Ilojinoin . . . Anji . . .*"

Several bullets had riddled the pages of the Marshallese Bible I found in a shell hole during the invasion of Kwajalein in the spring of 1944.

As I stooped to pick it up, the Japanese, who had been quiet for hours, started firing directly over our heads. I fell into the hole, on top of the Bible; my friend, John Bushemi, a few feet away, was hit several times. He died an hour later.

I looked at the first, inadequate novel I had published, "For John Bushemi, whose death must somehow be given meaning."

I turned off all the lights and went into my bedroom.

The pine forest was very beautiful in the night light. So was the orderly row of bookshelves. It had been a good day. I smoked a cigarette in the soft darkness feeling something rare in my life. I felt at peace with myself and nearly content.

On the train to the city the next morning I finished a long memorandum on the story line.

The basic idea resulted from my warm memory of Don Chappell's close relationship to the Alvillar family.

I had kept thinking of the father's trusting airplane flight to Cleveland, of the mother proudly displaying the 4-H Club medals, and of the sons, all three of whom were planning to go to the state university.

I remembered Arthur Alvillar, Sr.'s feeling. . . . If it weren't for Don here . . .

Okay. No Spanish-Americans in the pilot. The last thing in the world I want to do is stir up guilt feelings in anybody—or be counterproductive.

My family, the Lairds, were originally from—Bob Aurthur is right; I am a provincial man—Iowa, where they have been done in by drought, one of the hundreds of God-given disasters that can destroy a farmer.

They had come to the fictional county in the Southwest in which the series was to take place, and the agent—Cooper—had helped them get a fresh start.

At the time the story begins they are paying off the mortgage on the land they hold as sharecroppers and are putting away money to send their children to college. At first, there were eight Lairds (remember Xav and the three *c*'s?) and a dog named Jebediah.

Then Cooper discovers that a blight has attacked the Lairds' principal crop.

The blight, if allowed to spread, could cause great damage to the crops of the other farmers in the county, but to stop it the Laird crop has to be destroyed, and that is going to wipe them out.

The agent feels that his job is to convince the antagonist— who still owns the land on which the Lairds are living—and the rest of the farmers in the county that the welfare of the Lairds is the concern, even more, the *responsibility* of the county. . . . Talk about your creeping socialism.

Leonard Appleton had said, "I've got ranchers that have an annual income of a quarter of a million dollars, and I've got others—well, sometimes they don't have any income at all. And the welfare of one is just as important in my job as the welfare of the other. Both are—you might say both are my constituents."

When I got to Bob's office he had just come back from Brooklyn Heights, where they were either rehearsing or beginning to film or had just finished the pilot of *The Patty Duke Show*.

"How did it go?" I asked.

Bob said, "Harold Franklin once told me that if you don't want to be crucified stay away from crosses. Why didn't I listen?"

He pounded two bloody stumps on top of the jeweler's bench he uses as a desk. "Why didn't I listen?"

"Read my outline and stop bleeding."

"I'll read it, but first I'm going to call the commissioner of police and ask him to issue warrants for the arrest of several actors on charges of malicious mischief, disturbing the peace, inciting to riot, and breathing."

"It might work," said Bob. "What kind of blight?"

I said there were several. One is a disease called *roja blanca* that attacks rice; it comes from Cuba. (Of course!) When it is discovered in a field, the entire crop has to be burned. Another—ring rot—gets into potatoes. Same result; burn the crop. A third—cyst nematode—infects soybeans. Again, destruction.

"But doesn't the government help out farmers when that happens?" asked Bob.

"Nope. If they don't plant *anything*, they get paid for it. But if they do, and it has to be destroyed, nothing. Not even a condolence card."

"It might work," Bob said again. "The burning I like, but isn't there something more dramatic than soybeans, potatoes, or rice? What other kinds of things could there be?"

Here, gentle reader, is where our hero made his first mistake, one that eventually caused internal wounds that . . . Well, even now on a damp day . . .

"Well, there's something called a burrowing nematode. It attacks orange trees, kills them the way the trichinosis bug kills humans, same family, and if the nematode gets in a grove they have to bulldoze out every tree and burn the entire grove. They put all the trees in a huge pile, and . . ."

Merlin observed a look in His Majesty's eyes that caused him to realize that despite age, failing eyesight, and deterioration of the brain cells, he had not yet lost his magical powers.

"That's good. I like that," Bob said.

"But," I added quickly, "the disease has so far—in the United States anyway—been confined to a certain section of Florida."

"*Could* it appear in the Southwest?" asked Bob.

"Yes. I've had a couple long talks with a man named Mullin, he's a plant pathologist at Gainesville, Florida. One of the ways the bug travels is by latching onto a host plant.

They take every possible precaution, state border inspection and things like that, but some dame could pick up an infected plant in Florida, take it back to the Southwest, stick it in the ground near an orange grove, and in a year or so . . . Of course Mullin was a little leery about creating a panic in the Southwest. . . ."

"Burning an orange grove could be a great pictorial effect," said Bob. "The bulldozers and the fire and the Lairds and their kids watching everything they've worked for go up in flames. And the county agent knowing there's *no* other way. That could be very moving. . . ."

"How does Stanwyck fit into all this?" Bob asked.

I said I hadn't figured that out yet.

"That's one of the problems with this show," said Bob. "We've got two stars, and both have to have *star* parts. Especially in the pilot. That's both an advantage and a disadvantage."

He picked up the original dictated notes that had by that time been mimeographed; he read what I had written about the Stanwyck character.

". . . Several words describe her—lusty, gusty, rough, realistic, feisty. Her family, like the county agent's, has been in the Southwest for several generations. They still have a ranch somewhere in the vicinity. She is perhaps fifty."

In Hollywood I had asked Cooper how old I could make the home agent. He discussed it with Stanwyck. She had said, "I don't care. He can say I'm fifty, if he wants to. Let him make me whatever age fits the part and that's how old I'll be."

Bob continued reading, "She says of herself, 'I didn't put on a skirt until I was fourteen years old, and then my mother sent me East to round off the rough edges. All you have to do is look at me to see that *that* didn't happen. . . .

" 'I went to Miss Patchen's School for Young Ladies in the Blue Ridge Mountains. I was damned good on the rifle range. . . . Oh, yes, they taught us how to shoot. Miss Patchen was a great believer in the theory that a young lady should know how to defend herself. . . . How right she was, but I never found a rifle especially useful in this area. . . .

" '. . . After a while I came to New York where I met up with—well, he was thirty. Elderly, I thought. And was forever taking a nip of bourbon.

" 'I was never sure what he did; he kept saying he had "connections downtown." It turned out his office was a rat's nest on West Forty-eighth Street, and he spent his days bilking widows and orphans. . . . We had some lovely years together, though, almost fourteen of them, and then—I guess he knew he'd bilked his last orphan or widow—he up and died on me. . . .

" 'If you have it like that for a while and if you've got any sense you realize you were luckier than most people, and you don't try it again. . . .

" 'Eventually, I came back here. Everybody in the family was dead. Except my Mums. Which is like saying I was back living in a house with a platoon of Marine recruiting sergeants. Mums started doing battle with the world the day she was born, and at eighty she still gets up every morning and puts on her battle gear. . . .

" 'I heard there was something called a home agent, and I decided to go to school and, after I'd learned how to read and write, try to learn how to be one of those. . . . I was forty-five years old when I got my degree. . . .' "

Bob put down the folder and said, "Suppose her husband didn't die; suppose he walked out on her, and when this show opens, he walks back. Right after Cooper's discovered the blight. . . .

"Their relationship—Cooper's and Stanwyck's, the way we've talked about it—it's the kind in which Cooper has turned to her for advice. All kinds of problems, personal ones and professional ones, and now all of a sudden when he's got the biggest problem of his life on his hands, what to do about the Lairds, she's off gallivanting with her husband. . . ."

Instead of having my tongue pickled and sent to the Diner's Club I said, "It could work."

I went to another office and in a couple of hours typed up what Bob and I had agreed on. It took a lot of pushing and pulling to meld the Cooper-Laird story with the Stanwyck story, and I was afraid that in writing the script, the problem was going to be even more difficult, maybe even insurmountable.

Since I foresee a large textbook sale for this volume— and, kids, you're going to have to buy a new edition every few days if you want to stay in *this* class, because in the textbook racket it's revisions, revisions, revisions—I would like to add a note that will interest those of you who, like myself, want to make $50,000,000 without lifting a finger. What looks like an insurmountable problem in the beginning in the end always turns out to be insurmountable.

I took what I'd written back to Bob, and he made a few minor suggestions for changes. . . . There is no such thing as a major change in a television script. What happens is not surgery; it's whittling.

Cooper came to Bob's office a little before lunchtime, and Bob told him the story. In the telling the part of the county agent (Cooper) grew larger and larger and that of the home agent (Stanwyck) got smaller.

"I like it," said Cooper. "I've got a few suggestions for minor changes, but . . ."

Bob, Cooper, and I had dinner that night at a Chinese restaurant. It was a relaxed, friendly dinner. Those people— although they all look alike—certainly know how to fill you up.

We talked some more about the outline, and Bob and Cooper said that they were sure the meeting at C.B.S. would be a great success.

"They're going to love it," said Cooper.

At one point Bob said, "I feel very optimistic about this series. For two reasons, one because I'd like to watch it, and also I'd like to write for it. I think a lot of writers are going to feel the same way."

Later, over the Chinese cookie course, Bob said that he had just seen Fellini's 8½, which had recently opened in New York.

"It's a beautiful film," he said, "a work of art, and it has something to say about society. Nobody makes pictures like that in California, and it isn't that none of them have any comment to make. People like Steve Allen and Brando, they're always joining committees for some cause or other, and I ask them, 'Look, if you feel so strongly, about the bomb, for instance, why don't you make a picture about it? How come the *French* made *Hiroshima, Mon Amour?* That's a picture that should have been made in *this* country.' Nobody ever seems to have an answer."

"I've got a lot of comments I want to make," said Cooper, "and as soon as I'm important enough, I'm going to do it."

A moment passed.

"The reason I mentioned it is that I think this series gives us a chance to make a comment on society, a real one," said Bob.

"It has to," I said.

"And if C.B.S. doesn't go along, we'll take it to another network," said Cooper.

Later that evening I had drinks with Harold Franklin, who had spent a large part of the afternoon with Joe Jacobs and other officials at United Artists, discussing my contract.

The mutual option clause had caused some concern, but Harold had remained adamant. "There was only one actual heart attack," he said, "but you'll get the clause. You won't get rich out of this, but you're going to be very well off."

Journal, July 8, 1963. Dear Diary: Tonight H.F. told me I was going to be very well off. . . .

It has been my observation that your good writer is your very-well-off writer, and y.v.w.o.w. is always getting himself quoted in the book and financial sections of the newspapers— lately often the same section—on matters like whether it's better for the future of American Letters to invest in American Motors or American Tel. and Tel.

As for the swimming pool, etc., while Thoreau didn't have one, he did, after all, have a *pond*, and in those days that was practically the same thing.

I spent part of Tuesday conferring with Cooper on his ideas, and while Bob and Cooper told the story to Dorso, I went to the Gorham and started work on the outline that was going to be presented to C.B.S. the following afternoon.

By ten o'clock Wednesday morning—300 minutes before H-Hour—I was finished. I took the 12½-page outline to the U.A. offices, but Bob was out.

When he came back, I could tell that he had either been at the dentist or had been working on another of U.A.'s series.

He read the outline.

"It's good," said Bob, "but you've given them too much on the one hand and not enough on the other. But nothing that can't be fixed."

I glanced at the clock across the street; it was then a few minutes after twelve.

When Cooper arrived a little while later Bob gave him the outline, and he read it.

"I love it," he said. "They're all going to love it."

"It's too long," said Bob. "For a presentation like this, the outline shouldn't be more than four or five pages at most."

"Maybe it's a little long," said Cooper.

"This won't take any time at all," said Bob, "and remember, Merle, this won't have anything at all to do with the script you write. This is just to get the approval of the brass so that we can proceed to the next step."

"Nothing at all to do with the script you write," said Cooper.

Bob's secretary brought in some hatchets, saws, scalpels, pruning shears, rusty razor blades, and old hairpins.

Voice One: Now we'll put Abby's head on Ruthy's body. . . .

Voice Two: And instead of putting the last scene first we'll put the third-act curtain at the end of the first act, and then . . .

Voice One: Hand me the pruning shears and the Scotch tape.

Voice Two: This looks like it would make a better arm than a leg, and, besides, the agent's uncle has already got two legs . . . while . . .

"Va-room! Ka-room!" said Cooper.

"What?" I said.

"Va-room! The bulldozing may remind some of them at the meeting of *Hud*," said Cooper, "and the minute that happens . . ."

"We thought they could dynamite out the trees," said Bob.

"But they wouldn't," I said. "That's the whole point. They bulldoze and burn."

"Are you sure they couldn't dynamite out the trees?" Cooper asked.

"Well, I'm not *sure* they couldn't. . . ."

"Anyway," said Bob, "this has nothing to do with the script you write."

"Not a thing," said Cooper. "Va-room! Ka-room!"

At ten minutes to three Cooper said, "We aren't going to have time to make any copies; so I'll just act it out. Which is better anyway."

Dorso came in, looking rested, tanned, and cheerful.

"It's a beautiful story, Merle," he said. "Jack and Bob told me about it yesterday. They're all going to be very happy with it."

We walked the three blocks from the U.A. offices to the C.B.S. building at 485 Madison Avenue.

The meeting was to be in Michael Dann's office, and we waited in the foyer for a few minutes, and then the receptionist said, "Mr. Dann is ready now."

Dann, a short, rounded man, rose from behind what must be one of the largest desks on the island of Manhattan; I kept thinking of the desk that Chaplin sat behind in *The Great Dictator*.

Dann greeted Cooper, Dorso, and Bob. Dann and I, who had never met, shook hands.

Other high-priced executives there were Larry White, still looking pale, a man named Frank Shakespeare, about whom I remember nothing else, and a dark melancholy man who was, I believe, head of the network story department. He looked like several people with advanced degrees in English literature I have known, none of them well.

For a few minutes there was the usual, uneasy exchange of male jokes that always precedes getting down to business.

Dann said that Jim would not be present, and he made several frivolous comments about Bob's getup. Bob was wearing an orange sports shirt, a more-or-less tan summer suit, and the soot-sprinkled white sneakers.

Dorso laughed and then, getting serious, said that Cooper, Bob, and I had come up with a great story line, a comment I found surprising since, twenty minutes before when we were throwing together the outline, *I* didn't know what it was about.

A good deal of Dann disappeared behind his desk, and

everybody else except Cooper seated himself. Cooper stood directly in front of the desk.

Dann suggested that Cooper explain to the other executives what a county agent was and what he did.

Cooper said, "Well, in the first place he's a dedicated man . . ."

I took a look around the office. Wall-to-wall carpeting. To be sure. There were three windows to Dann's right and three behind him; venetian blinds were drawn on those to the rear of his desk. They face on a brick wall.

It was hot, but the air conditioner was turned off during the meeting. Several telephones were hung behind the desk, and they were not turned off.

Dann answered calls on all the telephones as Cooper told the other executives the nature of the man he planned to portray for twenty-six weeks during prime time on the C.B.S. program schedule for the 1964-1965 season.

When Cooper finished with his description of county agents, he placed the wounded pages with the story line on Dann's desk and said, "We haven't had time to make copies, but it's a wonderful story line, and I know you're all going to love it."

Dann nodded and then the rest of the executives nodded, too.

Cooper began by explaining each of the characters in the story; then he described the setting, including the art colony, ". . . wildly modern but also beautiful. The architect was a disciple of Gropius, Frank Lloyd Wright, and Philip Johnson. The townspeople may laugh at it, but the students from the Harvard School of Architecture come to study it. . . .

"Now let me tell you about our two regular girls. One is the office assistant. Her name is Lydia Willard. The other is a girl from the East, who's teacher and a student at the art colony, a real bitch on wheels, a perfect foil for Lydia and the county agent.

"She's a graduate of Vassar," said Jack. "That's one of the things about this series. Nobody's a . . ."

I believe he started to say, "Nobody's a hillbilly."

Instead he said, "Nobody's a jerk. Not even the Lairds. They're sharecroppers, sure, but the father wants to send the kids to college, and Jack—I'll call the county agent Jack— he doesn't have a name yet—anyway, Jack—the Laird boy; he's sixteen, idolizes Jack—and I'm going to do everything I can to help the boy and the oldest girl—she's seventeen—get to the State University, where I went. And Abby—that's the part Barbara's going to play—Stanwyck—she went to the State University too."

Cooper was sweating.

Dann was answering more telephone calls, receiving verbal messages and documents on crinkly paper from several secretaries, crinkling and studying the documents, noisily opening all the drawers of his desk and noisily closing them, passing a box of King's Ransom cigars, suppressing a yawn or two, not suppressing a yawn or two, packing and unpacking and repacking a dispatch case that was open near his desk.

The other executives took notes on what Dann was doing and, on occasion, glanced at Cooper.

". . . I go back to the Lairds and tell them what I've found out," said Jack. "They've got to burn the entire grove, every single tree. . . . The kid—he's the one who thinks that I'm the greatest invention since the wheel—the kid he looks at me and he hates me. There goes college; there goes everything. Finished. Wiped out. . . . I *know* that, but I *have* to tell them. *That's* my job. . . . I hate myself. And all of a sudden these people—they've loved me, respected me—they hate me. I'm surrounded by enemies.

"And the old man, old man Laird, he looks at me, hating my guts, and he says, 'Get off my land.' "

Dann pried open the most reluctant drawer of his desk and took out a crinkly piece of paper.

With a flourish, he wrote something on it. Then he turned the paper over on his desk and put his hand on top of it.

Cooper's performance was magnificent, but I hated every character, every incident, every line, and, especially, every ka-*room*.

I knew damn well what Dann had written:

"If C.B.S. has a brain in its corporative head, it will invest those millions in U. S. Savings Bonds."

Cooper read the last paragraph, "Everybody in this play has found out something he didn't know in the beginning. . . . The home agent—that she can't go back to a wasted life. Me—I've found out that when the going gets rough you can't count on anybody but yourself. . . . To paraphrase a very wise man, 'making a decision isn't easy, but once you've done it, you're committed.'"

Cooper looked up. He was greeted with total silence.

He took a handkerchief out of his pocket and started to wipe the sweat from his face.

Vice-presidential throats were cleared, vice-presidential feet were shuffled, hitherto-ignored vice-presidential itches attended to, vice-presidential coughs coughed.

"That's it," said Cooper.

Dann snapped his dispatch case shut. The others didn't move.

The eyes of Michael Dann vice-president in charge of making public pronouncements, traveled the room. Everybody's eyes were on the piece of crinkly note paper.

"Five minutes ago," said Dann, "I wrote something on this piece of paper."

He reached down, picked it up, and turned it over.

His handwriting is large and clear; he had written, "A great story."

Then, for the benefit of the nearsighted he said, "I think it's a great story, just great, and that's what I wrote on this piece of paper five minutes ago."

Dorso smiled and said, "Of course you did, Mike. It *is* a great story."

Cooper, still wiping his face, said, "I told you it was a great story. Isn't that what I said at the beginning? It's a great story."

Bob looked at me and smiled.

Dann turned to each of the executives and asked for his executive opinion. After some thought each in turn volunteered that it was a great story.

"What a fresh approach."

"And no violence."

"That's what's so refreshing—well, among so many other things."

"That's one thing that's refreshing—no violence."

"And they're all so real."

"The characters, all of them. They're real."

"That's the important thing," said Dorso. "These are *real* people. Jim knew that when we had that wonderful meeting in California. . . . This is a series about real people with real problems that everybody faces and can understand and sympathize with. *That's* the whole point."

I was wondering if I might not get Harold to call Joe Jacobs again. . . .

"Are you going to want copies?" Cooper asked Dann.

"We don't need any. It's not necessary. Everything's going along just beautifully."

"This whole thing is going to be something new in television," said Cooper. "There's never been anything like it before."

Dann asked the lesser executives if they had any criticisms or suggestions.

Since by that time it was clear that we were dealing with a classic of the caliber of *Othello,* the criticisms were minor. "Well, maybe the handkerchief scene is a *little* too long, although it's a beautiful scene, and since Desdemona and Iago and the Montague family—especially Juliet, her wanting to go to college and all is so moving—maybe the handkerchief scene, which is a beautiful and essential scene, is too *short.* . . . Although on the other hand . . ."

"It has all the elements I've always said you need in a pilot," said Dorso.

Dann turned to Bob. "How soon can you and Merle finish the script?"

"Not me," said Bob. "I'm the creative consultant. Merle's the writer."

Dann swiveled his chair in my direction.

"In other words, you're the only one who can screw it up."

"If it's screwed up, it'll be Bob and me. If it's a triumph, it'll be me," I said.

We all enjoyed a hearty chuckle.

On the way back to the U.A. offices—the afternoon had got muggier—Dorso said, "Well, another triumph."

"When I walked in there and saw all those executives and no Jim Aubrey," said Cooper, "I felt the adrenalin rise, and I tell you before I had my . . ."

"Analysis will do that for you," said Dorso. "That's the purpose of analysis. Before my own highly successful . . . But this was a triumph. An absolute triumph."

Bob and I were walking a little ahead, and since I wasn't sure whether Dorso meant his analysis was a triumph or the meeting was, I looked at Bob. I could tell he wasn't sure either.

"I went right ahead with it," said Cooper.

"And you were wonderful," said Dorso. "Wasn't he wonderful, fellows?"

Bob and I said that Cooper was wonderful.

"Sometimes I ask myself," said Dorso, "why *I* am needed."

I turned and breathlessly waited for the answer.

"I am needed," said Dorso, "because I get shows on the air."

"I went right ahead with it," said Cooper. "I didn't let anything stop me."

"And when Mike Dann wrote on that piece of paper," said Dorso, "it was a triumph, an absolute triumph."

When I got back to the Gorham, a pleasant surprise was waiting. The accountants, who run almost everything already, and just you wait, had finally let go with the hundred bucks for my academic triumph on *Invitation to Learning*.

I called Evan and suggested dinner.

"My charge account again?" he said.

"No. Château Henri IV. At Sixty-fourth and Madison."

The dinner was superb, and so was the wine, and so were the stingers. And, incidentally, the whole thing was dirt cheap, only $99.98, minus the tip.

"But your meeting *was* a triumph," said Evan. "Wasn't it a triumph, *garçon?*"

The *garçon* nodded and added another ten dollars to the check.

"You are going to be the richest writer in all the world," Evan said. "You will be able to lend money to the Maharajah of Kooch Behar, and yet you are morose."

"I didn't care for that, 'In other words, you're the only one who can . . .'"

"You're perfectly right," said Evan.

"Bob said that is just television-executive humor. Well, if it is, I don't like television-executive humor."

"You're perfectly right," said Evan.

"Humor-shmumor. I should have got up and said, 'Fellows, find yourself another writer.'"

"You're perfectly right," said Evan.

"I could have gone back to Brewster, my integrity intact, and all of my friends would have congratulated me, and . . ."

"You're perfectly right."

"Look, I may have had a quart or two of stingers, but I will not be condescended to, goddamn it."

"This priest has been having trouble with his parishioners," said Evan, "and he's new to the community. So he goes to this rabbi, who's an older, more experienced man, and he says, 'Rabbi, my flock is full of complaints, and I just don't know how to handle them.'

" 'My flock is like lambs,' says the rabbi. 'Never a trouble.'

" 'Would you mind if I sit in on one of your sessions?' asks the priest. 'Maybe I could learn something.'

" '*Mon plaisir*,' says the rabbi, who is a man of the world. 'Step behind the curtain here. . . .'

"The first woman to rush in is Mrs. Cohen.

" 'Rabbi,' she says, 'the trouble I have from Mrs. Shapiro, you shouldn't know from it. Firstly, her children she never feeds and her husband she gives him supper from out of a can and he's lucky to get even that because she's running around with other men all the time.'

" 'You're right, Mrs. Cohen,' says the rabbi, 'you're right.'

" 'A kosher house she doesn't keep; she mixes *milkadicka* and *fleshadicka* dishes, and about you, Rabbi, she talks about everybody, but about you, what she says it chops my blood like water. That you eat pork, even on Yom Kippur.'

" 'You're right, you're right.'

"In a few minutes Mrs. Cohen gets up, unburdened, smiles and says, 'You should live and be well, Rabbi, and your feet I could kiss you're such a Solomon.'

". . . Then Mrs. Shapiro rushes into the room, 'Rabbi! I just saw Mrs. Cohen leave, that *kourva,* that she lifts her skirt for every man in the neighborhood.'

" 'You're right, Mrs. Shapiro. You're right.'

" 'Her husband, TV dinners she throws on the table if he's lucky, and her children, I swear to you if I didn't sneak them a piece of bread and chicken fat they would starve. Everything they call a mother nowadays.'

" 'You're right, Mrs. Shapiro, you're right.'

" 'But all that I could stand and not a syllable would pass my mouth, but when she starts talking about you—my heart it tears out in little pieces. That you smoke on *shabbos,* that you do dirty tricks with the women in the *micvah*—the rest I can't tell you I'm embarrassed.'

" 'You're right, Mrs. Shapiro, you're right.'

"A few minutes later Mrs. Shapiro rises, heaves a sigh of relief and says, 'Good-by, Rabbi, if we'll live and be well I'll come again to see you next week. If not, the week after.'

"Mrs. Shapiro leaves and the priest comes out from behind the curtain. He's furious. 'That was disgraceful,' he says. 'Mrs. Cohen tells you those horrible stories about Mrs. Shapiro—and what do you do; you nod and tell her she's perfectly right.'

" 'And then Mrs. Shapiro comes in and tells you worse stories about Mrs. Cohen, and you keep saying, "You're right, Mrs. Shapiro, you're right." Both women can't be right. I tell you you're a disgrace to your cloth. A disgrace.'

" 'You're right,' says the rabbi, 'you're right.' "

I came back to Brewster on Friday and throughout the weekend managed to ignore the fact that I had a script to write.

There were distractions. My guest was a woman of whom I am usually fond. I have known her for sixteen years and was married to her for several of those—but she brought her two murderous cats.

Saturday morning at seven—we had been up until three—I was jolted awake by a game of leapfrog the cats were playing on and under my bed.

Believe me, it's almost as hard to kick a cat as a pigeon; I've tried both.

My two-footed guest, Elinor Green, made one further mistake. She did not leave until Monday morning. My theory about weekend guests is that they should arrive—catless and childless—on Saturday afternoon, late, and leave Sunday afternoon, early. Which is one of the reasons I have that large poster in my living room, an old Brazilian folk saying, "Guests and corpses begin to smell after forty-eight hours." Unhappily, none of my guests read Portuguese.

It was after eleven on Monday when I finally got rid of the guests and around to a shower. The bathroom floor was sprinkled with a substance called, I believe, Kitty Litter, which kept turning up under toe for the next ten weeks.

Kitty Litter had been the original grounds for my divorce.

After the shower I went outside, kicked a few trees, spoke harshly to a ubiquitous bluejay, and grabbed a worm away from a pushy robin.

I finished another pot of coffee and then checked on the three monkeys I keep chained to desks and typewriters in the basement. They were still working on *The Beverly Hillbillies, Petticoat Junction,* and whatever the new spin-off will be.

I walked around the typewriter, wiggled my ears at it, kicked it in the keys—typewriters are easier to kick than cats and pigeons and it doesn't hurt as much as kicking a tree—and then I insulted it. "You know what you are, don't you? A *machine*. And nobody really likes or trusts a *machine. . . .*"

The typewriter waited patiently, knowing who would win in the end.

I sat down and waited for *the characters to take over.*

I keep reading about writers who claim that in their novels and plays and quatrains the characters eventually take over for them, which sounds like an ideal arrangement.

But it has never happened to me.

Around four—it was two hours before cocktail time—I started to work. "The quick brown fox . . ."

Eventually I picked up the bits and pieces of the story line and started putting them in order but making no major changes.

I had been warned by both Bob Aurthur and Jack Cooper that any major changes would require our going back to the network for another conference with the vice-presidents. Never.

"But I thought that . . . well, didn't you both say that the outline we gave them didn't matter, and, afterwards, it could be changed? . . ."

"If we make any changes in the story line now, we're in trouble," said Cooper.

Okay, no changes.

Late that night I finished the expanded outline and the next morning mailed one copy to Bob in New York and another to Cooper in North Hollywood.

During the rest of that week and the next two I developed the fictional county in which the series was to take place and wrote about the people who lived there.

Nobody asked me to do it, but—for better, for worse—that is the way I go about any extended piece of work.

I always put down all the major facts about the principal characters from the moment they are born until they appear —the kind of childhood they had, their education, the houses they live in, their tastes in other people, what they do with their spare time, and how each got involved with the others.

A few rare times I have even discovered those secret places where a character lives.

Calhoun County is as large as the state of Rhode Island. The landscape is filled with wild and vivid contrasts. In the background are the Padres Mountains, topped by snow. In the foothills, cattle range and feed in a never easy struggle to survive. Below the grazing land is the desert, demanding reds, promising grays. The mesa sprawls in exotic abstract formations.

There is a great openness about the territory and about the people who inhabit it. They are gregarious, warm, and friendly.

The county seat, Rio del Oro, has 12,000 inhabitants. Five years ago it was one third that size. . . . The rapid increase is largely due to the Army installation nearby.

The main street of Rio del Oro is a combination of the several cultures, Anglo, Indian, and Spanish-American. . . . There are saloons built early in the century for cow hands, harness shops, and chili parlors.

We cannot escape the tourists who are endlessly taking pictures of each other, and, when they can remember, the scenery. For them there is a haberdashery that stocks J. Press suits and Italian shoes, a woman's shop as elegant and high-priced as Neiman-Marcus, a bookshop that has all the latest books, *and* the *Kenyon Review,* plus all those fancy paper-backs that everybody buys but nobody reads.

Rio del Oro is not drab. Many of the houses are mass-produced, but many are genuine adobe. The town exudes vitality, but there is never a feeling of bustle. There is plenty of time for everything—a cup of coffee, a casual conversation, even good manners. . . .

In most of contemporary society privacy is impossible. Somebody invariably seems to be looking over our shoulder, and often we are stared at not only through binoculars but by closed-circuit television. . . . Nowadays, most people appear to be terrified by privacy. Otherwise we would have not arranged things as we have.

In Calhoun County, however, privacy is abundantly available. The county agent, the home agent, and the county agent's uncle are, for example, fond of people, but there are many times when they need to be alone.

"I have never found the companion that was so compatible as solitude."

At the time I was reading Thoreau almost exclusively—the journal, the *Familiar Letters,* and *Walden.* I don't know why.

Evan and Hope Taylor came up several evenings during that two-week period, and Evan suggested that the county agent's surname be the same as the county itself. Cooper had earlier suggested the given name, Ev, for Everet.

As always, I consulted the thin pink and blue volume that I keep in my study, between *Bartlett's* and *Who's Who in America, What Shall We Name the Baby?*

"Everet, Everett, Everard, Evers . . . Strong or brave, as the wild boar [Teutonic]. . . . The boar was, in primitive days, a respected antagonist."

Fine—although the *boar* part worried me a little.

I wrote;

The name of the county agent is Everet Calhoun. **Almost** everybody calls him Cal; a few strangers call him Ev. **Not** many.

His grandfather was one of the earliest Anglos to arrive in the county.

Benjamin Calhoun was a man of honor—the best and the rarest kind of pioneer, interested in building rather than looting. He believed in public service and was for a time lieutenant governor of the territory. When the territory became a state—let us say in 1915—he was one of the first U.S. senators.

He once said [*obviously* I was reading Thoreau], "For what is the purpose of a man's life if not to make the world a better place?"

That inscription is at the base of the statue of Benjamin Calhoun which stands in the town plaza.

Cal's mother could trace her ancestry back to the Conquistadores. . . .

His father was decent, hard-working, and kind, but unable to deal with the complexities that had become necessary to survive during the hectic boom times of the 1920s. . . .

Most of what Cal's grandfather had accumulated—both land and money—gradually fell into the hands of the antagonist's family, the Sloanes. They were members of that most demanding of religions, the Dutch Reformed Church.

. . . It is part of the Sloane way of life to get theirs while the getting is good. . . . Pull up the ladder, mates, I'm aboard.

Sometimes Eric Sloane [the antagonist] may prove to be right; Cal may be wrong. . . . Cal, however, learns from his mistakes. Eric would like to but rarely does.

He is a rigid man. . . . The insensitive and unobservant often mistake rigidity for strength. Not so. . . . A rigid man senses the weakness within himself, and once he takes a position he can't change it. He is too afraid he would reveal uncertainty, which he equates with weakness. . . .

To Eric, ideas are black or white, good or evil, and people are either rich or poor, successes or failures. . . . He has never seen The Joke; he doesn't even know there is one. The sound of laughter embarrasses him; he was born middle-aged.

If one brick were to be removed from the wall he has built around himself, the whole façade would collapse. We will see that happen in a later script involving his wife, Nan, and his three children.

Cal sees life as complex, subtle, strange, and forever puzzling. Since he is—in general—fond of people, they amuse him. . . . Decisions are never easy because there are always too many elements to be considered. How can you ever know you're right? Well, you can't. But you have to give people the benefit of the doubt. Not for their sake, for yours.

There were no fun and games in Eric's youth, his parents were Dutch-English, and were hard-working, successful farmers. Eric was the eldest son. Thus, by the laws of primogeniture, Eric, merely by being born, inherited his father's entire estate, and he was never allowed to forget the responsibilities involved. He worked harder and longer than anybody else.

Cal was taught the uses of leisure, the joys of occasional idleness, the rewards of thought, the value of questions.

Cal and Eric were never close, but when they were boys there was a rivalry between them. Cal rode superbly. Eric never had a pony or a horse. He did play football; he was a well-muscled boy, full-grown at sixteen.

But even at sixteen Eric put on a mask before he got out of bed in the morning. . . . He had no intention of letting anyone know where he lived. He still hasn't.

Cal is much more open, frank, and outgiving; he usually expects the best of people and is often wrong. . . . Eric always expects the worst of people and is often right. . . .

Cal threw the javelin at track meets; Eric was a shot-putter. Cal swam free style; Eric swam breast stroke. . . . Cal, without seeking popularity, had it; Eric sought it and never achieved it.

. . . Cal learned very early not to reach out to find in

somebody else what he should have in himself. . . . The sciences always interested him; he has a probing mind, but he always knew that he could never spend his life in a laboratory. He is too fond of the outdoors. . . .

One afternoon while I was still working on the notes Cooper called, ecstatically happy:

Cooper: "Merle, I was walking down the hall at Television City, and I bumped into Aubrey and Mike Dann. Aubrey said, 'I hear you've got a wonderful story line. When am I going to hear it?' "

Miller: "Uh-huh."

Cooper: "Dann said, 'Not until it's on film.' "

Miller: "Uh-huh."

Cooper: "But Aubrey had a look on his face of 'Ah, come on, guys.' "

Miller, to himself: *That* I would like to have seen.

Miller, aloud: "Uh-huh."

Cooper: "And so I said, 'Okay, Jim. I'll read it to you.' It was lucky because I just happened to have your lengthened version of the story line right in my hand."

Miller, to himself: And your cello.

Miller, aloud: "You certainly were lucky."

Cooper: "This time I did practically no ad-libbing. I just read what you'd written, and Jim smiled *all* the way."

Miller: "*All* the way?"

Cooper: "All the way."

Miller: "Uh-huh."

Miller, to himself: I'll bet he didn't smile *all* the way; if you want my opinion the only time he smiled was when the

Lairds' grove is set afire and they throw a few of the kids in. That's when he smiled. If you ask me.

Cooper: "What you've written is so beautiful, Merle, and when I finished I asked him if he had any suggestions, and you know what—he didn't, not a single suggestion of any kind. . . . And later, Mike Dann told me this was the first time he could *ever* remember when Aubrey didn't have any suggestions. He said Aubrey usually has about a hundred. . . . But that's because what you've written is so beautiful, Merle."

Miller: "Uh-huh."

Miller, to himself: Perhaps I have misjudged Aubrey; just because he can chin himself and is handsomer than I am and a whole lot richer. If what Cooper says is true, the man is not without taste.

Cooper: "Merle, there's wonderful enthusiasm around town. Just wonderful. They *know* this is going to be another *Defenders.*"

Miller: "Not even one suggestion?"

Cooper: "Nope. Not one. . . . God bless you, Merle."

I had scarcely finished the second verse of "God Bless America" when Cooper called a second time. He had just received the character sketch and description of Everet Calhoun.

Cooper: "I haven't finished reading it yet, but I love it. I love everything about it. It's sophisticated. And real. And I love all the stuff about his grandfather. And I love the fact that the county is named after me. I love it. I haven't finished it yet, but I love it. . . . God bless you, Merle."

Miller: "Do you have any suggestions?"

Cooper: "Not a one. It's just perfect."

Miller: God bless you, Jack."

As one grows more secure in life the charitable organizations one supports are generally the solid ones, and the ink was not yet dry on the monthly check to the Birch Foundation—a somewhat larger contribution than I had planned—when the telephone rang yet again.

Another California call, this one from a friend who also knows Cooper. "Jack's walking on air; he says you've done a simply wonderful job, and he couldn't be happier, and he thinks you're a wonderful, wonderful writer. You're going to get rich out of this one, Merle, which is nice. Anybody that works as hard as you do deserves to be rich. Jerry Wald worked as hard as you do, and he was rich. . . ."

I had made up my mind to have four machine guns in my air-raid shelter instead of the two I'd originally planned when the phone rang once more.

This time it was only Bob Aurthur.

Aurthur: "Cooper just called me. He thinks you're doing a wonderful job."

Miller: "God bless you, Bob Aurthur."

Aurthur: "When you start getting all that money you will be known as Mellow Merle Miller. No more carping criticism of twentieth-century society, no more being *mean*. You will realize that if you can't write something nice, it is better to write nothing at all. . . . And as a mellow writer of tender, heart-warming prose, the *Reader's Digest* will be waiting in line to publish anything you write, including your laundry list."

Miller: "Well, you know what I've always said, your good writer is your very rich writer."

Aurthur: "And when you write your next novel, which will be in the tender, heart-warming style those of us who love you have always known you had in you, I want the dedication to me to be uncluttered."

Miller: "God bless you, Bob Aurthur."

That night, after I had sung all four verses of "Jesus Loves Me, This I Know"—I fell into an untroubled dreamless sleep from which, if I had the sense I was born with, I never would have awakened.

On the twenty-fourth Bob Aurthur telephoned—is it any wonder A.T.&T. declared an extra dividend at the end of the month?—to say that he had received a mimeographed copy of all the notes and was impressed with them.

He suggested that I do a book explaining how a pilot is pasted together, making use of all the notes, the telegrams, the telephone calls, and the conversations.

"It could be published around the time the show goes on the air," he said.

I thanked him for the idea, which is one of the reasons this book is in part dedicated to Bob.

It is a sentimental gesture and, like so many sentimental gestures, it saves money. Better a dedication than a share in the royalties.

"By the way, have you heard from Cooper lately?" asked Bob.

"I talked to him day before yesterday, for more than an hour. Twice."

"He say anything special?"

"Just that he loved everything I had done and that he didn't know what they'd do without me and that everybody else loved everything. . . ."

"I suggest you call one chapter of this book, 'No Comment' or possibly, 'On Working with an Actor,' " said Bob, chuckling.

"When you get around to telling me," I said, "then perhaps we could both chuckle."

"Have you seen yesterday's daily *Variety?*"

I confessed that, regrettably, that unique publication, as important a part of the culture of Hollywood as its faith-healer surgeons and its Southern Baptist psychoanalysts, seldom reached my pinewoods.

(This is to distinguish it from the weekly *Variety* which is published in New York and which is delivered to me every Wednesday.)

"I think this will interest you," said Bob, and he began read-aloud a 1500-word interview with Cooper, much of it in English.

Cooper said that he had been in show business for thirty-seven years, that his first two television series, *The People's Choice* and *Hennesey,* in addition to contributing to the strength and general welfare of the Republic had made him a millionaire.

" 'Cooper was . . . never just an actor on TV; he is also producer-director and general behind-the-scenes factotum.

" 'All of which is probably why he was able to sell his newest series to C.B.S.'s Jim Aubrey sans pilot or anything else, just an idea. Cooper took fifteen minutes explaining his series idea to the C.B.S. prez and Aubrey replied, "It's on." Thus came into being a multimillion-dollar series for 1964-1965 in which producer Cooper will show actor Cooper as a county agricultural agent. . . .' "

Bob paused.

"How do you like it so far?"

After a brief but thoroughgoing consideration I said, "Well, for one thing, the lyric style is reminiscent of some of the earlier Yeats and for another it has an air of earthy realism that is all too often lacking in present-day journalism, especially the part where President whatshisname says 'It's on.' Would you mind repeating *that* part, beginning where it says 'Cooper took fifteen minutes . . .' "

"Well, there's a lot more to come," said Bob, "but since U.A. is picking up the tab . . ."

Aurthur read that part again, giggling more than I found seemly, and then went on to read how " 'At one point in the subsequent negotiations, C.B.S. indicated they preferred a 13-week firm deal instead of the 26 weeks Cooper wanted. Replied Cooper: "My star is too expensive." ' "

There was a lot about Cooper as a child star, from when he started in Our Gang comedies at $50 a week to when Metro signed him in 1931 for $1000 a week.

" 'In TV it has always been a more robust financial picture for the young vet. Partnered with George Burns and Irving Brecher in the *Choice* series, they received a $1,000,000 down payment on its syndication. Partnered with Don McGuire in *Hennesey*, they got $600,000. And the latter show will gross $25,000 a show in reruns in five more years, Cooper estimates. "I never had many partners, so there wasn't too much cut out of the pie."

" 'For his new hour-long series, he is partnered equally with C.B.S. TV and U.A. TV. If the past is any criterion, the rich may get richer on this one.' "

Bob continued reading how *Cooper* had first thought of the idea, how *Cooper* had done all kinds of research about county agents and about how *he* had gone to Arizona, New Mexico, and Southern California in pursuit of the truth, and how *he* had discovered what were referred to as interesting vignettes—one about a hardy pioneer who wouldn't sell his land to the Army for its White Sands Missile Base, so that he lives right in the center of what is a missile range—and so on.

Bob stopped reading again, still laughing merrily.

"Is that all?"

"That's all. . . . By the way, Cooper's name is mentioned sixteen times and there are thirty additional references to *he*, *his*, and *I*, all of them referring to Cooper. Merle, I fail to see even *one* mention of your name."

"Of course not," I snapped in a friendly fashion. "Jack understands my feeling that these days the only way you get your name to be a household word in the literary racket is you *shun* personal publicity. You keep saying all the time how distasteful you find it, and you write letters to people like Sainte-Beuve, who writes under the name of Leonard Lyons, saying that the mere thought of seeing your name in print . . ."

When Bob hung up he was either laughing or he had a fishbone caught in his throat. I hoped the latter.

About a half hour later Cooper called; it was one of our short, forty-five-minute conversations.

At one point he said in, I felt, a worried manner, "I guess you've seen the article in yesterday's *Variety*."

I said that I hadn't but that I had heard about it and that I understood it was awfully good publicity for the series and that made me awfully happy. . . . (In other words, "You're right, Mrs. Shapiro.")

That was the new Merle Miller talking, or Rabbi.

The old Merle Miller, the snarly one—you'd have hated him—would have said, "It has, however, been read to me, and I want to congratulate *you* on *your* going to New Mexico and *your* uncovering all those interesting vignettes and *your* selling the idea to Aubrey . . . and now *you* write the pilot."

"It made me awfully unhappy," said Cooper, "and I called up *Variety* and complained."

Old Merle Miller: On account of they only mentioned your name sixteen times?

New Merle Miller, to himself: Y.R., M.S.

New Merle Miller, to Cooper: "Oh, you did? Called them up? Complained, did you?"

Cooper: "I complained to them because they didn't even mention your name at all, and I don't want you or anybody else to think that that's the way I treat my writers. I was embarrassed."

Old Merle Miller: I'll bet.

New Merle Miller, coast to coast: "Oh, shucks, Jack, I don't care about things like that."

Cooper: "Well, I do. I called them up and read them the riot act, and the reporter apologized, said he was sorry, but they just didn't have the space. . . ."

Later that evening, over our third helping of dessert, Hope Taylor and Evan commented about the article.

(I like something sweet after dinner and Hope has a very tasty recipe: Blend in an electric mixer one pint of chocolate ice cream, a touch of vanilla extract, three ounces of vodka, three ounces of creme de cacao. Fold into chilled parfait glasses, and if your guests really have a sweet tooth top off with brandy, flambé.)

Evan said, "The *Variety* story is just another example of the writer getting the short end of the stick."

Hope said, "Imagine making a million dollars on a series about a talking dog? Merle, you have two dogs . . ."

Evan said, "All through the ages writers have been taken advantage of. Elizabeth had her courtiers write all sorts of sonnets and things and then she said that *she* wrote them. So go argue with the girl who pays the executioner's salary."

"And $25,000 gross on every rerun of *Hennesey*," Hope said.

"It did win all sorts of citations from the A.M.A.," I said, "and—"

"I know," Hope said, "and the Navy considers it the sea-going version of *Le Médecin malgré lui*. Still, it *is* only a half-hour show."

Evan said, "Even Catherine the Great kept a stable of writers, and when she didn't have them otherwise occupied they wrote long tracts on the glory of Catherine and all the Russias. But guess who got the by-line in the Moscow edition of *Variety?*"

"Merle," said Hope, "the county agent series is going to be a full hour. You're going to be a very, very rich writer."

"If they ever acknowledge that the series has a writer," said Evan.

"They had a space problem," I said.

Hope said, "Yes, it is odd about *Variety's* space problem. C-o-o-p-e-r, M-i-l-l-e-r," she said, spelling it out.

"You see?" Evan said. "There aren't *that* many extra letters."

"Perhaps Evan is right," I said. "History past and present seems to bear him out. Did I ever tell you about the time David Shaw and Bob Aurthur were working for David Susskind, writing the *Mr. Peepers Show?*"

"You want to tell us, and we are willing to listen," said Hope.

"One day they were both slaving away at their typewriters —or so Bob Aurthur claims—when the door opened, and a couple of B'nai Brith ladies peered in, shepherded—although I don't think that's quite the word—by Mrs. Susskind, who said, 'And this is where my son David the Producer keeps his writers.' "

Journal, July 25: Finished the county agent notes today; the last two paragraphs.

. . . Nan Sloane [Eric's wife] . . . the only secrets she keeps from her husband are the important ones—like her thoughts, like the mysteries of her interior being, like the state of her soul.

For the moment, that's all. And probably far more than enough. . . . I guess there is nothing to prevent me from writing the script, although I am sure I'll try to think of something.

I am pleased with the notes, let's leave it at that.

Got a note this morning from an individual in the U. S. Information Agency saying, ". . . After careful consideration it is our opinion that the volume in question does not reflect favorably on the United States and thus . . ."

The volume in question is *That Winter,* written some fifteen years ago by me. A Yugoslav firm wants to publish it, and there is a fund set up—I guess by the U.S.I.A.—so that if the volume in question *does* reflect favorably on life in the U.S., the author in question, me, can get the *dinars* in dollars. Which makes a lot of sense. Otherwise, the *dinars*—in this case 30,000 of them—have to stay in Yugoslavia. And the author must spend them there.

I wrote to the U.S.I.A. individual telling her that she and her colleagues needn't read any more of my volumes; my aim as a writer is not to reflect favorably on life in the U.S. It is to reflect truthfully on it, and my truth is seldom if ever very favorable. And so on. . . . Wrote another letter to the Yugoslav publisher saying publish away. . . . I'm told I can have a great time in Belgrade on 30,000 *dinars*. And after I finish the script, I may want to spend a little time in Belgrade, quite a little. Like the rest of my life. I understand that at the current favorable rate of exchange 30,000 *dinars* is $1.25 or thereabouts.

I mentioned the Yugoslav publisher to Elinor last weekend. . . . She reminded me that when we were on our honeymoon—because of conflicting time schedules we went on our honeymoon before we got married—I was lecturing in, among other places, Toledo, Ohio. I mentioned *That Winter* in the lecture, favorably no doubt, and when I'd finished there was the usual question period during which a lady rose and said, "I happen to have read Mr. Miller's book, and he's missed the point of it.". . . Wait until she reads it in Serbo-Croat.

The chairlady in Toledo said to Elinor, "And when were you two children married?"

"We're going to be on Saturday," said Elinor.

No wonder it didn't last.

When I told my mother that I was being divorced, she was not at all surprised. "I knew it wouldn't last when she came to the wedding in that red dress."

Besides, the marriage took place at Ethical Culture, in New York. Algernon Black, a leader, did the deed.

Black asked the bride and me how we stood on segregation.

Against it.

Had we ever voted Republican?

We hadn't.

Had we paid our dues in the American Civil Liberties Union?

We had.

"I now pronounce you man and wife," said Black.

Mother came up afterwards, and I inquired how she felt

about the ceremony. "I'm sure it was all very interesting," she said, "but are you sure you're really married?"

> . . . Talked to Cooper today; he's leaving on Thursday for Las Vegas; they're taping a TV show he's doing with Danny Kaye. Cooper's enthusiasm for the project is higher than ever. He said, "I hope that just because I don't have any criticism you don't think I'm not involved; I'm totally involved. I just don't have any criticism."
>
> Evan called this evening. Talked for half an hour. He's enthusiastic, too. Said, "What's important about this is that the agent is a man who does something for people. And there's very little of that anywhere, especially on television."
>
> I told him about René Bertholet at Pindorama. René had said, "The need to do something useful—something socially important—is one of the most basic of human needs. That is why your Peace Corps is so important. For most people there simply isn't an outlet."
>
> . . . Have promised Cooper and Bob the script on August 6.

The script was not finished on August 6. Naturally.

Faced with a situation like that there are many alternatives; I know because I have tried them all.

One is to call your agent and ask your agent to call the editor—in this case Bob—and tell him that you are attending a funeral. This is the last resort of a scoundrel, and also nobody ever believes it.

Hope Taylor says that while she was my agent my mother died fourteen times, my father nine, a sister once, and a brother twice. . . . Hope exaggerates. It's a well-known fact that my mother and father are in perfect health, and I am and always have been an only child.

Besides, I couldn't call my agent because my agent was on *one* of the 1352 Greek islands.

Another alternative, which is even more dastardly, is to send a telegram to the editor.

On August 6 I sent a telegram to Bob Aurthur:

SCRIPT IN HANDS OF TYPIST STOP SHE HAS HAD AN ATTACK OF
CHILDBIRTH AND NATURALLY UNABLE TO TYPE STOP HOPES TO
RECOVER TODAY STOP WILL HAVE SCRIPT FOR YOU DAY AFTER
TOMORROW STOP SEE YOU THEN AND BEST WISHES HOPE YOUR
HEALTH HOLDS UP YOUR FRIEND MERLE.

I was about to get back into bed and pull the covers over
my head when the telephone rang.

I figured there hadn't been time for Bob to get the telegram; so I answered.

Just to be on the safe side, though, I used the voice of the
Chinese houseboy I intend to hire as soon as I can find one
who isn't *soft* on Communism, "Flied lice. . . . Mell Millel
lesidence."

Bob said, "A telegram is a coward's way out."

"You are talking to the plesident."

"Will I really have it on Thursday?"

"I swear on my mother's . . . Yes, Bob. Have I ever
lied . . ."

"Never. Except when you're writing a script," said Bob.
"How is it?"

"Roberto, it will absolutely knock you on your bonanza."

"In other words, it needs a lot of work. Well, don't worry;
first drafts always do. . . . How are you otherwise?"

"Otherwise I am broke."

"Still? How much have they paid you so far?"

"Nothing."

"You mean you've been working since June 3 and this is
August 6 and you still haven't been paid anything?"

"Not a cent."

"That is incredible, absolutely incredible. Where in Christ's
name is your agent?"

"In Greece. Everybody at the William Morris Agency is in
Greece. Except for those who are in Spain."

"Everybody?"

"Well, I think there's one switchboard operator. I *may* be
able to get in touch with her."

"Call her," said Bob, "and tell her to tell U.A. that unless they come through with the money right away, no script."

"She might get mad at me," I said, "and if she did, she might tell some of the big shots like Abe Lastfogel and Nat Lefkowitz, and they might decide they don't want to handle me any more. I mean they just don't handle anybody and then . . ."

"Lastfogel is in Spain and Lefkowitz is in Greece," said Bob. "It's the season, and as usual you are being taken advantage of. Look, you've done the story line, and *that's* what C.B.S. gave the go-ahead signal on. And you've written *eighty-three* pages of notes. Which everybody thinks are great. . . . For God's sake, Merle . . ."

"Well, I wouldn't like to get kicked out of William Morris."

"Your trouble, as I may have mentioned before, is that you have to be loved," said Bob. "*I* don't have an agent."

"I guess none of you people at U.A. have to be loved," I said, "which in a way is lucky because . . ."

"Call that switchboard operator."

I asked for Art Fuhrer, the William Morris lawyer who was handling all the negotiations for the county agent project.

Eventually a girl with a very soft voice whispered, "This is Mr. Fuhrer's office."

I gave my name and said, "I desire to speak with Mr. Fuhrer."

"He's in conference," she whispered.

"I could have told you that," I said. "How long will he be in conference?"

"I'm not sure, but I believe most of the day."

I did not whisper.

"Will you tell Mr. Fuhrer that I want him out of conference within the next fifteen minutes and I want him to call me in Brewster, New York. *Right away.*"

"Well, I'll tell him, but I'm not his real secretary. I'm his vacation secretary."

"But I'm his real client. *Right away.*"

Eleven minutes later Mr. Fuhrer called and in the calm, reasonable manner for which I am justly famous I screamed, "I've finished the goddamned pilot script but have no intention of delivering it to United Artists until I get some goddamned money."

"But that's unreasonable," said Mr. Fuhrer.

"You bet it is. No money, no script."

"But, Merle, this is a matter of good faith; you'll get your money. These things take time."

"Since June 3?"

"A lot of people are on vacation, you know."

I said, "Art, you have perhaps been told by Harold Franklin that I have the highest horse . . ."

"I'll call you right back," said Mr. Fuhrer.

An hour later he called back. He had talked to Joe Jacobs at U.A. and Fuhrer said that when I walked in with the script a check for $5000 would be waiting for me.

Evan and I worked the rest of the day and the next on the script. At dinnertime on the second day, Marion Harris, a Brewster housewife, arrived to type the last pages.

At one point while I was hotting up some leftover gruel I called in to Marion, who was typing away in the study, "How do you like the script?"

"It certainly smells good," she said.

A little after two the next morning the last pages had been typed and proofread.

I sent a night letter to Cooper in Hollywood:

SCRIPT IS FINISHED AND TO BE CONSERVATIVE I THINK IT IS BEAUTIFUL ANY WILD BELLS QUESTION MERLE.

Look, I was tired.

I read the entire sixty-three pages twice before falling asleep.

It had many things wrong with it—we'll come to those—but it had several virtues. It was honest; it was simple; and it was about problems and people that John White, Don Chappell, and Leonard Appleton would understand.

That morning at six-thirty Evan drove to New York and delivered the script by hand to Bob Aurthur.

I came to New York around noon, and Bob and I had lunch, after which we went to his office and went over the script, page by page, line by line.

Bob is the best script editor I've ever worked with, even when harried. That afternoon, he got a telephone call saying that a person associated with *The Patty Duke Show* threatened to commit suicide.

"Tell him I said nothing would give me greater pleasure," said Bob. "If he needs any help, call me back."

He was consulted every three seconds about three other pilots he was working on, *Mark Dolphin,* by N. Richard Nash, *Pioneer, Go Home,* by N. Richard Nash, and *Kibbee Hates Fitch,* by Neil Simon.

People kept rushing into his office saying, "But, Bob, you don't seem to realize" . . . "Wolf! Wolf!" . . . "The sky is falling! . . ."

Naturally, none of those things were of the slightest importance to anybody who got a passing mark in crayons in kindergarten.

But the script.

Bob said there were too many Lairds; he was right. So I did away with the three youngest children—they were too small to fight back—and the dog, Jebediah. . . . If Jebediah had lived I might at this very minute be sitting in my sauna.

"Too much talk, not enough action. You can cut. Here and here and here. And you can speed it up by . . ."

"Okay. I'm with you. . . . Okay, although I rather liked that part where . . ."

"So do I, but this is a pilot. . . . And, Merle, you have one major fault as a dramatist which while it may not necessarily be fatal . . . You *cannot* keep secrets from the audience."

"Where? I was very careful not to . . ."

"For one place, here. You're talking about the waiter at the Art Colony, and he's also a painter, and you say *he* looks proudly at *his* paintings. But since the audience can't read the stage directions, how do they know the paintings are his?"

"Well, that one little teensy . . ."

"And here and here . . ."

"Why do you hate me, Bob Aurthur?"

"And Sid [Stanwyck's husband] is just too obvious, too much of a schmuck. The audience is going to know from the beginning that she'll stick with her job rather than go away with him. That's okay, but make him more attractive. . . . Otherwise, it's an excellent first draft."

"But it needs a lot of work."

"It needs a little work."

The next morning, Bob and I—still bleeding—had another conference, and he suggested several more changes.

The accumulation of changes meant reworking the entire script and having it ready for Cooper when he arrived in New York the following Monday, August 12.

"Can you do it?" asked Bob.

"No, but I will."

"Don't knock yourself out," said Bob.

"I hope Jack likes it."

"He will. It's a good part for him. But remember, Merle . . ."

" 'Actors are not people.' "

"Besides," said Bob, "in the end there's only one person in all of this that's got to be pleased. Jim Aubrey. And don't ever forget it."

I said that I wouldn't, but I did.

Evan drove me back to Brewster that afternoon, and on Saturday we started making the changes Bob wanted, and, as always, making a few improvements that we wanted.

Hope Taylor and a mutual friend, Christopher Chase, came up on Sunday, and late Sunday afternoon and in the evening we all worked at separate typewriters.

We finished around midnight.

"Be sure you get the script to Cooper by ten in the morning," I said to Hope.

"Don't worry," she said. "He'll love it. I think it's one of the best things you've ever written. And I'm *not* your agent. I probably won't see you until after you get back from your reunion, so good luck in Iowa. And give my love to your mother."

"I didn't know you had a mother," said Chase, "but then I guess everyone does. . . . Anyway, give her my best."

"I may see you again before you go," said Evan, "but in case I don't, say hello to Dora for me."

I took a long walk that night through the pinewoods, over one stone fence and then a second, across a grove of larch and birch trees, and down a friendly hill.

I finally reached a familiar brook and sat down.

I heard the sound of the brook, the erratic beat of my heart, and Dora's voice:

"There are only two kinds of people in the world, Merle, those who get ahead and those who get by. . . . You'll be late for school, Merle; Lester Good is never late for school. . . . Merle, Lester Good swam across the Y pool five times and Lester told Mrs. Good that you didn't even . . . Lester Good not only gets straight A's in all his studies and then some, he swims like a fish and is on the basketball team and the football team, and Coach Dickerson told Mrs. Good, and she was at the Eastern Star the other night, and she said that Coach Dickerson said . . . Merle, you're going to ruin your eyes; you've always got your nose stuck in a book. . . . And I simply will not allow you to read at the table. . . . And nobody ever got rich by reading a book, Merle. And that's all I've got to say on that subject."

"No, it isn't," I said.

"Merle, don't sass your mother. Nobody likes a sass box. Lester Good . . . Your trouble is you won't face the facts, and that is all I've got to say on that subject."

"No, it isn't."

"Merle, you are getting gray. . . . Lester Good is forty-five and he hasn't got a gray hair in his head. I am seventy-eight years old and don't have a gray hair in my head, and when your Great-Grandfather Winders was ninety-three . . . We don't gray in the Winders family; we never have. . . . Face the facts, Merle; face the facts. And that is all I've got to say on that subject. . . . When I was at the Eastern Star meeting the other night Mrs. Good said Lester never misses a day at the Y. . . . Face the facts, Merle. That's what separates the sheep from the goats. . . ."

"And the men from the boys and the Goods from the Merles," I sassed. "Okay, Mums; I am getting a little gray here and there, and I am losing the teensiest bit of hair here and there, and between the two of them, they will lick the platter clean. . . . I am going to be one of those unusual bald men with gray hair. But, Mums, I am going to own my own pool, my own cabañas and Finnish sauna. . . . And next Saturday night when I get up at the 'new' Tallcorn Hotel . . .

"Ladies and Gentlemen, Fellow Classmates, Friends, Enemies . . . I'm glad to be back; I don't mind being back. . . . Put it this way. If I hadn't still been suffering from Brazilian jungle rot at the time I got Mary George's letter . . ."

Mary George Garrington was reservations chairman for the twenty-eighth reunion of the Marshalltown High School Graduating Class of 1935.

Her letter said, "In our preliminary discussion the opinion has been unanimous that the capstone of the whole observation could be provided by our esteemed classmate from the East."

Capstone? I looked it up, ". . . the crowning point, most important moment, decisive factor."

Had I ever been any of those before? Never. Would I ever be asked again? It seemed unlikely—except at the Emmy Awards next year.

So I accepted Mary George's invitation.

In March who ever thinks August is going to happen?

"There are only two kinds of people in the world, Merle, those who plan ahead and those who do not plan ahead, those who save money and those who squander, and a penny earned is a penny saved, Merle, and Lester Good has got a hundred thousand dollars in life insurance alone. If he should pass on, his mother will be sitting pretty. . . ."

"Look, Mums, if Jack Cooper likes the script, and he's going to love it . . ."

". . . Lester never married, Merle; he just never found Miss Right; some of us, of course, got married at Ethical Culture in New York—and I'm not mentioning any names, Merle. . . . And Lester is just the *best* cook. His recipe for lady fingers took up practically the whole woman's page of the *T-R* [*Times-Republican*] last week. . . . And that's the last word you'll get out of me on that subject."

"No, it isn't."

"It's none of my business, Merle, but what in the world are you going to talk to them about at the reunion? . . . Lester Good made the nicest little talk at the Star meeting the other . . . And everybody will have an eye on what you're saying."

"I thought I might . . ."

"A thing like that will simply fall flat on its face here in Marshalltown, Merle. You might be able to get away with a talk like that in New York City, but here in Marshalltown . . ."

I said good night to the brook and started back to the glass house.

I took two Miltown that night but didn't close an eyeball.

Toward dawn I got up, made some coffee, and settled down with my horoscope for the week ahead.

I got to the Pierre a little after eleven that morning.

"Merle, you look wonderful," said Cooper. "You must have

had a good night's sleep. Your friend brought the script a little while ago and I haven't quite finished reading it."

He made no comment on what he had read but I could tell he hated it.

I stood by the window. The view of Central Park was magnificent, but I hated it. I hated Central Park, and I hated the Pierre Hotel and everybody who was staying there.

I began making a list of all the people and things I hated and all the people and things that hated me. A very long list.

Finally Cooper said, "I've finished it, and it's beautiful."

I tore up the list, turned, and asked a question I have asked once or twice before in my life, "Did you really like it, Jack?"

"You've done a beautiful job," said Cooper. "It may need a little expansion here and there, things you and I know but people who haven't read the notes won't know. Nothing major."

Cooper and I spent the rest of the day discussing the changes and Bob joined us in the late afternoon.

He had already read a copy of the new script, and he said, "It's at least two hundred per cent better than it was on Friday."

That was a statement I didn't wholeheartedly go along with, but I kept my mouth shut. Nobody likes a sass box.

The three of us talked for some time, and I said that I'd get up early the next morning and do the changes.

As I left to go to the Gorham, Cooper said, "It's going to be a wonderful pilot, Merle, and Jim is going to be very excited."

I did go to bed early that night—about six, if you want to know—and slept beautifully.

I got up at five the next morning and by three in the afternoon had rewritten and pasted together a new version of the script, which I sent to the U.A. office by messenger.

Then I walked to the Biltmore Bar to have an early drink with John Willey, my book editor.

"Is there such a thing as a quadruple vodka-tonic?" I asked the bartender.

"I could serve you two doubles."

"Start out with one double," I said, "but stick around. You're going to do a land-office business."

John observed that I seemed more distraught than usual and inquired why.

I mentioned the forthcoming trip to Iowa and added, "And then there's the goddamn script."

"But I thought you finished that last week," said John, "and now when you get back from Marshalltown you can get back to work on the new novel."

"John," I said, "you may have heard that playwrighting isn't so much writing as it is rewriting, but a *television* pilot . . . However, Bob Aurthur and Jack Cooper are going to be delighted with the new draft which I just finished, and it is only about the eighth draft, and so . . ."

"One editor is better than two editors," said John, "but still."

"And they've sent a copy air mail to Dick Dorso, who's in California. I have to go to U.A. tomorrow and find out what he has to say."

Who, John wanted to know, is Dick Dorso?

That took some time to explain—nine or ten doubles' worth—but when I had finished, John nodded.

"Two editors are better than three editors," he said, "but still."

I said, "But even if Dorso likes it, the script has to go to Larry White at C.B.S., who is Director of Program Development . . . and if he likes it, it has to go to Frank Shakespeare, who I don't think is a relative, and if he likes it, it has to go to all the other vice-presidents in charge of, and if they like it, there's a vice-president in charge of talking named Mike Dann, and if he likes it then it has to go to a man named James T. Aubrey, Jr."

"I have to catch the five-nineteen," John said.

"In other words," I said, "it's like you have to get unanimous raves from *Playboy, Partisan Review, Confidential, Captain Billy's Whiz-Bang,* and the Marshalltown *Times-Republican* before you decide whether or not to publish a book, and you have to agree to make all the changes any of them want, and for most of them you have to spell out the hard words like c-o-u-n-t-y a-g-e-n-t. . . . And then . . ."

"Good luck in Iowa, Merle," said John, "and give my best to Dora."

The next afternoon I went back to the U.A. office for The Message.

It was about three when Bob's secretary said, "It's Mr. Dorso."

Bob got on the phone in his office, and Cooper got on the one just outside.

I just sat there, with my hands in my pockets.

"Isn't that wonderful," said Cooper.

Bob said to me, "He likes it."

Cooper said to me, "He thinks it's just wonderful."

Bob said, "Uh-huh, uh-huh. . . . The fair scene. He loves the whole idea of the fair. ⸳ . ."

Cooper said, "I love the fair scene, too, Dick; the fair scene is a wonderful scene. . . . Uh-huh, uh-huh."

Bob said, "Uh-huh, uh-huh. He thinks it has flow."

Cooper said, "Uh-huh. Uh-huh. And form. He thinks it has form. Dick thinks you write about people, Merle. . . . Yes, that's true, Dick. Wonderful, Dick. Uh-huh. Uh-huh."

Bob said, "Uh-huh, uh-huh. . . . That's no problem, Dick. . . . It's nothing, Merle, ten minutes' work."

Cooper said, "Yes, yes, isn't that a wonderful scene? He thinks the scene with Abby and Sid is wonderful."

I rose and said, "Since you're discussing the *script*, you obviously don't need me."

I made an exit that John Barrymore could have learned a lot from if he'd been there, but nobody seemed to notice.

I walked to the water cooler—strode? stalked? stormed?— and said to it, "The last person a man like Dorso wants to talk to about a script is the writer. Am I right?"

The water cooler blooped.

On my way to the conference room I passed the reception area several times, but since it was filled with actors, they had their minds on more important things, mirrors.

A few minutes later Bob and Cooper came into the conference room; Bob said, "Dick is still on the phone."

Cooper said, "He thinks it's just wonderful, Merle."

Bob said, "He says to tell you he's very enthusiastic."

I said—a little repetition never hurt anybody—"If Dorso has anything to say to me, let him say it to me."

Bob said into the phone, "Here's Merle. Tell Merle."

Dorso said, "Merle, it's marvelous. You are a screen writer. I was worried about the way you were going to introduce Abby; having her at the fair judging the 4-H dress contest—

doing her job—that is just wonderful. You write about people. It has flow, form, style."

Merle Miller: "Why thank you, Dick. Did you really like it?"

Dorso: "I love it."

Miller: "Well, it is . . ."

Miller, to himself: At last I've come across a tennis player who at the same time is a fine judge of literature.

Dorso said, "I've told Jack and Bob, I've got two very minor suggestions. Just minor, and they don't even *happen* until Act III."

Miller: "Not until Act III? . . . You like everything up to Act III? . . ."

Dorso: "Yes, and that wonderful scene at the end of Act III when Zac Laird orders Cal off his land? We just can't cheat the audience by interrupting that wonderful scene with a commercial."

Miller: "I'm with you, Dick, with you. And you like everything up to Act III?"

I returned the telephone to Bob, and he and Cooper and Dorso talked a couple hundred dollars' worth longer.

Finally Cooper put down the phone and said, "Dick says, 'God bless you, Merle.' "

Bob said, "He really liked it, Merle."

I said, "Well, it does have a lot of flow and form."

Cooper said, "It's about people; that's the important thing. You write about people."

Cooper said, "Well, after talking to Dick, there's just no question. Aubrey is going to love it. . . . I'm going to do the same thing I did before. I'm going to read it to him. I'm sorry you won't be here, Merle. But it doesn't matter. I'm going to read it aloud to him."

Bob said to Cooper, "We'll talk about it later."

Before leaving for the airport—by bus; I was paying for it—I dropped into the U.A. offices to say good-by to Bob and Cooper.

The colloquy that had begun the afternoon before was still going on.

". . . I'm just going to have Larry call a meeting tomorrow with Jim, and then I'm going to read it to them," Cooper was saying.

"Jack, you're out of your mind," said Bob. "We're in the middle of contract negotiations. You get Aubrey and those other guys in a room and they're going to *have* to find fault. That's not the way to do it."

"It's worked twice . . ." said Cooper.

"It won't work this time. We didn't promise them the script until Monday. Let's have it mimeographed, and then we'll send it over to them the way we have the others. They'll make little notes. We'll get the notes, and those that are valid I'll give to Merle. Let's not make a production out of this because if we do we're in trouble. Big trouble."

"Bob, you're wrong. I've done it twice before, and that's how we got this far."

"Jack, you're beginning to believe your own press notices, which is dangerous. If you do this you're out of your mind. . . ."

I cleared my throat and said, "Well, fellows, if you'll excuse . . ."

"God bless you, Merle," said Cooper, "and don't worry. They'll love it, and I'll call you. Give my love to your mother. . . . Bob, look . . ."

"Good luck, Merle," said Bob. "You'll need it. Say hello to Dora. . . . Jack, you're making what is possibly a fatal mistake. Take my word for it . . ."

I spent the night at the Flying Carpet Motel near the Chicago airport.

The room had everything, air conditioning, Muzak, nine or ten television sets, FM radios, AM radios, a rose garden, and, best of all, a sun lamp in the ceiling of the bathroom, flooding the whole place with vitamins and minerals and tanning you, too. Talk about service. By the time I got to Iowa I would look like a bronzed, gray-haired, bald Greek god.

While I was sitting under the sun lamp I picked up a newspaper left behind by a previous occupant. In it was a column by Louella Parsons that had appeared a couple of days before. The headline was in 86-point type, the size used when declaring war or peace:

STANWYCK JOINS COOPER. "—All the time my Barbara Stanwyck Show was on TV it played opposite Jackie Cooper's popular *Hennesey* from start to finish and I say—If you can't lick 'em, join 'em," said Barbara Stanwyck right after I confirmed that she and Jackie Cooper will be teamed in a new one-hour television series.

The deal between Jackie Cooper Productions, Inc., and Barbara is the most important made with a femme star for a complete series since Shirley Booth started *Hazel*.

Don't blame me for being curious about the type of stories which combine Stanwyck and Cooper.

I learned that Barbara plays a county home agent, the distaff counterpart of Cooper who plays a young county agent who are the source of help on all farm and ranch activities of the Department of Agriculture.

So far the show has no title—but shooting starts in September for CBS-TV beaming.

I sent a telegram:

Evan Rhodes 1 Minetta Lane N.Y., N.Y. SEE LOUELLA COLUMN AUGUST 13 REPEAT SEE LOUELLA COLUMN STOP NOW THAT LOUELLA BELIEVES IT DON'T YOU QUESTION I BELIEVE IT STOP THEY ARE GOING TO WANT ME TO WRITE ALL TWENTY-SIX SCRIPTS STOP AS PER DISCUSSION THINK YOU OUGHT TO GET LEAVE OF ABSENCE FROM N.Y.U. AND HELP ME OUT HELP ME OUT HELP ME OUT HELP ME OUT MERLE

After I went to bed I counted my blessings and sheep, but the sandman didn't come.

I hadn't been back to Marshalltown for more than a few days at a time since at sixteen, after finishing high school, I fled to the State University of Iowa and from there to London, New York, and other celebrated spas.

At sixteen I hated the people I grew up with, and, it goes without saying, my parents . . . However, I've already written about that, and the general subject is one that has engaged a few other novelists from time to time.

What did I think now? Did I still hate my parents? At forty-four? Was I still estranged from the town I grew up in, the people I grew up with? At going on forty-five?

Was Thomas Wolfe right? Can you or can't you?

My mother and father met me at the airport in Des Moines, and it is true that at seventy-eight my mother didn't have a gray hair in her head. . . . Later, after prolonged investigation in dark closets, I found a little brown bottle which said, "Does She or Doesn't She?"

My mother kissed me and my father shook my hand.

My mother smiled, presumably pleased with the bronzed Greek god who stood in front of her.

"Your face is as red as a beet," she said.

I walked a little ahead so that she could get a load of the brand-new Tripler sport jacket, the sea-island cotton shirt I'd picked up at Harrods in London, the slacks from Brooks, and the pair of Italian shoes, handmade.

My mother observed this masquerade and remarked, "Your Uncle Kenneth in Texas is a millionaire several times over."

She looked at the new Mark Cross bag my father was carrying for me.

"How much did that set you back?"

Since she had long ago taught me never to lie to my mother, I told her.

"Well . . . your Uncle Kenneth. It is one thing to earn money. It is quite another to know the *value* of money. To look at your Uncle Kenneth you wouldn't think . . . Those clothes I used to buy you when I was out in the public all day at the J. C. Penney Store . . ."

My father, a taciturn man by nature and necessity, winked at me and I shut off my hearing aid.

I spent the formative years of my life in J. C. Penney clothes. My mother was then a clerk—"I'm not assigned to any department; I just more or less *rove*"—and got things at a discount, which everybody in town knew.

The night of my graduation—May 29, 1935—I had on a blue serge, double-breasted Penney suit.

A few days earlier I had with the calm logic that has grown calmer with the years pointed out to Mother that boys like Earl Keyser, Neil Naiden, and Jacob Eige would be wearing single-breasted suits from Gildner's.

"That's all very well if you can afford several suits," Mother said, "but money doesn't grow on trees in this family and from the looks of things never will, and a double-breasted suit is *warmer*. That's why they make them that way. Chest colds and all."

And so I walked the last mile to get my diploma burdened with honors—the Shirley Scholarship Award, Salutatorian, The Most Intelligent Boy, The Best Debater, *Societas Praemi Virtutis*—and—the double-breasted suit.

"What are you doing these days, Merle?" Mother said.

"Well, an actor named Jackie Cooper—"

"At the Eastern Star meeting the other night . . ."

Will Earl Keyser be fooled by your Tripler jacket? I asked myself. Will Jake Eige be humbled by your handmade shoes? Did the emperor get away with his robe?

". . . right out in front of the store with them *on* and not another stitch."

She had at last caught my fancy.

"What's that?"

"Jean Seberg," said my mother.

Miss Seberg is the most celebrated "former Marshalltown-ian"—I'm quoting the *T-R*—since Billy Sunday. She is much prettier than Sunday and likely has more talent.

"Her husband," said my mother, "the one before she divorced that Frenchman, two before the one she's married to now, or three. I'm not sure, although I asked Jean's father —he's just the nicest man—and we give him a lot of our trade, and Jean's mother is in . . ."

"*Who* didn't have a stitch on?"

"Well, they, Jean and he, they went into Gildner's, and as I was telling you he was buying a pair of underwear shorts, and he marched right out in front with them and not another stitch on to show Jean. Now maybe they do that in Paris, France, but not in Gildner's right here on Main Street and everything. . . ."

We were getting into town. There was a sign by the road, "The coming of the Lord is nigh. Are ye ready?"

We were sitting at the kitchen table having coffee. Mother had got up early that morning—in my youth she had got up at five; now she lazes around until six or so—and made cinnamon rolls.

She was saying, ". . . your Cousin Hollis; he's in the construction business, you know, in Davenport, and I don't know, of course, and it's none of my business, but your Aunt Leta says he's coining money hand over fist. . . .

"Your last book . . . the one that . . . well, I haven't read it all. Did that sell many copies?"

"Not many."

"How much do you make out of a book like that?"

Since this was territory we had covered in some detail many times before I said, "Mom, I finally am going to make a lot of money, really a lot."

She started to rise but she sank back into the blond wood chair. I had caught *her* fancy. I think for the first time ever.

"Merle, tell me."

I told her about the series, and she listened—another first —and I said, "Jackie Cooper is going to play the lead."

"I like Jackie Cooper," she said. "I remember him when he was this little boy when you used to be head usher at the Casino, and now he's in the Navy."

"And Barbara Stanwyck's going to be in it, too."

"Which one is she? I'm not sure I know which one she is."

"When I was at the Casino," I said, "she used to be *Stella Dallas,* and she was on the telephone a lot in *Sorry, Wrong Number.*"

"How much do you think?" she asked.

"I wouldn't be at all surprised to wake up some morning and find myself a millionaire."

"You don't mean to tell me."

As I went into the bedroom to spruce up for the first round of the reunion, she was on the telephone, ". . . No, Edna [Lester Good's mother], I never pry into Merle's affairs, but he just said cool as a cucumber, 'I woke up one morning and found myself a millionaire.' Jackie Cooper *and* Barbara Stanwyck and . . ."

Registration and coffee hour were from one until four in what Mary George had called "our beautiful new Fisher Community Center."

I got there a little after two, afraid I'd be early, but when I opened the door it sounded as if everybody else in the class had already signed up.

I closed the door again, from the outside.

An elderly Studebaker drove up; a voice shouted, "Aren't you Merle Miller?"

I confessed.

A ruddy-faced, middle-aged man got out of the Studebaker and started toward me.

"Remember me?" he asked. A question I was to hear many times during the next day and a half.

"Of course," I said. "Of course I do."

"No, you don't and no reason you should. I'm George Day."

I remembered him then. George Day, Class of '36, had been one of those rangy, competent boys with a depressingly high mechanical aptitude.

My mother used to say, "George can fix anything."

I can break anything. Then, and now.

"What are you doing out here?" asked George.

"Just getting a little fresh air. . . . You see, I'm afraid I won't recognize anybody."

"Look at people's eyes," said George. "No matter how much their faces have changed above and below they won't have changed much around the eyes."

Wearing the smile I plan to wear at my execution I marched into a room bulging with strangers.

"You *do* remember me," said a woman with hopeful blue eyes. "You stood me up for dates, twice."

"That doesn't single you out from a lot of other females I've known," I said, though not aloud.

"I sat behind you in French for three straight years . . . and if it hadn't been for you . . . How else could I have passed?"

"Grayce Rowlette," I said. *"Comment tally-vu?"*

"Once you left me at the end of the sidewalk," said Grayce Rowlette, "and didn't even say good night."

Grayce, who was voted the Peppiest Girl in our class, looked awfully prosperous and throughout the reunion remained very peppy.

I recognized Joann Oppenheimer at once; she had been a handsome girl but is an even handsomer woman. Blanche Hooven—her mother ran the bakery where I used to have to ask for day-old bread—had been a pretty girl; she is a beautiful woman. So is Emily Akers, who was elected The Biggest Bluffer and now has seven children. Dale Tincher, The Best Athlete, had lost a lot of hair. He was totally bald. Howard Falb, who looked about twenty-two, had turned into a very handsome man.

"And I didn't even *notice* him in school," said Grayce, with some rue.

A lot of what had happened to people physically had to do with their income. In addition to smelling better the well-to-do age more gracefully than the poor.

"How many books have you written?" asked Barbara Hatcher.

"Nine," I said modestly, "and I've just finished the pilot for a new television series that concerns itself with . . ."

"I haven't read a single one of them," said Barbara, a statement to which I have never found a satisfactory reply.

"Do you remember what you wrote in my yearbook?" said Emily Akers.

I confessed that I didn't.

"It was the strangest thing," said Emily, "and for the longest time it shook me up . . . made me very sad . . . for the longest time. . . . You wrote, 'Brains may win admiration but never friendship.'"

She paused and then she smiled and I saw that she hadn't changed much around the eyes.

"Do you still think that?"

I felt the smart of salt in my eyes but managed to say, "I'm not sure."

"We were all trying to offer you friendship," said Emily, "but the harder we tried, the more you withdrew. You wouldn't let us be friends. . . ."

"Have you been crying?" asked my mother.

She had picked me up after registration and was driving me back to the small farmhouse in which she and my father have lived for the past ten years. The house is set on the crest of a hill, and the view is spectacular, though I'm not sure that my mother has ever noticed.

"I need to stop at the liquor store and get a bottle of vodka," I replied.

"*Vodka.*" She made it sound subversive.

Later, when I was having a third drink, she said, "Do you drink vodka all the time?"

"Not all the time," I said. "Sometimes as much as an hour passes and I don't touch a drop."

"Ho, ho," she said. "Ho, ho, ho, ho. Some of us have developed a sense of humor."

When my father went to mix himself a second drink, a tablespoon of rye in warm water, she said, "Monte, you aren't having another drink?"

"That's the way it looks," said my father.

"You know what Dr. Earl said . . ."

"Dr. Earl said two or three small drinks wouldn't hurt me," said my father, who is seventy-six. He put an extra tablespoon of rye in the drink and started back to what in some households might be described as an easy chair.

"Well, if you want to kill yourself, I'm sure it's quite all right with me."

"Your mother's trouble," said my father, "is that she crosses all her bridges ninety-nine times before she gets to them."

"Ho, ho," said Mother, "ho, ho, ho, ho. Aren't we *all* witty this evening."

Then she went to see if the steak was done. It wasn't. It hadn't been frying much more than an hour.

". . . Would you like some more steak, Merle? . . . You haven't eaten enough to keep a bird alive. I was telling Edna . . . She and Lester went on their vacation to California two years ago I think it was; Lester is always a good boy to his mother. . . . And they went right on the set, and she said Rock Hudson was just as nice, just as common as an old shoe, and Lester . . . I said Jackie *Cooper* . . . And, Merle, if you'd just played your cards right, *you* could have been a child star along with the best of them. I remember—and you weren't more than five at that if a day. You were Governor Bradford. In *The First Thanksgiving*. And you said, 'We'll have dinner out here under these trees.' I'll never forget if I live to be a million. Do you remember what the *T-R* said?"

"As I recall, they said, 'Nothing like it has ever been seen in Marshalltown before.'"

"No, Merle, that was when you played *Träumerei* on your little violin when I was being installed as Most Worthy Matron at the Star, and you sang, 'Fleecy clouds are drifting by. In the sky, in the sky.' Singing *and* playing, and if you'd just played your cards right . . ."

That night there was a "social mixer" at the Elks Club and it was greatly aided—as so many things are—by the considerable flow of alcohol, although nobody got falling-down drunk.

I told a great many people the story of my life; a great many people told me the story of theirs. What had brought us all here anyway—more than a hundred of us, more than half the class—except a raging curiosity?

Howard Miller (no relation), who played basketball, said, "You look thin."

"I've been in the jungles of Northeast Brazil, the most dangerous," I said, ". . . and I caught . . ."

"I've worked for the Minneapolis and St. Paul for twenty-one years now," said Howard, ". . . a brakeman . . . the run between Marshalltown and . . . that kind of work you run into a lot of interesting people. . . ."

Claude Ahrens, not a classmate but married to one, Dorothy (Dolly) Hey, is a manufacturer. He and Dolly live in Grinnell, Iowa.

Claude, Dolly, and I talked for a long time, largely about Claude's friend, Roswell Garst, the Coon Rapids farmer who was Khrushchev's host when the Russian Premier was in Iowa in 1959.

"Garst thinks the first job is to get people started eating," Claude said. "We've got to teach the Russians, the Chinese, whoever wants to know, how to produce a lot more food. I don't suppose Garst thinks of himself as a crusader, but he is. . . . You'll have to meet him; you two would get along. There are a lot of people like Garst around, people who are concerned, who care. . . ."

I told them about René Bertholet saying that the need to do something useful is a basic human instinct.

"Of course it is," said Claude, "and the most inarticulate people have a surprising appreciation for the . . . good and the beautiful."

I explained about the TV series, and Dolly said, "I certainly hope it can be like that. Because it seems to us—most of what we see on television—we're not great television fans —but most of it, it's not for us. Or for the people we know. In New York—Claude and I get there several times a year— in New York so many people seem to think the rest of the country is a—well, a great big oblong statistical blob."

Claude said, "I hope you can pull it off, but . . ."

I folded shortly after midnight, on schedule.

It was nearly dawn when I fell into a troubled sleep, once more worrying about the capstoning, 192 reservations . . . There I was on the podium, struck mute, and my zipper open.

At breakfast—eggs and bacon and raisin-bread toast and French bread and another batch of cinnamon rolls, baked that morning—I said, "Jackie Cooper will probably call me later today or tomorrow."

"Jackie Cooper," said my mother, her hand going to her hair. She is a woman who dresses for important telephone calls. "What's he calling about?"

"Just to say hello."

And to tell me that the C.B.S. meeting was a triumph and that Jim Aubrey loved the script and . . .

"You must be very close; well, Merle, this time see that you play your cards right. . . ."

As I showered I remembered the last time I'd been home, shortly before the Late Unpleasantness over quiz-rigging, an activity that outraged a great many people, particularly those on whose networks it had taken place.

My mother had been sitting in front of the crystal ball watching *The $64,000 Question.*

When the program was over, she was silent for a moment; then she sighed volubly and said, "Merle, if you'd just played your cards right . . . When you did those interviews on the radio station down in Iowa City. Your voice . . . You could have been another Hal March."

That afternoon there was a tour of the high school. I went early and alone. Hadn't I always?

I walked across the viaduct. Stone's Café was just below.

I'll bring you back a blueberry pie, Dean Leyendecker.

Past the Anson School where I had played Governor Bradford, "Lucius, you will bring the maize; Alroy, you will shoot the wild turkeys. And never fear the Indians. God will protect us with His might."

I lingered briefly in front of the new offices of the Marshalltown *Times-Republican.*

When I was a boy the editor had been a misanthropic old man devoted to the philosophy and works of Machiavelli. He also printed my early creative efforts, mostly poetry. At fourteen I had already developed a profound poetic instinct. Has the present high school generation in Marshalltown come up with a bard who can pen anything comparable to my *The Bridge?*

> Life is a bridge,
> And we walk upon it . . .

The rest is gone, all gone.

There was a new addition to the high school, but the old part hadn't changed. The chemistry lab still smelled of rotten eggs, humiliation, and defeat. It was only through the kindness of the teacher, Edward D. Knock, that I managed a C in either chemistry or physics.

Next door was the room in which Norma A. Kringen taught ancient history. While doing research for a term paper on that remarkable Sicilian, Cagliostro, I came across a book that I still cherish, Bolitho's *Twelve Against the Gods.*

I recognized that Bolitho and I were soul mates from the first sentence on, "Adventure must start with running away from home."

Finally I sat down at the desk from which I had listened with fascination to the lectures on journalism. For Ruth Outland, journalism was the study of mankind, and she had the odd notion that the purpose of a sentence was to communicate an idea or an emotion.

At the end of the year she asked each of us to put down what we felt we had got out of the course. I wrote, "I've always wanted to know how to write, and now I do know how."

The official tour of the high school was anticlimatic.

I sat for a long time on the back steps of the high school. It was a beautiful afternoon, the air clear with the promised crispness of early fall.

From close by came the moan of a train sounding.

I often went down to the railroad station when I was a boy. There were two good passenger trains, one at nine in the morning, the other at seven-thirty in the evening. On the latter people were often still eating dinner when the train stopped to take on water—but almost never any passengers.

I thought of me, small and ignorant and anxious, and I thought of all the trains and planes and ships I've traveled on since my escape from Marshalltown. I thought of the young Italian in Fellini's *I Vitelloni;* I thought of the Indian boy in *Pather Panchali.* I knew then what my capstoning speech would be.

When I went home to dress, my mother said, "You haven't even thought about your speech. I don't suppose it means a thing to you, but *I* have to live in this town."

"I've thought about it," I said. "I'm going to talk about people who have to leave home and why they have to do it."

"Why *you* had to I will never know, not if I live to be a million. We gave you everything you ever . . ."

"Except maybe a happy childhood," I said, I hope not unkindly. "My father was always walking out . . ."

"Only twice, Merle, only twice. . . . Besides, what's the difference between his leaving home and *your* leaving home? . . . And Mr. Cooper didn't call; so maybe they've changed their mind, and you're in the prime of life, Merle, and you have to plan for your old age. . . ."

I thought of Cooper saying, "At least they let you have a childhood."

"Mom," I said, kissing her on the forehead, "you're crossing my bridge before I get to it."

At cocktails before the capstoning dinner at the new Tall-corn Hotel there was dancing to the music of a juke box.

After dinner, Jake Eige, our class president, asked the members of the football team, the basketball team, and various other groups to stand up. Then he introduced me.

I rose, stood at the microphone at my table, my hands trembling, my forehead wet. I wasn't sure I could make an audible sound, and for some time after the applause ended, I didn't.

I looked at the 384 expectant eyes and said, "Well, we beat the rap, didn't we? . . . So far."

I was pleased with the laughter.

"I note by the yearbook that you elected me The Most Intelligent Boy—which you'd hardly think was an elective office. The Most Studious. And The Most Individual. I looked on that last with suspicion at the time, and I haven't changed my mind.

"I'm grateful though. I always have been. But, if you want the truth, what I wanted to be was The Best All-Around Athlete, The Most Popular, and The Cutest. The way when I used to go to the Y.M.C.A. camp at Pine Lake I always wanted to be The Best All-Around Camper. It took me thirty some years to realize why that didn't happen. I *wasn't* The Best All-Around Camper. . . ."

Fifteen minutes later I got to the point.

"There are people who have to leave home, who are born displaced, who are aliens with no place to register. And there are people who are—I am told—born at peace with themselves and their environments. Which is better? Who knows? They're different; that's all.

"To be sure, those who leave home paint most of the world's pictures and write its books and its plays and compose its symphonies. And make most of the world's wars and its miseries.

"I had to leave home. I never once doubted it. I believe I started packing when I was about two years old. . . . There are lonely boys and lonely girls in every town in the world who have to get away. Maybe some of your children are among them. If that is true, don't try to stop them. You'll both get hurt—and for no reason. Besides, you'll fail.

"I'm sorry Marshalltown is no longer a passenger-train stop. The sound of a jet in the sky will never—not for our generation—have quite the mournful promise of a train sounding."

I looked at my audience. Not a sound.

"I once wrote in a novel, 'I used to walk down the street, and I was surrounded by enemies, and every face I saw was my own.' . . . That was some time ago. I look now around this room and see a variety of faces, many of them friendly, almost all of them friendly. Have you changed? Or have I? . . . My nearest neighbor in my town in New York, a friend named Lydia Rahlson, is Finnish, and she says, '. . . The yoo-hoo you yoo-hoo into the forest is the yoo-hoo you get back.'

"She's right, you know.

"Very late in his troubled life Mark Twain, who was in India, said, 'All the me in me is in a little Missouri village halfway around the world. . . .'

"I've spent a good part of my life running away from that truth and hating this no-longer-so-small Iowa village in

which—of course—is all the me in me. . . . I no longer do.
I no longer can. I no longer hate. . . ."

In the peroration I spoke a placebo that may also be the
ultimate truth, "Nobody's got it made, neither those of us
who leave home nor those who stay.

"A better writer than I once said, 'All lives when viewed
from within are a series of failures.'

"We have lived through a depression, a series of wars,
and God knows what personal anguish. And we have all
learned, I suppose, that a broken heart at forty causes as
much pain—no more—as a skinned knee at fourteen. 'Man
is born; he suffers; he dies.' . . . This insignificant golf ball
in the galaxy will not be much changed by our brief presence. And should anyone ask—almost nobody ever does—
what we accomplished—we might reply in the words of that
French cleric whose name I forget. When asked what he did
during the French Revolution he said, 'I survived.'

"I am glad I came home again; thank you for asking me."

I sat down, and 384 hands started applauding.

On Sunday morning I was lying in bed, reliving my triumph of the night before.

At around ten I heard my mother's voice saying, "Jackie
who? Oh. Jackie Cooper? Merle, it's Jackie Cooper. He's
calling from Long Island, New York."

"Give my love to your mother," said Cooper.

"Mother, he gives you his love. Jack, what happened? Did
you read the script to the brass at C.B.S.?"

"Bob will tell you all about it. I'm in East Hampton with
Bob now. He'll tell you all about it. . . . They've all read the
script, including Jim."

"Did they like it?"

"Oh, yes. They liked it very much."

The Little Voices leaned close to my right ear, "You're
in trouble, kid. You may have been a triumph in Marshalltown, but on Madison Avenue you laid an egg."

Jack said, "They had a couple of minor suggestions. Nothing major. They said in the first place there wasn't enough humor, and I said, of course, there wasn't, that this was a first draft. And then they said that the problem isn't *big* enough. So I said, 'We'll make the problem cancer and sit around and laugh.' "

"An *enormous* egg," said the Little Voices.

"But it's nothing major, Merle. Nothing you and Bob can't do in a very short time, a week or less. I'm going back to California; I've got to start lining up the cast. . . ."

"Give my best to Bob and have a good trip. See you."

I stood by the phone for a while, and my mother said, "They've changed their minds. I knew the minute he didn't call yesterday . . ."

"Oh, no," I said. "Everybody loves what I wrote. Cooper is going to California to line up the actors, and they thought it was—funny."

"And you're going to get all that money?"

I nodded. ("You're a big boy now, and big boys don't cry. Nobody likes a crybaby; you're a regular little man now, Merle.")

"Well, I'm glad," she said, "because it's always been one of your big troubles, Merle; you were always counting your chickens before they were hatched. That time you were in California and they wanted you to sign a contract and write movies and you could have been rich then, but you said, and I told you at the time if you recall, and that's all I have to say on that subject."

She looked closely at me, and then she said, "I've made you some pancakes for breakfast. Remember how your Dad and I used to say you were just like Little Black Sambo, you ate so many pancakes they were coming out of your ears, and we said you were going to turn into one if you didn't watch out. . . . Mrs. Good called, and she says she heard you made a very good little talk. What did you talk . . ."

"I told them nobody's got it made," I said.

"Dora sends you her love."

"You were a smash in Marshalltown," said Bob. "I can tell by the look of smug self-satisfaction on your face."

"When *you* finish telling *me* what happened in Marshalltown on Friday, I'll tell *you* what happened at C.B.S. on Friday. Who's the new writer on the series? Because I've got a few suggestions. It's right up Laura Lee Hope's alley, and Ethel M. Dell's."

"Nothing much happened at the meeting," said Bob, "and nothing was suggested that you and I can't do in a couple of days, and besides, there's no big rush. Take a few days' rest. You just finished the script and then flew off to Iowa to face all those elderly people you went to high school with. . . . You've just got time to catch the four-thirty train back to Brewster, and it's got a bar car."

"I'm going to take in a flick, Fellini's 8½."

"I wouldn't if I were you," said Bob, who was standing at the window of his office, looking down at Madison Avenue, "it'll just depress you."

"Why?"

"Because it's a work of art."

"You look rested," said Bob, when I next saw him.

"Well, you don't. Not that I've been asked, but I wouldn't have your job for anything in the world. Why do you do it?"

"I'd like to make $2,000,000," said Bob. "Shall we talk about what happened at the summit meeting at C.B.S.?"

"Go ahead."

"In the first place, what I didn't tell you, Jack called me not long after the meeting, he was nervous, to say the least. So I invited him out to East Hampton, and by the time he left on Sunday he was calmed down. But in the beginning he was going to take the show to another network; he wanted me to fly to California to talk to Dorso. It was crazy. . . .

"What happened is that up to now Cooper hadn't had any opposition at all, to anything. Until last Friday it had been fun and games. It had been just great to fly back and forth to the Coast and talk about the script, but now the chips were down. Now was the time to hire the actors and technicians.

"And the same was true of C.B.S. . . . Until the Friday meeting all they were in for was the money for the script. But now they had to make a decision, whether or not to give the go-ahead on an expenditure of maybe as much as $250,-000. . . . Besides, Cooper has been giving interviews like the one to *Variety* saying it took him only fifteen minutes to con Aubrey into . . . and *Cooper* wants a guarantee of twenty-six weeks instead of thirteen because *his* star is so expensive, and he wants creative control, which he hasn't a chance of getting. . . . And so on Friday, they let loose, no holds barred."

"Besides, they didn't like the script."

"Not much. They want . . . well, a few changes."

"Who's they?"

"Larry White, Oscar Katz, he's another v.p., Frank Shakespeare, *and* Aubrey. Mike Dann wasn't there; he was in Europe."

"Historians will certainly want to make a note of that," I said. "But *they* want a whole new script."

"I'll let Dorso tell you," said Bob. "He's talked to Aubrey . . ."

Dorso looked tanner than before, and there wasn't a bag or a gray hair to be seen anywhere.

"Everybody is very pleased with the way things are going," he said, "very."

I began to take notes on the several hundred changes all the pleased everybodys would want.

"C.B.S. feels that Cal's problem isn't big enough," said Dorso, "and I'm with them on that. The way the script is now, all Cal stands to lose is his job."

I thought but did not say, In my youth that used to be quite a problem.

"C.B.S. feels there ought to be some physical menace, too," said Dorso, "and I'm with them on that."

I thought but did not say, I could be wrong, and correct me if I am, but at the conclave in Dann's office—less than a month ago—several of the individuals present said that one of the many things they liked about the story line was that there *wasn't* any violence. . . .

"C.B.S. feels that Cal ought to be more of a hero," said Dorso, "and I'm with them on that. . . .

"C.B.S. feels that Cal ought to display more physical courage, that maybe everybody in town wants to run Zac Laird off his land, and Cal stops them. C.B.S. described the town's feeling toward Zac and Cal—and I'm with them on this—as a lynch mob attitude."

I looked at Bob, who was back on his Canadian exercises.

"We need just one additional scene," said Dorso. "What C.B.S. wants is a kind of *friendly* lynch mob scene."

Later in Bob's office, I said, "Roberto, I always got high marks in English, and I've been writing full time—or as Dora says I haven't had any regular work—for thirteen years now, and I get paid for my arrangements of words on a page, not a princely sum, but still . . . And you were graduated from the University of Pennsylvania with what I'm sure were adequate marks. In your mind, just what is a *friendly* lynch mob scene?"

"Very simple," said Bob. "It is a scene in which the potential lynchers are *friendly*. Any other questions?"

That was when I made my first note of the day.

"What are you writing?" asked Bob.

"I've just had the inspiration for the opening paragraph of the next novel I'm going to write. Like to hear it?"

"You are being counterproductive, but go ahead."

And so I read, " 'Someone must have been telling lies about Josef K., for without having done anything he was arrested one fine morning.' "

3

Everything
is television

"No amount of polishing will make a mirror of
the brick, sir."

ZEN BUDDHISM

I sat on the terrace for most of the next day, watching the black and white cows in the field just beyond the stone fence that separates my land from my neighbor's.

The Little Voices didn't give me a moment's peace:

"Anybody could write a friendly lynch scene if they just had the time, only don't have any Puerto Ricans in it, because they make people feel guilty, and it can't have any dirty words like water, and we all tell little lies and eat a peck of dirt before we die because we are in *The Beverly Hillbillies* instead of Birmingham, and the only good Indian is a dead Indian."

I first met Bob Aurthur in Southern California's response to the palace at Versailles, the Beverly Hills Hotel. We had a drink in the Polo Bar, and I told Bob I liked a movie he had written; he said he liked a couple of my novels, and we were friends from then on.

A year passed, and in July 1959, the phone rang. I made my usual mistake. I answered it.

It was Bob. He said that in the fall he was going to be executive producer of a one-hour live dramatic series on N.B.C. It was to be called *Sunday Showcase*.

Bob wanted me to write for it and asked if I could come to New York to discuss it with him.

"Will it involve going west of the Painted Desert?" I asked.

"Merle, you won't even have to cross the Hudson."

Bob and I had lunch at Absinthe House, and he plied me with Mickey Finns.

"I've got a lot of good writers lined up," he said, "Gore Vidal, Reggie Rose, who's going to do a two-part play on Sacco and Vanzetti . . ."

"Well, I do have an idea," I said, "it's been kicking around in my head for a long time . . . almost fifteen years."

I first saw Ira Hamilton Hayes on a bright morning in 1945. I was in Washington, D.C., on an assignment for *Yank*, the uncompromising weekly magazine published by the Army. Joe McCarthy, the New York editor, had sent me to Washington to find out if there were any atheists in the foxholes down there.

Three Marines, one of whom was Ira Hayes, had just been flown back from Iwo Jima to help sell War Bonds. Iwo Jima had recently been secured at the cost of one Marine for every square foot of real estate.

The three Marines had been among the six in what was already the most famous photograph of the Second World War, the one taken by the Associated Press photographer, Joe Rosenthal. It showed the American flag being raised on top of Mount Suribachi.

Ira and the two other Marines had come to the White House to give what was said to be the original flag to President Truman. . . . Other original flags turned up in many places; eventually, they were almost as common as splinters of the True Cross during the Crusades.

During the presentation I stood not far from Ira, a dark, haunted-looking man. I could tell that he had been drinking.

A few weeks later a *Yank* correspondent who had been on Iwo Jima told me that the Rosenthal photograph was not, as everybody thought, a picture of the original flag raising.

The first flag, which had been brought to the top by the Marines who fought their way up the hill, was small and shabby, and it was hung on an iron pipe. A picture like that wouldn't hardly sell one War Bond.

When Rosenthal, several other still photographers, and some movie cameramen arrived a few hours later, they substituted a large, clean, and more inspirational flag on a proper pole.

Since the original flag raisers were either dead or otherwise occupied, in the restaging, six men who happened to be in the vicinity were used. Ira Hayes, who was laying wire nearby, was one.

"They flew a lot of brass out from Washington to find the guys who did the restaging," said my *Yank* friend, "and it took some digging even to find out their names. A lot of people thought they shouldn't be identified. They were sort of symbols. . . . It didn't bother the other two guys much, but it bugged poor Ira. He thought the picture was a phoney."

After the ceremony at the White House, Ira and the other two Marines were sent across the country on a bond-selling tour. Everywhere they went they were greeted as heroes, given keys to the city and wined and dined and wined.

In the midst of the tour the Marine Corps announced that at his own request Ira was being sent back to the Pacific to rejoin his outfit.

It seemed unlikely that the Marine Corps would grant the request of a man who was a private first class . . . That turned out to be a lie, a small one. Ira was sent back to the Pacific because he had been drinking heavily during the entire tour.

During the years that followed I kept clippings of what happened to Ira—arrested in Chicago, drunk and disorderly, hired by Dean Martin to take care of the Martin children, arrested in Los Angeles, D. and D., thirty-nine arrests in Phoenix, D. and D. Phoenix is eighteen miles from the Pima Reservation where Ira lived.

The famous picture was used as the basis for the 500-ton Marine Memorial Statue in Arlington Cemetery. The bronze figure of Ira is thirty feet tall.

Ira went to the dedication, and Vice-President Nixon made a speech, and many more pictures were taken, and that night Ira got drunk again.

Then he went back to the reservation, and on a bleak January night in 1955, Ira Hamilton Hayes died. He was thirty-one.

The official cause was exposure.

"And that is perfectly true," I said to Bob. "That may be the only truth. Ira died of exposure to publicity, public relations, and propaganda. . . . Everybody did what he thought he had to do, and he did it with the best of motives. A machine was set in motion, and the machine created a myth, but it helped destroy Ira."

Bob Aurthur had served with the Marines at Iwo Jima and knew about Ira and the flag raising.

I told Bob about the Pimas, the only Indian tribe in history that had never fought the white man, and had been in the valley of the Gila River in Arizona since before the time of Christ.

"They were probably the first Indians in this country or anywhere else to irrigate their fields," I said, "but then the white man came along . . ."

A little more than a hundred years ago the Pimas were persuaded to move onto a reservation, and in return the federal government agreed "to advance them in civilization and protect their rights."

At the time the Pimas were irrigating the entire area and were promised first priority on use of the water of the Gila, "as long as the grass shall grow and the rivers shall run. . . ."

Less than twenty years later white settlers upstream from the reservation started diverting water for their own use, and by the time Ira Hayes got back from the war there was almost none left for the Pimas.

"The Pimas have protested," I said, "but they are patient and don't have feelings like you and me, because if they did, they'd have put white people on reservations 'to advance them in civilization and protect their rights. . . .' "

"When can you leave for Arizona?" asked Bob.

That was a very long time ago, Virginia, and in those dear dead days beyond recall if a producer and a writer agreed on an idea, they went ahead and did it.

"I could get you an airplane ticket this afternoon," said Bob, ". . . and you could . . ."

"You said I woudn't have to cross the Hudson."

"You don't. You can write the play from *secondhand* material, although instead of *telling* people about the Pimas being stolen from . . . we could *show* it, which is what drama is all about. . . . We could tape the show at the reservation and in Phoenix, and *that* has never been done before by anybody."

Yes, Virginia, there were pioneers in those days. Of course, the budget for the show was only $100,000, not the yearly budget of $6,000,000 that Mike Dann had announced for *Calhoun* and then said would earn $9,000,000 for C.B.S. *alone*. People weren't so nervous about a mere 100 G's and they could *afford* to be adventurous and maybe try something new. But that was long, long ago—way back in 1960.

I spent two weeks in Arizona during which, in addition to going to the Pima Reservation every day, I attended the convention of the National Congress of American Indians.

I met a great many articulate and witty Indians. One night during the convention a young college graduate and I were discussing the McCarran Act. We agreed that it should be repealed.

"Although," he said, "I sometimes think that my people

might be better off if we'd had a *somewhat* more restrictive immigration policy."

There are green fields hemming every side of the Pima Reservation. The irrigation ditches are overflowing and the crops are lush—corn, barley, citrus fruits, and cotton. A retired Texas oil man whose ranch was not far from the reservation told me that he could pump enough water every day to take care of a city of 50,000.

I thought of the barren Pima Reservation many times when I was in Northeast Brazil.

Manuel Ferreira da Silva, the settler at Pindorama I mentioned earlier, was describing the difference between his life as a worker on a sugar plantation and his life as a settler at the cooperative.

Manuel said, "It is the difference between heaven and hell."

It is the same in Arizona.

The soil on the Pima Reservation is mostly sand; tumbleweed is the principal crop.

The first thing I saw was a huge water drum set in the middle of the scorched land. A narrow pipe extended from the drum to a primitive faucet where a line of horse-drawn wagons was waiting. The horses were emaciated. So were the people, especially the children.

The faucet was the sole source of water for more than a thousand Pimas. For many of them driving to the faucet takes at least half a day; the wait and the drive back to their homes takes the rest.

The faucet had no handle. It had to be turned on and off with a pair of pliers. I asked a young Indian about that.

"We wished to fix it," he said, "but they told us that would be interfering with government property."

The house in which Ira Hayes spent most of his life was built of mud bricks and wood posts. It had one room, and the dirt floor was covered with old carpets. The room had no ceiling, only bare rafters. In the middle was a wood-burning cookstove, and nearby were a roughhewn table and four straight-back chairs. There were four beds.

The bed that had been Ira's was near the single window that looked out over a graveyard in which members of the Hayes family have been buried for several hundred years.

The graveyard was the last thing Ira saw before going to sleep and the first thing he saw when he woke up. He wanted to be buried there, but he wasn't. He was buried in the Arlington National Cemetery in Washington, in sight of the Marine Memorial Statue.

A little away from the cemetery is the small white church Ira attended; as a boy he thought he might want to be a minister. His favorite hymn was called, "What Would You Give in Exchange for Your Soul?"

I spent some time with Ira Hayes's father, a small, defeated man with the good manners that seem to be natural with the Pimas.

We sat near the cookstove, and he showed me the newspapers he had saved, "Ira Hayes Day at . . . American Legion Post Honors Arizona's First Citizen. . . . Mayor of Chicago Greets Heroes of Iwo Jima. . . . President Truman Greets . . . Vice-President Nixon Shakes Hand of War Hero Hayes. . . ."

Ira's father looked at the naked rafters. "Ira always hoped that after the war he would be able to put a floor in the house and a ceiling, but that was not to be. . . . And he would say, 'When we get the water that belongs to us my mother will no more have to pick cotton.' . . . I do not believe the water will ever again be ours."

Ira's father said that sometime before Ira's death the Arizona state legislature finally gave the Indians the right to vote.

"A white lady came to see Ira," he said. "She wished that

he would come to be a guest of honor at a place in Phoenix, and she said he must make a speech asking the Indians to vote. She stood here in this room and Ira said to her, 'I thank you and I am most honored.' He was a polite boy; he was always polite. . . . And then he said to the white lady, 'I am not qualified to vote because I have not registered. I am not going to register, and I am not going to vote.' The white lady did not ask why, nor did I. Ira spoke not much, but when he came back from the war there was a great hurt in him. He did not say why."

I went to see Judge David Johnson, a Pima elder. The judge's house was a little larger than Ira's, and his wife made coffee for us.

When she brought the coffee she said, "When they were little some of the boys used to make fun of the old people, but Ira never did. He never made fun of the old people."

Judge Johnson said, "Ira didn't want to go to Washington when they dedicated the monument, but we said that he must. We said that it was important for him to be there, important for *us* because he was an Indian. And we said that he must not drink. He went, and he drank, and when he got back, there were people, his own people, who were ashamed of him and who spoke to him with unkindness. I knew that he would not go away again. . . . Everybody, his own people, too, made use of him. . . . What he wanted for himself he did not say, I do not believe he was ever asked."

I wanted to hear some Pima music, and before leaving went to a small museum on the outskirts of Phoenix. The curator played many recordings. One had the voice of an old man, accompanied by a gourd and a drum:

He sang first in Pima, then in English.

"Where is it raining?
Out behind the hills it is raining now.

Where is it raining?
Oh, where is it raining now?"

Just those four lines over and over and over again.

I thought of the dry river bed on the Pima Reservation,
and while I knew that symbolism is what closes on Saturday
nights, it seemed to me that Ira's thirst and the dry river
bed . . .

That is one of the reasons that writers go to the original
source, to find just such unifying elements. It was the reason
that Cooper and I had gone to New Mexico.

The story I wanted to tell about Ira was a simple one. It
was about a simple man who ". . . hears a different drummer. Let him step to the music which he hears, however
measured or far away."

In a sense, that's what the county agent series was all
about, too. A dedicated man who believes that the human
being comes first.

In New Mexico Cooper and I had hoped to find a situation
that would have shown the county agent and his ideologies
in action. We thought we found it when we heard about old
man Prather ordering the whole U. S. Government off his
ranch.

The county agent in our story would have been the one
man, maybe the only man, who recognizes that Prather's
right is the most basic one of all, and he would have been
ready to risk his job and his position in the community to
fight for that right.

But that was before it was pointed out what a *familiar*
story the Prather one was.

In the five months between my return from Phoenix where
I did the research on Ira Hayes and the following March
many people tried to keep Ira's story, called *The American,*
from being broadcast.

The first threat came from a writer named William

Bradford Huie, who had written a book called *The Hero of Iwo Jima.*

It was the longest account of what had happened to Ira— or what Huie said had happened to Ira—published up to that time.

At a conclave in Bob Aurthur's office attended by Bob, two N.B.C. lawyers, Huie, and myself, Huie volunteered that since he knew more about Ira than anybody else he would be happy to collaborate on the script.

I glanced at Bob, who was shaking his head.

I said I would think it over.

I finished the first draft of the script without Huie's help.

Bob read it and said, "I like it. But to produce it will cost as much as *Ben Hur*, and it will run for twenty-four hours, and while I admire the way you have dramatized the history of the Indians from the Stone Age on . . ."

After two story conferences we decided that the script should be concerned only with the last few months of Ira's life, and as for the water problem, the camera would be used to point that up.

Four drafts and we were ready; the fifth draft was the one that went on the air. So far as I know Bob hadn't shown it to a single vice-president at N.B.C., nor had anyone written on a crinkly piece of paper, "a great story."

John Frankenheimer was hired as the director; he is a tall, brooding man of great talent and energy whose work I admired.

Lee Marvin, a fine actor, played Ira Hayes, and Steven Hill, a talented character actor, played George Pitt, a fictional Pima and a friend of Ira's.

On Monday, January 17, 1960, Frankenheimer, Claude Traverse, the unit manager, later the production manager of the Brazilian project, and several others went to Phoenix to pick out locations.

Until then, the Pima Tribal Council and the Pima attorney, Z. Simpson Cox, had promised every cooperation when we came to tape the show. Frankenheimer gave Cox a copy of the script.

Late Friday night I got a call in Brewster from Cox in Phoenix. He said that he and the Tribal Council were very upset about the script, that it showed Ira as "just another drunken Indian" and that there were numerous technical errors.

I said that I would gladly correct the technical errors.

"It's really not at all the sort of script we expected," said Cox. "We're disappointed."

I hung up and called Bob Aurthur.

He had already heard and said, "I hear the Pimas won't let us inside the reservation to tape the show. Cox has told the city officials of Phoenix that we're out to harm the Indians and we won't be allowed in Phoenix either. . . . Other than that . . ."

"But why?" I said. "Why?"

Toward dawn the Little Voices answered. They pointed out that shortly after Bob and I had the conference with Huie, it had been announced that *The Hero of Iwo Jima* had been sold to a movie company.

The movie people who were producing the film, eventually called *The Outsider* and starring Tony Curtis as Ira, were opposed to the television project.

"Has it occurred to you, Lame Brain," asked the Little Voices, "that the movie people might have gone to the Pimas carrying muchum wampum? And they can also hand out a lot of parts, not to mention bright-colored beads and trinkets. Did you bring wampum when you went to Phoenix, Dim Wit? Not a sequin."

On the following Wednesday—who says miracles never happen?—Claude Traverse called from Tucson.

I was in Bob's office with John Frankenheimer; we were trying to decide whether or not the show could be done in a studio in New York, and if it could, how much rewriting would be involved.

Claude said that he had driven from Phoenix to Tucson and that Tucson hated Phoenix the way St. Paul hates Minneapolis. Tucson would be delighted to have us tape the show there. What's more, every location in the script could be duplicated in Tucson, and only a half mile from town was the San Xavier Indian Reservation. It looked exactly like the Pima Reservation, even down to the water faucet I'd written into the script.

Although many of the San Xavier Indians are Pimas, their Tribal Council had promised to help.

"What's the catch?" asked Bob.

"There's no catch," said Claude. "If you want to do it, it's all set."

Is it any wonder that every time there's a presidential election I write in the name of Claude Traverse, the favorite son of Driftwood, Oklahoma?

On February 16, run-throughs for *The American* began in New York in a Lower East Side rehearsal hall, and on the following Friday, the coldest day since the end of the Ice Age, Bob, Frankenheimer, Marvin, several other actors, and I went in a bus to a rock quarry about forty miles north of New York City.

The scene we shot that day was the only one we did not tape in Arizona.

Shortly after the end of the war Ira had re-enacted the flag raising in a movie, *Sands of Iwo Jima*, a realistic war picture in which John Wayne played a Marine who single-handed clears some 100,000 Japanese off the island.

The scene I wrote had nothing to do with the filming of that movie.

In the beginning, the director of the imaginary movie yells, "Cut! Cut! Cut!"

Six actors were raising the American flag on a wind-swept hill.

As the scene was written, one of the actors is out of place, Lee Marvin as Ira.

"Gentlemen," shouts the director, "we all know that those were not real shells or bombs, but our job is to pretend they are. Because that is what acting is. . . . Now which one of you was out of place?"

After an interminable moment, Ira, who is drunk, raises his hand.

"Chief, it was you?" says the movie director. "Well, *we're* wrong then; we have to be wrong. The chief was there, but *we* weren't. . . . Now, chief baby, I want you to check me out on this. Because I want every Marine who was on Iwo to say, 'That's it. That's the way it was.' No bands playing —none of that—I want this to get to people. Now, chief baby, where were you when they raised the flag?"

"It was a long time ago," says Ira. "I don't like to think about it."

"Yes, I know—but we are here to think about it—we are spending $3,000,000 to make a picture about it. That is why we are thinking about it. . . . Now you're here on the left —and Nicolson's next to you. Right?"

"Nicolson's dead, sir. Nicolson was killed."

The director gives Hayes a look, then says, "You and five other men came up the hill—this way—against heavy opposition—mortars—machine guns—shell fire. . . . You hear that, special effects? Not firecrackers and popguns. *Mortars. Machine guns. Shell fire.* We are going to run all the special effects again after the lunch break. . . . Now, chief, you had the flag. How'd you carry it?"

"No, sir, I didn't carry any flag. Never. There was a flag already there. I kept saying to Nick—I said to Nick—'Why're they putting up that other flag and taking down the first one?'—and Nick said, 'That's because they're going to take some more pictures.'"

The director sees that Ira is drunk and says to the crew, "Okay. Take a break."

He turns to the actor playing Nicolson and says, "Keep an eye on him. If there's one thing I don't need it's a drunken Indian."

The actor and Hayes go to a bonfire near a tent, Ira takes a heavy slug from a bottle he has been carrying in his back pocket.

"It was funny," says Ira, "after the war—I went all the way to San Antonio to see Nick's mother—We'd sort of agreed—if anything happened to me—He'd go see my mother—and if anything happened to him . . . She was nice enough all right—but I could tell she hated my guts— It took me a long time to figure out why. . . . I was alive. You can't blame her for that—She wanted to know about the flag raising and all of that—and I was going to tell her how it really happened—but she didn't want to know—So I just let on it was the same as it was in the papers—I didn't like to do that—but Nick was dead and if you're dead I guess it doesn't matter how it really happened."

Ira starts to take another drink, and the actor says, "Look, Ira, it's none of my business—"

"You're right there—It's none of your business—Look, Nick—Stop snapping your fingers. . . . You're going to get us both killed before you know it. . . . Look, Nick—That's your one bad habit. Stop snapping your fingers."

Because he is an artist, Lee Marvin made the duality of time in Ira's mind understandable and moving. Part of the time Ira was on a movie location, and part of the time he was back on Iwo Jima.

After another slug from the bottle Ira says, "When that colonel flew all the way out from Washington, D.C., and said he was going to take us guys that were in the picture back for some War Bond drive—I said no—I said there must be some mistake. I said I hadn't had anything to do with raising any flag—I was just in the picture—that's all. The colonel, he said, 'To everybody back in the States—you're a hero.' And he said, 'It doesn't really matter. All that picture is is a symbol of all the guys that were on this island.' He had a nice smile on his face when he said that. He said, 'As far as I'm concerned, chief, every man here was a hero. And nothing else matters.' I said to him, 'Begging your pardon, sir, it matters to me. I can't go around the rest of my life letting people think I did something I didn't do.' . . . And the colonel said to me, he said, 'Ira, we've all got to eat a peck of dirt before we die—and tell a thousand lies. And this is a very small lie in a very good cause.' I looked very straight at him and I said, 'What's a small lie, sir? You'll have to explain that to me, sir, because I just don't know what a small lie is.' "

The next week we all settled in at a motel on the outskirts of Tucson. The technical people went through dry runs at the locations; Frankenheimer rehearsed the actors; I sat around listening to my lines, crying a lot.

There was a constant distraction. Bob kept saying— he is often not an easy man to like—that further cuts had to be made and that the funeral scene I'd written wasn't good enough.

"Steve Hill, who's acting it, liked it," I said, "and it made me cry."

"You cry when Frankenheimer says, 'Let's take it from the top.' The scene isn't good enough. It ought to sum up in one speech both the Pima water problem and the futility and waste in Ira's life."

From the time Bob first called me eight months before and throughout the entire taping of *The American,* he exercised a firm creative hand, which is one of the many functions of a producer. With the *Calhoun* project, because it was such a shoo-in, a producer was not assigned until the very last minute. We shall come to that.

The Phoenix newspapers that week were saying that all

of us, the writer in particular, were out to undermine the Constitution, do irreparable damage to the state of Arizona, and permanent harm to the Indians.

On Friday we were to go to the San Xavier Reservation for the first time. None of us was sure what the attitudes of the San Xavier Indians would be.

When the rest of the Indian fighters prepared to go to the reservation on Friday morning I became violently ill.

I telephoned Bob from my room and told the executive producer that my patient was in poor shape and started listing the ailments, "double pneumonia . . . triple hives . . . a fatal hernia . . . and a splinter."

"Listen, you," Bob shouted, "you got us into this and you're going to the reservation. On the lead horse."

When we got there my worst fears were confirmed. Lined up on one side of a dry river bed was what looked like the entire tribe. Some were on horseback, some on foot, some in wagons.

We stopped on the opposite side and got out of the station wagons and trucks. There was a long silence.

Bob pointed to our two stage managers, Sam Kirschman and Dick Auerbach, and said, "Go negotiate."

Kirschman and Auerbach, both wearing cowboy hats, started toward the massed Indians.

Halfway across the river bed Sam and Dick paused. Not a sound, not a breath from the Indians, not a movement.

Finally, Sam raised his right hand in a gesture of friendship, and his voice drifted across the dry river bed.

"We are Jewish," he shouted, "and we come in peace."

The shooting began the next morning at the Desert Inn, one of the most expensive watering places in the world; none of the guests was under ninety-four or worth less than a couple of million, and there wasn't an Indian among them. They cackled in well-bred whispers.

None of us was shaved and we spent most of the time

screaming at each other. In moments of stress Frankenheimer gets along on a vocabulary of one word, using it as a noun, a verb, an adjective, adverb, and very often, a dangling participle.

Bob expressed his concern to an employee of the inn, who said, "Don't worry. It's the most exciting thing that's happened to any of the guests since the crash."

The scene at the inn had to do with an Ira Hayes Day—there had been many—and its purpose was to make a contrast between the luxury of the inn with its swimming pool and the wagons and Indians lined up at the rusty water faucet at the reservation.

In the scene Ira talks to a visiting congressman about the Pima water problem and asks for his help.

The congressman, a decent man, says, "Ira, in this state water represents power and profit and political strength— and a word that stands for all those things is a *dirty* word. Nobody wants to hear a *Pima* talk about water. . . . It makes people feel guilty. . . . Now this luncheon given in your honor today. By having it a large number of people have afforded themselves the welcome opportunity to feel that they have fulfilled their patriotic duty, and nothing in the world makes people feel more noble than that. But help you get your water? Never."

For those of you who will use this textbook in the Advanced Course, Television II, it will be interesting to note that *guilt* was not then a dirty word.

Late in the afternoon on the second day of shooting Bob went back to the motel to see if there had been any messages.

When he returned to the reservation, he was pale.

Just inside a decaying brick house (one room, all of them were) Frankenheimer was rehearsing a scene with Marvin, Steve Hill, and two other actors.

Bob walked up to me and said, "Joe Rosenthal [the A.P. photographer who took the picture] is suing. He claims we're saying his picture was posed."

"For much?"

"A billion dollars or so."

I rose, my teeth chattering from more than the cold desert air.

As Bob describes the moment, "Right in front of my eyes a fighting liberal made the transition to a bitter iconoclast."

Nonsense. I have never been bitter.

"I hate all photographers," I said. "I also hate all Marines, but above and beyond that, I hate all Indians. . . . You know something? We should never have done this show."

"Go to hell," said Bob.

We changed a couple of lines in the script in an attempt to placate Rosenthal and the Associated Press. Rosenthal sued anyway.

That night at the motel while Bob was convincing the governor of Arizona that we meant the state and the Indians no harm I wrote the funeral scene Bob had been asking for.

I wasn't ready to write it; I didn't feel like writing it, and there is only one reason I did write it.

It was going to be taped the next afternoon.

On location there is never a final script until the last scene is shot. John Frankenheimer had suggested several changes in the script from time to time, but he never insisted on any.

"My job is to direct what you write," he said.

In that area, never a problem. Frankenheimer later wrote, "It was the happiest professional experience of my life up to now."

The discerning reader will be quick to note directional differences when we get to the filming of *Calhoun,* but we will reserve that pleasure until a later chapter.

All of the San Xavier extras were on hand for the taping of the funeral scene, the young children, the girls and boys in their teens, their parents, and the old men and women of the tribe. They were all brushed and in their Sunday-go-to-meeting clothes.

Frankenheimer placed them in a *ramata,* a handmade shelter that had a beautiful simplicity. It was where the Tribal Council met.

Not far away a replica of the memorial the Pimas had erected for Ira had been constructed; next to that was a flagpole. A Zuñi law student dressed as a Marine stood next to the flagpole. At the end of Steve Hill's speech—Steve had got it only that morning—the Zuñi boy was to run up the flag.

It was late afternoon, and the orange sun brought out the strong, warm colors of the mountains in the background.

Frankenheimer talked to the Indians for a while; he told them to imagine they were attending a memorial service for Ira Hayes and asked them to listen to what Steve Hill was saying, "because," said John, "it's important."

Then Frankenheimer talked to Steve for a minute, went inside the tape truck, and gave the cue to begin.

Steve waited. He looked at the distant mountains and at the green fields just below. He looked at the dusty reservation; he looked at the sad, small huts, and, finally, he looked at the Indians in the *ramata.*

Then with the deliberation with which all Indians speak, he began.

"I once called Ira Hayes a symbol," he said, "but he was not that. He was never that. History will, I suppose, call him a hero—but he was never that either. He was a man. He had the strength of a man and the weakness of a man.

"Ira was a gentle man, a good man, a trusting man. He believed in God, in honor, in courage, and in truth. To him a promise was a sacred thing. In all his life he tried never to break a promise.

"Ira Hamilton Hayes was given a great many things, but nobody ever gave him what he wanted most. It was very little, really. He loved the land—this land. As indeed we all do. And he wanted enough water to farm this land. As indeed we all do."

Steve paused and looked at a very old man standing

near the *ramata*. Tears were running down the old man's face.

Steve looked at the children, at the parents, at the old people. Many of them were crying. Steve was talking about them, about their frustrations, their tragedy.

"Ira Hamilton Hayes was promised water," Steve went on. "All of us have been promised water. But the promise has been broken. It has been broken many times. It is broken still.

"Ira was one of us. He shared our dreams, our anger, our defeat, and our patience.

"Once we were all proud of Ira Hamilton Hayes. Later, some of us were ashamed of him. We shall none of us ever be ashamed again."

Steve stopped and waited for the flag to be raised.

It wasn't. The young Zuñi had forgotten to act. He was crying, too.

Bob wrote about that moment, "*This* was why we had come twenty-five hundred miles. Suddenly, as we always knew it would, the original hopes for the project became fully realized. Not a play to match *Hamlet,* not even the greatest play ever done on television, but a fleeting moment of absolute truth, so rarely caught anywhere, and especially rare (and so easily lost) among the other nineteen-thousand-odd yearly hours of television."

From the very beginning *The American* had been a controversial play. We had run into opposition from officials of the Indian Bureau, Senator Barry Goldwater, Stuart Udall, then a congressman from Arizona, the Pimas, and even some people in the National Congress of American Indians.

William Bradford Huie asked for an injunction against the network, and up to the final hours before the show was to be aired it was touch and go—N.B.C. was standing by with some organ music—and then Federal Judge E. J. Dimock found in our favor.

In the end, the creative people directly concerned with the project were able to exert enough pressure to get the play on the air.

The show went on, and as always, a great many people liked it, including some critics, and a great many people and critics did not. N.B.C. got hundreds of letters, mostly approving, more letters I am told than any program in its history up to then.

So far as I know it didn't help the Pimas much, but then its purpose was to state a truth—what I thought was the truth anyway—and fifteen million people were said to have heard it.

The cows were being led into the barn.

I thought of Bob saying, "Write the pilot [*Calhoun*]. Sure it will suffer from the disease of the committee system, but then you'll get maybe a dozen other chances to say what you really want and be reaching a mass audience, too."

I got up and started back into the house.

The next morning Evan and I set to work on yet another draft of the script.

It included—well, not exactly a friendly lynch scene; it was sort of a—it wasn't even really a lynch scene; it was what you might call—a crowd scene, but *tense*.

What happens is this:

The ranchers of Calhoun County discover that there's a blight in the orange grove of Zac Laird; he's the share-cropper. This news causes the ranchers to panic.

Do they go to their county agent, the man in a Stetson and a dusty pickup, to find out what the blight is, how it can be prevented, how fast it spreads, and how the spread can be stopped?

That is what most farmers and ranchers in this country have been doing since the beginning of the century; it is, as I've said, what a county agent is all about.

No, the Calhoun County ranchers, enticed to stupidity by our smart antagonist, Eric Sloane, gather in front of Laird's blighted grove, prepared to drive him off the land.

When Calhoun hears of this, he rushes to Zac's place and makes an eloquent speech telling the ranchers that just be-cause Zac is a *foreigner*—in that version of the script the Lairds came from Texas—Zac nevertheless deserves a fair shake, just like the rest of us because when you come right down to it, that is what this nation is all about. . . .

The angry ranchers wait politely until the speech is done and then disperse. They are as ashamed of themselves as if they had cheated on their income taxes.

When the scene was written, my only wish was that John White and every other county agent in the country and all the men in the U.S.D.A. I'd talked to would be out bowling the night the thing went on the air.

That afternoon I called Harold Franklin. "Will I be able to take my name off the pilot if I don't like it?"

"I imagine so," said Harold, "but why worry about a thing like that now? Wait until you see what's on the screen; then decide. . . . You know what your trouble is, Merle?"

"I cross my bridges ninety-nine times before I get to them."

"I couldn't have put it better myself," said Harold.

The real question is how I was able to sit down and write a scene that I didn't for a moment believe.

Several excellent reasons:

a) I am greedy.

b) I am greedy.

c) I am greedy.

Besides, I assured myself that the scene would be dropped. Once *anybody* saw it on paper he *must* realize how preposterous it was in the context of what a county agent really is.

The one scene that was *never* seriously questioned was the tense crowd scene.

Dorso loved it; Cooper said it was beautiful; Larry White said it would play; Bob Aurthur said it needed tightening.

Within a week I was beginning to think it was an okay scene, and by the time the October Madness set in, I was convinced that it was probably the best scene in the script.

On the afternoon of September 10, Evan drove me to the city for a meeting on still another draft of the script—the eleventh.

The meeting began with Dorso saying that he loved every single change I'd made. Larry White said he had, too, and

Cooper, who had flown in from the Coast, said, "The changes are just beautiful, Merle."

"Now this meeting has nothing to do with you personally, Merle," said Dorso. "We love you, and we love the script."

Larry White placed his chin on the back of his hands, which were resting on top of the table in the U.A. conference room.

Bob said, "I've told Merle that this will be the last draft he's going to have to write. This *is* going to be the pilot. If it weren't going to be the pilot, we wouldn't be doing this, right, Larry?"

White kept his eyes closed.

"Larry, for God's sake," said Bob.

White opened his eyes and started to raise his head, then changed his mind.

"You do agree with me," said Bob.

"I'm the kind of fellow that likes to listen," said pale Larry White.

"Is it or isn't it the pilot?"

White, not raising his head, moved it in what might have been a nod. On the other hand it might have been a shake. Put it this way, no jury is ever going to convict White on a head-moving charge.

"Okay," said Bob. "Now suppose we discuss what needs doing, and it won't take long."

"None of the thoughts I have are major," said White. "I think the confrontation scene between Eric Sloane and Calhoun doesn't come soon enough."

"I agree with you there, Larry," said Dorso. "The confrontation should come earlier. Maybe Eric should be in the tease instead of Nan [Eric's wife], although maybe both of them should be."

"Suppose Eric has been away some place," said Cooper, "and he's coming back. In an airplane. . . . We all know that Eric has a private plane because of that beautiful description that Merle wrote of Eric's hangar and landing strip . . .

narengrr . . . narengrr . . . narengrr . . . the sound of a
plane, and we all look up, and it's Eric, and he looks down
and sees the blight, and right off, we've got something going
. . . narenggr . . . narengrr . . ."

"Beautiful," said Dorso. "That's a beautiful idea. Don't
you think so, Larry?"

White made a movement with his head.

"Maybe Stanwyck should be in the first scene," said Dorso.
"After all we don't meet her until Jack gets to the fair, and
we're already about four minutes into the show."

I started to say, "But a little less than a month ago you said
you loved having Stanwyck at the fair, doing her job. That
was the day you said I was a great . . ."

I did say, "What would she be doing in the tease?"

"Well, she could be helping Jack," said Dorso. "You know,
she could be—handing him tools, a shovel, a pickax, things
like that, and then—and here's the point; here's where the
conflict comes in—she doesn't do something that Jack asks
her to do. Because her husband has come back and she's so
excited about that that she lets Jack down. That ties the two
stories together right from the beginning, and we've got our
audience involved with our two stars."

Toward the end of the meeting White said, "The length
of the script doesn't matter. This is a script to be read, not
acted. I've got a script by Jerry Weidman at my office right
now, and it's 130 pages long."

Jerome Weidman, the novelist, had gone to C.B.S. with
the idea for a series about a real estate woman in Connecticut.
After more than a year of conferences, not, I imagine, much
different from the one described here, the real estate woman
become a male reporter on a metropolitan newspaper. Which
is often the case.

I don't know who thought of the series title, which is a
shame, because it is an example of the creative thinking that
makes you realize that the network people are worth every

cent of the hundreds of thousands they each pull down every year. The title was *The Reporter.*

After the meeting in the U.A. conference room, and again the next morning, Cooper and I went over the script, line by line, word by word.

"This time make it as long as you want to," he said. "Put in lots of description—the fair scene, for instance, really describe the fair, the way you would in a novel because it's very beautiful, and when we go to Texas to do the filming . . ."

"But I thought we were going to do the filming in Las Cruces, and I've already written John White at the university. You said . . ."

"Texas has got everything we need," said Cooper, "actors —they've got a lot of wonderful little theaters, especially the one in Dallas—and they've got some wonderful fairs, and it's cheaper . . . and we've got to have this script finished in time to get the final approval from C.B.S. and catch the last fair in Texas."

"Is this really going to be the last draft?" I asked.

"This is the one we'll go with," said Cooper, "and it will be very beautiful. Hunt Stromberg on the Coast was saying after the August meeting, 'Maybe we need another script.' I said, 'It won't be another script. It'll be another network.'"

I got red as a beet and said, "Thank you, Jack."

"I stick by my writers," said Cooper. "And when you get your little duff out to California . . ."

"When I was in California last June," I said, "before I wrote the first draft of the script, you said it should be kept down to under sixty pages, which I did, and Dorso said that you shoot a pilot a little bit short, and now . . ."

"The script you write has nothing to do with the script we shoot," said Cooper. "We've got a lot of talented directors interested in this project, and they've read your notes, and when the time comes, you and the director and I will decide what goes on the screen, and nobody will interfere.

"When Mike Dann got back from Europe and found out

that I'd read your script to the brass at C.B.S. he said to me, 'Never show anybody a first draft, and besides, us bastards don't know how to read a script anyway.' Mike said that Pat Weaver had taught him to 'Stay up all night and argue with the creative people, but in the morning let them have their way.' Mike said, 'Otherwise we wouldn't have had a *Playhouse 90*'. . . . Merle, you and the director and I will decide what goes on the screen. And nobody else. Take my word for it."

Bob Aurthur was flying to California the following Wednesday and wanted to take as much of the final script as was available with him.

Evan and I drove back to Brewster, and for the next few days worked all day every day and most nights as well.

On Tuesday the first fifty pages of what we thought would be the final script were sent to Bob, and the next morning he took them with him to Hollywood.

Late that afternoon the next thirty pages were dispatched to New York with a young man named Dennis MacMenamin, who was painting my house at the cost of a thousand dollars a minute.

Those pages were to have been flown to California in a special pouch that the William Morris office sends to Idlewild every weekday afternoon.

Every weekday afternoon but that one.

Dennis called from the city to say that the office was deserted. It was Rosh Hashana, and apparently even the switchboard operator was away.

Dennis sent the package air mail from the main post office and I sent Cooper a telegram:

NEW YORK TOTALLY SHUT DOWN WILLIAM MORRIS CLOSED STOP FORGOT IT WAS ROSH HASHANA HOLD YOU AT LEAST HALF RESPONSIBLE STOP WOULD THE PONY EXPRESS HAVE GONE THROUGH QUESTION MERLE

On Friday the final pages of the script—it turned out to be 119 pages long—left Brewster. It was a miserable early fall evening with a heavy rain and an impenetrable fog.

By the time the pages were ready, the Brewster post office was closed. I called the local candy and stationery store to find out if they had two dollars' worth of stamps in their machines. After a lot of dimes it turned out that they did.

Kay Flanagan drove her taxi through the rain and the fog, licked two dollars and thirty cents' worth of five-cent stamps, pasted them on the package—"There was just enough room for the address to show"—and bribed a trainman on the New York Central to take the envelope to the main post office in New York.

That night the glass house blazed with electricity, a huge fire in the fireplace, and self-satisfaction.

The final draft of the script had been finished, not my script, not anybody's script, a script that from the beginning had suffered from "the disease of the committee system."

But as soon as it was approved by the network, then Cooper, the director, and I would get together and decide what we wanted on the screen. At last the creative people would be in charge.

The weekend was beautiful. The air was clear, the sky dark blue, and the leaves were at their best.

Dennis drove Evan and me to Danbury, Connecticut, where I bought a new Volkswagen convertible, pearl white with a black top.

I couldn't at the moment afford it; in four and a half months I had received only the original $5000, but now that the final draft was finished, another $2500 would be paid, and when the filming began I would get the final $2500. And then there would be the royalties of $1000 every week, plus the additional six scripts that my contract called for with "the most favored nations clause," which came to another $60,-000 within the course of the year, and there was always the possibility of being script editor at $1000 per week extra, to begin.

To be sure, I still didn't have a signed contract, but Harold was back from Greece.

As we were driving back to Brewster in the new convertible Evan said, "What do you think of the script?"

"Well," I said, "despite the fact that it's longer than *The Decline and Fall,* it's funnier, and the ending is upbeat, and I am delighted with the way the *tense* crowd scene turned out. I was afraid that this show wouldn't have a message."

"What is the message?" asked Evan.

"That you shouldn't hate Texans," I said.

"A thought that I shall certainly take to heart," said Evan.

"Although," I said, "if the pilot is filmed in Texas, then the Lairds, as the *foreigners,* will probably come from New Mexico, but since they are all Anglos and therefore have no guilt, I don't see how anybody can fail to be uplifted, cleansed, and purified."

"You're right, Mrs. Shapiro," said Evan. "Anyway, the fair stuff is good, and so are the scenes with Cooper and Stanwyck and the 4-H Club kids. At least we've saved that. And the epilogue with Daphne Rinehart [the art teacher-painter who was, along with the assistant home agent, Lydia Willard, to be Cooper's continuing love interest] is funny and exciting. Anyway, this isn't the script you're going to film. This is just the selling script."

I said, "I have always wanted to know how to be a salesman and now I do know how."

On Monday I finished an article about the Iowa reunion for *Show* magazine and worked on the journal, which had been neglected for several days.

> *Monday, September 23.* Bob Aurthur said today that a series represents a year's work for almost everyone involved, the writers, the producers, the stars. Four hundred and fifty thousand dollars is now being put up to film the pilot of *Calhoun* but so much more is at stake. You bring a play onto Broadway and if it flops you've lost $150,000, maybe $200,000, and maybe a couple of months out of the lives of the people involved. Bob didn't include the writer in that; he may have been working five years on the idea. In a pilot, because the profit can be so huge, everyone gets nervous.
>
> The weekly budget for *Calhoun* is $145,000 for each show, one of the largest budgets, maybe the largest in the history of C.B.S. and of television. Say *Calhoun* runs a year, thirty-nine weeks. That's about $6,000,000 next year alone, not including the summer reruns, thirteen weeks of those, usually. . . . Cooper's take for his services as an actor is $10,000 a week. He gets another $3000 a week for Jackie Cooper Productions, Inc. Half a million for him next year alone, again not counting the summer reruns. . . . And the folks at William Morris will get $14,500 out of every show. Another $600,000 a year. I've asked around at U.A. about their take and even read a few letters when people were out of the

room, but I can't find out what their haul is. More than William Morris, I'll bet. And good old Mike Dann says the series is going to make $9,000,000 for his network. Not next year alone, but then everybody gets more loot the second year and by the third year, well, does Brink's have enough trucks?

I've heard certain pessimists tell each other that it's not like the old days—"We're still making plenty of colored beads, but the Indians have run out of land," and, "The cotton gin has simply ruined tourist class on the clipper ships from Africa."

What those poor-mouths don't seem to recognize is that there's a new mother lode that beggars anything we've ever known, the air waves. We're still the land of opportunity. And next year, the three networks that have got hold of the air waves that I'm told belong to me, not me personally but me the public, are going to make at least a billion dollars. Up till now I haven't had my share, but *Calhoun* is going to change all that. . . .

In the late afternoon Cooper called from North Hollywood. The final pages of the script had arrived, and he said, "I'm ecstatic, I can't tell you how ecstatic I am. I just love it, and I've already mimeographed the first fifty pages. Every draft has been beautiful and this is the best of all.

"The fair scene, I love the fair, the way you've described it, it's just the way we talked about it in New York. And when Cal is driving with the 4-H Club kids in the pickup, and we're all singing, 'I went to the animal fair . . .' It's just beautiful."

"I thought maybe . . ." I said.

"Merle, it's marvelous. When Cal gets on TV to warn the country about the blight and we see the reaction of everybody to what he's saying, I come out a real hero. Beautiful. I've got three members of my staff in the office right now, breaking down the script, discussing locations, the budget, everything. I'm sending you a list of the actors we're thinking about casting in the series. You should be ready to bring your little duff out here any minute. . . . Of course the script's a little long, and I don't want to show it to anybody just yet, actors I mean. Until we've cut it . . ."

"Jack, you told me to put everything in; you said the length didn't matter."

"Of course I did, and it's beautiful, and when you come out, which will be any minute now, we'll do the cutting. I'm going to line up the best director in the business. . . . Del Mann, David Miller . . . and God bless you, Merle."

I started packing, yet another unwise decision.

On Wednesday, September 25, Bob Aurthur called; he had just got back to New York, had read the 119-page script, and said he liked it.

"The length presents some problems, though," he said.

"I know that, but Larry White and Cooper told me to make it long, and I thought you agreed. This was going to be a *reading* script."

"The cutting won't be any problem," said Bob, "a couple hours' work, no more than that. I can do it this weekend in East Hampton."

"Would you like me to come to East Hampton?"

"You don't need to and don't worry about it. The only purpose of this script is to sell it to Jim Aubrey. That's why it has to be cut."

"As you know, my acquaintance with Mr. Aubrey is peripheral—"

"It doesn't need much cutting," said Bob, "and don't worry about it. It has nothing to do with what goes on the screen."

"Okay, Bob. Fine. I don't care what you send to Aubrey. But as soon as you've finished the cutting, send me a copy, and we'll get down to business."

That, students of Advanced TV II, was a mistake. Not the first, and, as you'll see if you go on to complete Graduate TV III, by no means the last.

I've said that Bob is the best editor in the business, and he is, but a writer should always be present when his child undergoes surgery. If the writer isn't—it's like sending your head out for a haircut. The barber may do a splendid job, but, oh, the shock.

On October 2, Bob called again; he had finished one cutting of the script, but further cuts appeared to be necessary.

"For whom?"

"Merle, don't worry about it," said Bob. "I'll finish the cuts in a few hours. . . . . I've told everybody I'm coming up to your place; so if anybody calls, say I'm walking in the woods."

Nobody called until October 8; Bob again.

"I've finished," he said, "and, Merle, when you read it, don't weep."

"Go on."

"Look, when I came back from California, everybody seemed to think that you couldn't possibly have any objectivity on your 119-page script and that I could cut it quicker. I said to myself, 'Okay. This is a craftsman's job and I can do it.' You said it was okay so I went ahead. When you read what I've done just keep in mind that this script has only one purpose, to sell it to Jim Aubrey. When Dorso threw it on Aubrey's desk Dorso said, 'This is the one you're going to buy,' and I think Aubrey will."

"How is it different?"

"Well, there's no tease; the material is still there, but the fade-out is gone. No tease."

"No tease. Any other emendations?"

"It was decided between C.B.S. and Cooper that, as they say, format-wise, there wouldn't be any epilogue. It would mean hiring another actress and an extra day's shooting and this show is already over budget."

"No tease and no epilogue," I said, "but otherwise it's still the same script."

"We had to drop the fair scenes because it would take a week to shoot and cost $100,000, and C.B.S. apparently never liked the fair much."

The county fair had been a focal point of the script, partly because it represented the traditional celebration of the harvest and also because it provided an opportunity for all the principals in the cast, Cal, Abby, Lydia, and even the antagonist, Eric Sloane, and his wife, Nan, to be part of a single event. In a rural community everybody takes part in the fair.

After a pause I said, "No tease, no epilogue, and no fair. Any other changes?"

"The flower show," said Bob, "but you already knew about that. No flower show."

"Excuse me just one second," I said. "I want to jot these things down."

I found a pen, and since there was no ink available, I dipped it into the rapidly deepening pool of my blood.

"Now let me just be sure I've got all this straight. No tease, no epilogue, no fair, and no flower show. Anything else?"

"Well," said Bob, "the search for how the blight got into the county. Everybody thought that was too long and too scientific. . . ."

"It does take a minute and a half," I said, "and since the county agent is basically a scientist, finding the source of the blight is as much a part of his job as it would be for a doctor to try to find the source of a disease, but no matter. So far as I can see none of the changes have been fundamental. Anything else worth mentioning?"

"There's no 4-H Club stuff any more," said Bob. "*Everybody* knows county agents and home agents work with 4-H Club kids, and besides . . ."

I thought, Robert Alan Aurthur is your friend, and whenever you have felt hostility toward him it has been laden with love, and it is now.

I managed to say, "Are there any other . . . ?"

"Since we took out the search for the source of the blight

I had to change the ending. At first it may look a little Frank Capra-ish, but everybody seems to think it will work. After the burning of Zac Laird's grove, after what you call the tense crowd scene, well, the people who have wanted to run Zac off his land are ashamed and . . ."

I believe I interrupted at that point and said, "You don't have to tell me; I wrote that scene many times under the pseudonym of Lloyd C. Douglas. They bring Zac calf's foot jelly and they do a lot of shit-kicking and then Aimee Semple McPherson steps out of a shining cloud . . ."

"Merle," said Bob, "after the script has been sold to C.B.S. you and Cooper and the director can make any changes you want. . . . I'll send you a copy."

I swam out of the pool of blood and tears in my study.

Evan was in the gracious living area of the glass house, sorting and packing all the county agent files, which had now grown to about four hundred pounds.

"The script," I said, "though shorter remains unsullied. Although the epilogue and tease have been deleted, the fair, and all references to the 4-H Clubs and . . ."

"Merle, you're dripping blood all over the carpet."

The script arrived the following day. I refused to read it.

Evan did, though, and when he returned from a five-hundred-mile hike in the woods, I asked how it was.

"It's shorter," said Evan.

"That all?"

"Didn't you tell me that one of Aubrey's complaints about the August 15 script was that Cal was a crybaby and Abby a pain in the ass?"

"That, according to Cooper, is an exact quote. And Aubrey or one of the moguls said that Calhoun should be a lot funnier, sort of Hennesey in county agent's clothes."

"This last version is a laugh riot. Cal's a basket case, and Abby is snipping away at what's left over."

I got up at four-thirty the next morning and read the script.

I hated it.

The main plot line of *Calhoun* had originally been simple.

Dorso once described and described well what the story was about: ". . . A head-on meeting between two forces, that of the individual personified by Zac, and the supposed good of the community personified by Eric Sloane. Cal, when faced with the inevitable fact that the man he opposes is right, then must turn around and convince the man he supported to destroy the very thing that he [Cal] had defended. . . ."

In the early drafts of the script Cal, on discovering the blight, is almost sure he knows what it is—the burrowing nematode—and what has to be done. To be absolutely sure, he takes a root sample to a plant pathologist at the state university. Cal's diagnosis is confirmed.

The pathologist, who is more scientist than humanist, tells Cal that the only way to contain the disease is to tear out every blighted tree, as well as several rows of healthy trees to create a buffer zone, and set them afire. The method is called "bulldoze and burn." I had got back to bulldoze and burn because the U.S.D.A. had told me that this was the only way.

"Is that the only way?" asks Cal, again knowing the answer

and knowing that "bulldoze and burn" means the end of Zac Laird and his farm.

The pathologist says it's the only way he knows about; however, new things are discovered every day. Who knows?

Eric Sloane and most of the community want Cal to do the burning immediately. The hell with Zac Laird. Why take chances? The blight may spread to their orange groves. But Cal insists on exploring every possibility to save Zac.

In the end, after telephone calls and telegrams to the U.S.D.A. and every nematology expert in the country, Cal is convinced that the bulldoze and burn method is the only way, and he must persuade—persuade, not order—Zac to wipe himself out.

Cal: "Zac says I'm the smartest man in the county. . . . Oh, I'm smart all right. The lady in the back row wants to know why her peonies don't bloom. I know the answer. How do you get rid of the skunk under the front porch? Ask Einstein here. Hornets in your kitchen? Bats in your belfry? Call 505-814-322. Open night and day. . . . But when a man's life is on the line—What the hell am I doing in this job anyway?"

That line was still in the script that Bob had cut; so was the essence of the situation I've described, but the simplicity was gone. So, I think, was the truth.

Cal's dilemma had been drowned in a swamp of sentiment, melodramatic posturing—the tense crowd scene, among other things—and a hoked-up ending.

These things had not happened all at once; as was said, it's never sculpting, it's whittling.

Who did it? Who was responsible?

It began in a suite in the Beverly Hills Hotel on a sunny day the previous June, the day Dorso said we all wanted to be down in Birmingham. I felt no need to be in Birmingham, but I did feel the need to say, "Either we do the script I can write [Prather], a script about a man defending a right I understand and sympathize with, or it's so long Charlie and no hard feelings."

The morning I finished reading the script Bob had cut I said to Evan, "Bob says that when Dorso put this script on Aubrey's desk Dorso said, 'This is the one you're going to buy.' Aubrey won't though; he's not a fool. So it's all over. You go back to your novel and I'll go back to mine. It's been a painful but enlightening experience. And I've learned something, I guess relearned something. You cannot beat the system. You cannot ever beat the system."

That afternoon Bob Kotlowitz, an editor of *Show*, called to say that they were buying my piece on the Iowa reunion.

"What changes do you want?" I asked.

"None," said Kotlowitz.

"Not even one?"

"I can't think of any."

"Well, there you are," I told Evan. "The bloody series is down the drain, thank God, but *Show* doesn't even want one . . ."

The phone rang.

"*Show* has changed its mind," I said. "They've decided that the capstoning speech should be given before a friendly lynch mob, and they want the setting changed from Marshalltown to the French Riviera . . . and they want me to make Dora a role Tuesday Weld could do . . . and . . ."

I picked up the phone.

"Did you read the script?" asked Bob Aurthur.

"Yes."

"And you hated it and didn't call me. Now I know how you feel when you give me something and I don't call you."

"Well, it isn't so much that . . ."

"I've got news for you," said Bob. "Jim Aubrey loved it."

"I don't believe it."

"It's been an hysterical couple of days around U.A. Everybody's been walking around saying that Aubrey probably hated what I'd done to your script, and we didn't hear, and we didn't hear, and finally, Dorso got Aubrey on the phone, and Aubrey said, 'I love it. I thought it was understood.' "

"Are you sure it was Aubrey?"

"He loved it," said Bob. "Of course there are . . ."

"A few minor changes."

"Let's have lunch on Thursday," said Bob. "There's nothing major."

I said I'd be in the city on Thursday.

"Congratulations," said Bob. "Start building that swimming pool."

A lot of champagne corks were popped that night, and at the height of the festivities I sent a telegram to Cooper:

SOMETIMES I THINK THERE IS A GOD STOP CONGRATULATIONS IS
ALL I CAN SAY AND SAY AND SAY   MERLE

But when the glasses were empty and there was no more wine, I said to Evan, "I don't care what Aubrey says. I still hate the script and what's been done to it. I want out. . . . What do you think I should do?"

"You've got a long history of walking out on things," he said. "You've gone this far. Why not stick around to the final curtain? If you want to write about the times, then look at it, all of it, and I have an idea that everything is television. But I can't make up your mind for you. This is one you'll have to decide for yourself."

I decided to go on.

Shepheard's, the oasis in the Drake Hotel where Bob and I had lunch on Thursday, has a bas-relief of the Sphinx's head above the checkroom. The walls are covered with dark green billiard cloth, and the constantly whirring ceiling fans are painted gold.

It is apparently got up to represent a room in the old hotel of the same name in Cairo, but it would never fool an Arab.

Most of the waiters are German. I tell you those people are getting in everywhere. They're like red ants.

One of them halted me at the door. He at once spotted me as a premature anti-fascist, measured me for a bake oven, then said, "We can't serve you like that."

"Naturally," I said, "first I have to be stuffed, then roasted, and you'd have to stick an apple in my mouth, pour brandy over me, and . . ."

"You are without a necktie."

The necktie I was given was the size and shape of a noose.

Bob had watched all this with pleasure. "Little whirlwinds seem to follow you wherever you go," he said. "What are you drinking?"

"Nothing, thanks." That was one of the days when in addition to the aforementioned around my neck a replica of John Calvin sat on my shoulder.

"I'm sorry you didn't like what I did with the script," said Bob.

"You know what Bankhead said when she saw the movie they made out of Tennessee Williams' *Orpheus Descending,* 'Tenny, darling, how awful for you. They've absolutely ruined a perfectly dreadful play.'"

"The purpose was to sell the script to Jim Aubrey," said Bob, "and it worked."

"And now they want a few additional changes," I said, "again."

"How would you like to come down to Florida?" asked Bob. "We're filming *Pioneer, Go Home* in Boca Grande, and we've got a whole hotel to ourselves. You could lie on the beach all day, and in a couple of hours . . ."

"We could make the few minimal changes."

I thought, Four months have passed, and the more things change . . . In July everybody said as soon as C.B.S. approves the story line, then you can go off and write anything you want, but later everybody said, "Now that C.B.S. has approved the story line, you can't change it." And now that Aubrey has okayed the script, all I have to do is make the changes he wants. When will I be able to make the changes I want? . . . You know the answer to that one. So go to Florida; it isn't the season, but . . .

"I should never have got you into this," said Bob.

I smiled, remembering, and said, "Go to hell."

"Can you come down with the rest of us tomorrow?"

I said I'd come down on Sunday night.

"The changes have to be back to Aubrey on Tuesday," said Bob. "We'll do them on Monday. No problems, and when we've finished, you go out to Las Cruces. They've decided to film there since there isn't any fair. Stay until the pilot is done and then get out. Take your royalty check every week but have nothing more to do with the project."

"Why?"

"Last week—Cooper *hated* the script, and he was sure Aubrey wouldn't buy it."

That gives Cooper and me something in common, I thought.

"I believe I will have a drink," I said.

"Frankly," said Bob, "he's lost all faith in you, and . . ."

I said, "The last time I talked to Jack on the telephone he was ecstatic. . . . Of course that was two weeks ago."

"So two weeks ago you were blood brothers. Cain and Abel were, too, and Romulus and Remus. Old ties diminish very quickly in Southern California. . . ."

Bob and I went back to the U.A. offices, and there was a meeting with Vice-President White, Dorso, Bob, and me in which the minimal changes were discussed.

Dorso kept saying things like Cal needed to be more flawed, have more idiosyncrasies as well as be more heroic and a little less unsure of himself.

Larry White, who sat up straight much of the time, said that he felt that maybe Eric was painted too black. Dorso said that he thought that was a virtue, although maybe we ought to have a scene in which Eric shows that he loves his wife.

Dorso said that maybe the scene in which Abby says good-by to Sid was too long; White said perhaps it was too short.

Bob and I went back to his office, and his secretary handed me a round-trip ticket to Florida.

Then there was a telephone call from Cooper in California.

"Jack," Bob screamed into the telephone, "I have nothing whatever to say to you."

Cooper: "--------------------."

"Jack, I think you're a ——. I don't want to talk to you."

Cooper: "--------------------."

"Jack, last week you were screaming and shouting and carrying on. You wanted to get rid of Merle, of U.A., of me, and now that C.B.S. has come through, you want to be my friend. I don't want to be *your* friend. I'll work with you, sure, but be your friend, no. You're a ——."

Larry White tiptoed into Bob's office.

"Who's he talking to?" he whispered.

"Cooper," I said.

What blood there was drained from White's face.

"Cool it," he whispered to Bob.

Bob said, "I'm not finished with him yet. . . . Jack, you're a ———."

The remainder of the telephone call was repetitious.

When it was over, Bob turned to me and said, "I said most of that for your benefit. I just want you to know that the only way the project can be saved is for you to come to Florida, make the changes that Aubrey wants, and then you and Cooper and the director can go off and shoot whatever . . ."

Four messages were waiting for me at the Gorham, all from Cooper.

"Is that Jackie Cooper the actor?" asked the night switchboard operator.

I nodded.

"His secretary says it's urgent."

"I don't want any further telephone calls from *anybody*."

"Not even Jackie Cooper?"

I shook my head.

"If he calls again, do you have any message?"

I looked at her for a moment, but even though I knew she has a son who's a buck sergeant in the Army I decided against giving her the message.

The next morning on the way back to Brewster I said to Evan, "I shall never speak to Cooper again as long as I live."

"Uh-huh."

"It's not that I feel the slightest hostility toward him personally. None. From his point of view he acted in a perfectly rational manner, and, besides, hostility is almost as bad for your liver as alcohol."

"Uh-huh."

"On the other hand, when he begs for forgiveness, I shall, well—since my successful analysis which I am beginning tomorrow—I do not need to be loved by one and all. I can afford to be choosy."

"Uh-huh."

"To be sure, I am a little angry, but that is a perfectly healthy emotion, and Freud himself stresses that it is better to get these things out in the open instead of letting them fester. That is why I will never have an ulcer."

"Uh-huh. Although, if you never speak to Cooper again, how will he know you're angry?"

"I'll take it," I said, grabbing the phone. "Jack, you're a hysterical . . ."

"Mr. Cooper has been trying to get you since yesterday," said Dorothy Fisher. "Here he is."

"Merle, old buddy, how are you? And thank you for sending me that sweet telegram. It made me cry. It was very thoughtful of you."

"Jack, you are a . . ."

"Barbara was saying only this morning what a sweet man you are."

"Jack, you . . ."

"Isn't it wonderful about Aubrey loving the script?"

"*I* do not love the script," I said. "I had nothing whatever to do with the cutting. . . ."

"Merle, old buddy, I was hoping you'd say that. Barbara kept saying to me, 'If you're unhappy, call Merle, call Merle.' Now all that is over; they've got their selling instrument, and it's been sold. Now's the time for you and me and the director and the other creative people in this project . . ."

"Not me. I understand you've got several other writers in mind, and that is just fine by me, because . . ."

"*That* was last week. I didn't like the cutting, and I was sure Jim Aubrey wouldn't either, but now that you say that *you* don't like the script, you and Stuart and I . . ."

"Who's Stuart?"

"The wonderful director, Stuart Rosenberg, the best there is. You will love each other. Do you know him?"

"I've met him."

The meeting had been at the screening of a pilot for a series called *Espionage;* I was there because Steve Hill, who had been in *The American,* played the lead.

Though I knew Mr. Rosenberg was considered a top director I was disappointed in the show and was trying to sneak out of the projection room because I didn't know what to say to Steve.

I was stopped by a William Morris man who said, "Merle, I want you to meet Stuart Rosenberg, who directed the wonderful pilot you've just . . ."

Since I didn't know what else to say, I said to Rosenberg, "You certainly were lucky to have a fine actor like Steve Hill."

"Thank you very much," said Rosenberg. "I'm glad you liked it. It was a very difficult pilot to direct."

"That came through," I said.

"Why thank you, aren't you nice? In the first place, of course, we had script problems, and I personally had to . . . And then halfway through the shooting the actress who was playing . . . And it was filmed in London, and you know the English, not to mention the fact that the two writers . . ."

"Stuart's got a lot of wonderful ideas," said Cooper, "creative ideas. He doesn't like the cut script either. As far as I can make out nobody but Aubrey liked it, but that's all over. Now the creative people are in charge, and we've got just fourteen days before we start shooting, and that means a lot of work, and, Merle, Stuart and I were thinking . . . If you want me to buy you a writer, two writers, the best writers . . ."

I wondered if they were having a *sale.* . . . In which case maybe I could pick up a bargain and unchain the monkeys. . . .

"Jack," I said, "if it's my script, it's going to be written by me and nobody else."

"God bless you, Merle," said Cooper. "I knew you'd say that. And that's the way I want it, and that's the way Stuart wants it. . . . By the way, have you ever read Ibsen's *An Enemy of the People?*"

Is it a quiz? I wondered. I quickly said that I had.

"What did you think of it?"

Since I hadn't the faintest recollection of what it was about, I said, "I liked it." . . . If the author's dead, you're always pretty safe with an answer like that. With live authors, you're equally safe if you hate it.

"I knew you'd say that. Stuart loves it, and I've just been reading it, and I love it, too."

I started to tell Cooper some of the more recent things I'd read but he interrupted, "Read *Enemy of the People* again. We're going to be shooting on the seventh or the ninth of November."

"*Enemy of the People?*"

"Stuart and I feel—well, look, read the play again and think about it in terms of *Calhoun*. I don't mean we'd want you to plagiarize or anything like that, but . . ."

I said that I'd read it but added, "I don't see what an Ibsen play . . ."

"At first I didn't either, but Stuart convinced me, and Stuart has a very beautiful idea. He's coming to New York this weekend; he's directing a *Defenders* and I'm coming with him. We'll be there on Sunday and we'll all get together. . . ."

"Jack, I'm going to be in Florida on Sunday. Bob's down there, and he asked me to come, and we're going to make the few changes Aubrey wants . . ."

"I want you to be in New York with Stuart and me. Bob's doing another show, and he'll have about fifteen minutes to give you. *I* think Bob is going to have a nervous breakdown because when he was in California for *several* days he only gave *me* fifteen minutes. I want you to come to New York on Sunday."

"Jack, who's the boss of this project? You? Bob? Dorso? Aubrey? Who?"

"Now that the sale has been made, I'm the boss," said Cooper.

Okay, I thought; at last we're making sense, no more trying to butter up the Aubreys, the Whites, the Dorsos. At last the people directly involved with what goes on the screen are in charge, which is the way it should have been in the beginning, but better late . . . And I've worked with a lot of directors and with one exception got along with them. Which is the way it should be.

I said to Cooper, "Okay, Jack. Be the boss. If you don't want me to go to Florida call Dorso and tell him."

"I'll do it. Right now. In the meantime read *Enemy of the People,* not with any thought of copying it, just the basic idea. It's a very beautiful play. Stuart's convinced me, and I know you'll agree."

I hung up and said to Evan, "Stuart Rosenberg has some kind of idea about *Enemy of the People.* What's it about, anyway?"

"It's about a Norwegian hothead," said Evan, "the worst kind. Maybe he was the right kind of hero for the end of the nineteenth century or maybe even in the 1930s. He goes around making speeches, alienating everybody. He's supposed to be the county medical officer, but instead of trying to persuade anybody the way Cal would this guy likes making enemies, and so they stone his house, and . . . Look, I don't know what Cooper said, but if he's thinking . . . Stockman, the sour ball in Ibsen's play—his first name is Gabriel, doesn't that give you a hint?—is the exact opposite of the kind of guy Everet Calhoun is supposed to be. . . ."

Evan would no doubt have said more if the telephone hadn't rung.

The call was from Dorso, who appeared for the first time to be out of breath.

"Jack just called me," he said, "and he said you're not going to Florida. That's not true, is it?"

I said that I didn't know.

"But Jim Aubrey *loved* the script," said Dorso, "and there are only those few changes, and I wish *I* could go to Florida, but *I've* got to . . ."

"Dick," I said, "everybody told me that once the script was sold, we could go ahead and do what we wanted. Now all of a sudden, two weeks before we shoot, everybody is saying we make a few changes and that's what we film. I think the script needs a lot of changes, and so does Jack, and so, apparently, does Stuart Rosenberg."

"Rosenberg wasn't the first director on the list," said Dorso. "In fact, he was about fifth on the list, but C.B.S. okayed him, and he started reading your 119-page script and then was told not to read that, that there were going to be cuts, and then when he read the script Aubrey bought, I gather Stuart didn't like it. I just don't understand why everybody is fighting success. If Jim *hadn't* liked it . . ."

"From here on in, I'm interested in what I like."

I discovered I was shouting.

"Now let's be calm about this," said Dorso, not being calm.

"As I told you in the beginning, you and I have to be frank with each other at all times, and that's the way it's been. I told Jack you were going to Florida. Jack just doesn't understand me. I guess because I never have told him that I loved him, and I've never told him that I hated him. He just can't understand that."

"Dick, let's talk about the script. Do you like it?"

"Jim has suggested some changes," said Dorso, "very few, but Jack is a sentimental man, and he doesn't understand me at all."

"Are you going to Florida or not?" asked Evan.

I put my hand over the mouthpiece of the telephone. "We haven't come to that. We're at the part now where Cooper is sentimental and doesn't understand Dorso."

"Nobody ever says, 'I love Dick Dorso.' I have two daughters . . ."

"There's an all-girl violin orchestra playing in the background," I said to Evan.

"I have to be objective," Dorso was saying. "I can't get involved emotionally. If *I* say I like something today, I can't turn around and next week say I don't like it. I have to be direct and honest at all times. It makes me much more comfortable with myself emotionally."

"He's on emotional comfort now," I said to Evan.

Dorso said, "I told Jack that he's a great actor, a very warm actor, and he's one of the few that isn't afraid to be sentimental, but I told him that when he tries to be a producer, that will just never work. Of course he never heard the producer part; he just heard the part about what a great actor he is . . ."

"Dorso's just nominated Cooper for next year's Emmy . . ."

". . . I am not for sale," said Dorso. "*I* cannot be bought. . . ."

I said to Evan, "Cooper may be able to buy me a writer or two, but Dorso is not for sale."

". . . I only compromise on the big issues. On the Negro issue, for example. I do it because it's more profitable emotionally. . . . Certain words have certain meanings today. Charm means false. Suffrage means the Negro, but I don't think of Negroes. I think of women marching around in bloomers. . . .

"Now I think you should go to Florida, Merle, and forget about *Enemy of the People.*"

I said to Dorso, "Cooper hasn't told me what he has in mind, and since he and Rosenberg and I are the three people who are going to be directly involved with getting this thing filmed . . ."

"I haven't read *Enemy of the People,*" said Dorso. "I don't have to read it. When Stuart Rosenberg and Jack first suggested this idea to Bob, Bob and I discussed it for ten minutes, then dismissed it. Because it's a whole new approach, and we'd have to go back to C.B.S. and get new approval, and, besides, Jim Aubrey likes the script the way it is, with the few minimal changes we've discussed. You should get on a plane on Sunday and go to Florida."

"Dick," I said, "Cooper and Rosenberg are going to be in New York on Sunday, and Cooper says he's the boss and that he wants me to meet with them. . . . Now which?"

"We can all four meet on Sunday," said Dorso, "you and Cooper and Rosenberg and I, and I'll explain to Stuart about the nature of a pilot. Then you can go to Florida."

After I hung up, Evan said, "Well, which is it to be, Florida or New York?"

"Both. But Rosenberg is the lucky one. He gets to hear the lecture on the nature of a pilot. . . . But, if I play my cards right . . ."

"You know what's going to happen, don't you? You're not going to Florida, and you're not going to stay in New York. You're going to wind up in California."

"Why?"

"Because there's already a half million involved, and a six-

million budget for the year. So I'm going to load up the car
with all the county agent files and notes and stuff you might
need when they start filming. Just in case."

Sunday was a malevolent day. The fog was dense, the
wind penetrating, and the sky gray and bitter. The fall
was over.

Evan and I drove to the city. I was armed with a memorandum explaining once more—I had a feeling Rosenberg
might not have read the notes—what a county agent was,
what the original concept of the series and the pilot script
had been, and what I felt had gone wrong with it. ". . . As
it now stands Abby, the home agent, emerges as a man-eater,
and Everet Calhoun comes up a weakling. . . ."

The memorandum also explained, diplomatically, the difference between Calhoun and the firebrand hero of *An Enemy of the People*.

Because of the fog, Cooper's and Rosenberg's plane hadn't
landed until dawn, and neither of them had had any sleep.

We had breakfast at Rosenberg's apartment, which was
bright, large, and expensively furnished. There was a balcony
overlooking the East River and Gracie Square. The two Mrs.
Rosenbergs, mother and wife, had prepared a magnificent
breakfast, scrambled eggs, bagels, lox, cream cheese.

Rosenberg kept saying, "I haven't had any sleep for forty-
eight hours," and Cooper kept saying how wonderful it was
that the creative people were in charge at last.

"Dorso's coming over," Cooper said, "but this time all we
have to do is listen."

After breakfast Rosenberg, Cooper, and I went to the study
and had some vodka.

Rosenberg turned on the hi-fi. I had two copies of the
memo, and handed the original to Cooper and the carbon to
Rosenberg.

Cooper read it and said, "It's just beautiful, Merle; it gets back to the concept you and I started out with. Don't you agree, Stuart?"

"I haven't had any sleep for forty-eight hours," said Rosenberg, who was on the second page of the memo. He put another record on the hi-fi, a Brazilian guitarist playing Bossa Nova.

"I don't understand a guy like Calhoun," Rosenberg said. "He sounds to me like a compromiser."

I said, "The job of the county agent is to persuade people; he's an educator. Leonard Appleton, one of the agents Jack and I met in New Mexico, said, 'I'm not inclined to rub people the wrong way.' That's on page three of the memo, Stuart. In *Enemy of the People* Stockman seems to go out of his way to do just that."

"Calhoun sounds to me like an arbiter," said Rosenberg, "and I don't like arbiters. I like people with convictions. I'm directing a wonderful script about blacklisting for *The Defenders.* . . . Suzy Parker read this [the *Calhoun*] script . . ."

"Suzy Parker?"

"Everybody in town has read this script, and I asked my wife to read it and nobody likes it. Suzy said, 'Stuart, what are you doing directing this piece of crap?' "

"Why are you?"

"Old Jack persuaded me," said Rosenberg.

"Stuart, you're talking about a cut script that neither Jack nor I like. That's why we're all here. The point is the kind of guy a county agent is and the kind of job he does. The memo . . ."

"I haven't had any sleep for forty-eight hours," said Rosenberg. "Now in television you've got to grab them right away. In the *Bob Hope Show* I've just done with Milton Berle— and, by the way, he's marvelous—we fade in and the screen is filled with a great big bloodshot eye. That's all. Just a great big bloodshot eye. An opening like that, and you've got the audience. . . ."

"I think it's a beautiful memorandum Merle has written," said Cooper.

"I can't direct a memorandum," said Stuart. "You open with something like a big . . ."

Dorso arrived. He said, "Now Jack and Merle have heard this, but, Stuart, let me explain to you my theory about the nature of a pilot."

It was one forty-five in the afternoon when I got back to the Gorham.

Evan had moved in what little luggage I had and ordered two hot pastrami sandwiches from the Carnegie Delicatessen.

"How did it go?" he asked.

"I thought the lecture on the nature of a pilot lacked its usual verve. For one thing, instead of fifty thousand Berbers headed toward Cairo there were only five hundred. So who needs Dick Daring?"

"What's Stuart Rosenberg like?"

"He's put on weight since he was directing under the name of D. W. Griffith, and he's got a little although not much more hair than when he was using the name Eric Von Stroheim, and he's shorter than when he was Max Reinhardt, but otherwise I found him unchanged, and he has come up with a startling new idea about a television show."

"A new spot for the bathroom?"

"No. He says you've got to grab them in the first *twenty* seconds."

"I never know where you creative people get all your ideas. How did they like the memo?"

"It made Cooper cry."

"I know, but how did he like it?"

"He said it was very beautiful."

"In other words, he didn't commit himself. How did Rosenberg like it?"

"He didn't really read it; he was too busy telling me about how much he and Suzy Parker hate the script."

"Suzy Parker? What part is she reading for?"

"I don't know, but he says Miss Parker thinks it's a piece of crap, and so does he."

"Why is he directing it?"

"Lox and bagels don't grow on trees."

I had scarcely bitten into my cold pastrami when the telephone rang.

It was Cooper.

"I just got off the phone with Barbara," he said. "I read her your memo, and we both cried, for more than an hour."

Talk about grabbing your audience.

"Did Barbara come with you to New York, Jack?"

"No, she's in California. She kept saying, 'I've been telling you to call Merle, call Merle'. . . . And when I read her the part where you say we all want the same thing . . .'"

Cooper began acting out my memo over the phone.

"'. . . A series that is distinguished, will please C.B.S., will sell to a sponsor. . . .' Well, she kept saying, 'I told you to call Merle.' And in the final paragraphs where you say, 'Can these changes—whatever we decide—be accomplished in time for the shooting date? Yes. Will C.B.S. be dismayed by the changes? I cannot believe it. If the creative people involved in this project—and that is all of us—cannot in the next week come up with a shooting script we are proud of and that C.B.S. will applaud then we are in the wrong business. But we are not. We are professionals, and we must do what we think is right. C.B.S. will be pleased; the people who look at *Calhoun* will be astonished.'"

There was a long silence.

Cooper said, "It's a very beautiful memo, old buddy."

Old Buddy was weeping a few tears, too.

"I just can't sleep," said Cooper. "I'm too excited, and we've got so much to talk about. Why don't you get your little duff over here to the Pierre?"

It was three in the afternoon when I got to Cooper's suite, and we talked until late in the evening. We seemed to agree on everything that needed to be done to the script, some tightening here, more humor there, an additional scene with Eric Sloane toward the end, a scene in which Calhoun tries to convince the county commissioners that . . . making Abby somewhat softer, and so on.

"What about *Enemy of the People?*" I said.

"Don't worry about that."

"But suppose Stuart doesn't go along," I said.

"He will," said Cooper. "We all want the same thing. We want a good pilot, and I've told him if he doesn't go along, he can step aside and we'll get another director. But I know he'll go along."

I said, "Of all the people involved in Calhoun, the two who have most to lose if it's a fiasco are you and I."

"That's right, Merle. They're only gambling with money. We have our integrity. Come to California, Merle."

"When?"

"Tomorrow night. With me."

"I didn't bring any clothes," I said.

"You won't need any clothes. You'll be writing. Working together we can do the revisions quicker and better than anybody else . . ."

"But there are a couple of interviews and things lined up for my book [*A Day in Late September*]. It's going to be published next week, and *Newsweek* wants to take . . ."

"It's a wonderful, wonderful book, Merle, and it will make a wonderful movie, and with you and me working together . . . Come to California."

"I'll have to check with Bob Aurthur."

"Bob has been working too hard," said Cooper. "In my opinion he's headed for a nervous breakdown. I told you he was in California for several days . . ."

"What about Dorso? He'll never . . ."

"I'll handle Dorso; you get your little duff out to California."

"I couldn't possibly leave before Tuesday," I said, "and then Evan will drive out to California in the car, so I'll have all the files and notes and some transportation when we're doing the filming."

"After we've finished the pilot, I want you and your buddy to take a tour of the Southwest, all over; visit some Indian reservations, some other county agents, and so on. You'll pick up a lot of story ideas; think of all the ideas you got in those few hours we were in Las Cruces in June. I know you'll want to be helpful to other writers, but when this thing gets under way I want you to be very, very generous with yourself. I want you to write *most* of the scripts. You need to get a little continuity in your life."

We cried a little, shook hands, and pledged eternal fealty.

I called Bob Aurthur in Boca Grande from the Gorham and told him what had happened.

Bob said, "Merle, the C.B.S. changes come first. What you and Cooper and Rosenberg do after that, whatever you do won't be any more than the changes you and Frankenheimer and I made in Tucson with *The American.* Come to *Florida.*"

"There isn't time," I said, which was true or not true, depending on how you look at it. "I'll make the changes you and Dorso and White and I talked about on Thursday, and then I'll make the changes Jack and I agree . . ."

"Merle," said Bob, "if you do this thing, the pilot will never be filmed. Take my word for it. It's dead, buried, done with."

"I've got to take that chance."

"Okay," said Bob, "go ahead, but I think you're out of your mind."

In the next three weeks a great many people said that, but Bob was the only one who said it directly to me.

I flew to California on Tuesday, and Evan and the Volkswagen, loaded with the four hundred pounds of material on the project and the electric typewriter, left on Wednesday morning for the five-day drive across the country.

I arrived at the Los Angeles airport with two shirts, both dirty, one brown suit, and an extra pair of brown shoes that achieve some importance in the narrative that follows.

Cooper had made arrangements for me to have a junior suite with terrace on the fifth floor of a unique establishment in North Hollywood called the Sportsman's Lodge.

The accommodations were a little larger than the glass house; the wall-to-wall carpeting was shoulder deep, and the empire-sized bed could have accommodated three early Farouks and several lucky Pierres.

The pool below was less than a block long, but alongside was a stream that was stocked with honest-to-God trout.

I had no sooner unpacked the portable, the books, the ball-point pens, and the brown shoes than I was gripped with the feeling of isolation and despair I feel every time I'm in Southern California. If everything is television, only television is more so, then Hollywood is American life, only more so.

I went to the studio early the next morning.

As it had been in June the lot was crowded with actors masquerading as cowboys, with executives wearing tans, looks of concern, and clothes from Carroll's, the Brooks Brothers of Beverly Hills.

In the distance I saw Ethel Winant, who was casting director for the *Great Adventure* series. Early in 1959 when I was in Southern California for my last *Playhouse 90*, Ethel had been casting director for that. She placed in a minor role in my play, *Dark December*, a young man who had trouble with his lines.

When I protested, Peter Kortner, the producer, said, "He'll be a big star one of these days. Mark my words."

The young man was Warren Beatty, who now is a big star and is playing in a movie called *Lilith*, opposite another big star named Jean Seberg, one of whose husbands was a sensation in Marshalltown, Iowa. The script of *Lilith* was written by Robert Alan Aurthur.

See how nature imitates art? How life is just like the movies?

I passed the space where Martin Manulis parks his car. When I first knew him he was the exuberant, extravagantly talented man who more than anyone else was responsible for the success of *Playhouse 90*.

The day I left California in 1959 I went out to Twentieth Century Fox Studios to see Martin, who had left C.B.S. some time before to become head of filmed television at the studio. He wanted to talk about my writing a script.

When I got there Martin introduced me to Gardner McKay, who was to play the lead in a series based on a James A. Michener story. McKay was the shyest young man I had ever met, and one of the handsomest.

After McKay left, Martin asked what I thought of him.

"He's very good-looking," I said, "but can he act?"

"That's not important," said Martin.

"Is the series going to be any good?"

"The series is sold," said Martin.

The difference between *Playhouse 90* and *Adventures in Paradise*—well, students, if you've gone along this far, you're nearly ready for your final exam, and it's going to be easy.

Quality doesn't have anything to do with anything.

Playhouse 90 was live and you cannot resell or syndicate it. *Adventures in Paradise* was on film and that can be resold and syndicated and resold to foreign markets and it all means money. *Adventures in Paradise* is, I am informed, still around on reruns.

That morning in October I lingered in front of the office of Robert Soderberg, who used to live down the road from me in Brewster and is now an official of Four Star Television, a producing company that Cooper wanted to head at the time of Dick Powell's death.

Cooper didn't get that job; another friend of mine, Tom McDermott, did.

Elinor Green, the woman to whom I was married, once said, "There are only two hundred people in the world."

There aren't that many, Elinor.

In Cooper's outer office I met a new secretary, Judy. She introduced me to Norman Kahn, who was to be associate producer of the *Calhoun* series. From the beginning Cooper thought that he would be the producer; he still thought so. C.B.S. had never agreed.

Kahn shook my hand and said, "It's been hectic up to now, Merle, but I want you to know that your being here has certainly given us all a feeling of security."

"Mr. Cooper's arranged for an office for you," said Dorothy Fisher. "I think you'll like it."

Thus began the saga of the offices, and if you know where to find it, class, it does have a moral.

The office assigned to me was a few doors down the hall. It was sunny, modestly furnished—a desk with one or two cigarette burns, a swivel chair, a gray rug, and a gray filing cabinet.

On top of the filing cabinet were several picture books about Turkey, and on the desk was a ceramic ash tray of irresolute shape. A camel was painted on it, or else it was a cow or a horse with two humps.

I had brought along some books, several thousand ballpoint pens (at least three a day are stolen from me), copies of the numerous versions of the *Calhoun* script, and my portable. Also the extra pair of brown shoes; they needed new heels.

I was still unpacking when I heard a key being tried in the lock. Before I could get to it, the door opened, and a handsome, very tanned man with white hair stepped inside.

He looked startled.

"Is this your office?" he asked.

"It has been for five minutes. Was it *your* office?"

He nodded. "Of course, I've been on vacation for ten days."

I started gathering up my belongings.

"I'm sorry," I said. "I'll get out."

"Oh no. It's perfectly all right. I'm sure, well, they must have assigned me another office."

"Are you sure you wouldn't rather . . . ?"

"No, no," said the man, "I'll just collect my things. By the way, my name's . . ."

I told him my name and we shook hands.

"Are you here for long?" he asked.

"I don't think so, but I'm not sure."

The man looked at the books on top of the filing cabinet.

"I was writing a script on Turkey, but I guess . . . Is there a Parker 51 in the top drawer of the desk?"

I opened the drawer and there it was. I handed the pen to him and said, "I'll leave while you get your things, and I'm sorry."

When I was at the door, the writer picked up the ceramic ash tray and said, "It's of no value, really. My daughter did it. She's nine."

"I'm glad I met you," I said.

"There've been a lot of writers in this office," he said. "They seem to come and go. Well, I'm glad to have met you, and I wish you the best of luck."

That afternoon I went to the office of Cooper's other secretary, Dorothy Fisher, to get some coffee. While there I noticed that a new edition of the county agent notes had been mimeographed.

Through an oversight a copy had not been sent to me.

Moreover, I observed casually that my name did not appear anywhere, not on the cover, not on the title page, not at the end, nowhere.

Later I mentioned this to Cooper.

He said, "When people get to the last page of those notes, they cry. I did myself."

The last page said, "For the moment that's all. And probably more than enough. I guess now there is nothing to prevent me from writing the script, although I'm sure I'll try to think of something."

"When people get to that paragraph," said Cooper, "not only do they cry, they all want to know who wrote it."

"A perfectly logical question," I said.

"I just can't understand how it happened," said Cooper, "your name being left off."

"Whoever was running the mimeograph machine was probably crying so hard he got careless," I said.

Some days later I arrived at the studio on a morning of stress and strain we're coming to.

I had left the key of my office with Judy, and when I asked for it she said, "But that isn't your office any more. You've been moved to Building B, Room 29."

"You mean somebody went into my office, unlocked my desk, packed my things, and took them to another office in another building, and didn't bother to tell me? And read my journal?"

"We didn't think you'd mind," said Judy. "Most people don't."

"Well, I do, and I'm not most people. By the way, and it's a matter of no importance, really, who has been moved into what was my office?"

"Mr. Cooper put Mr. Chambers in there because Mr. Chambers and Mr. Cooper are going to have to see a lot of each other in the next few days."

"Who is Mr. Chambers?"

"He's the producer," said Judy. "He's new."

"After you'd all read my journal, which was in the upper left-hand drawer, did you move that to Building B, Room 29?"

"Everything was moved," she said.

"And the brown shoes in the bottom drawer?"

"I don't know about the brown shoes," said Judy. "Did you see Mr. Miller's brown shoes, Dorothy?"

Dorothy Fisher entered stage left from where I was standing.

"They forgot to move your brown shoes," said Dorothy, "and then Mr. Chambers—I think it was Mr. Chambers, or else it was Mr. Kahn—found your brown shoes and brought them in here, and they were here just a few minutes ago. In this office."

"Oh, *those* brown shoes," said Judy. "I didn't know those were your brown shoes, Mr. Miller. I'm sure they've been moved to your new office in Building B."

"Room 29?"

"Are you sure?" said Dorothy Fisher. "Because those brown shoes were here not five minutes ago."

Building B is about a hundred and fifty feet from Building A but it might be a hundred and fifty miles. Room 29 is on the second floor. The climb up isn't too bad if you watch out for the splintered floor boards; the hall light was burned out.

I felt my way along the second-floor corridor and found Room 29. The skeleton key was a little tricky but I'm the never-say-die kind and in less than twenty minutes I'd conquered it.

As I opened the door there was the smell you get when you open a beach cottage after a rainy spring.

Compared with the hallway, the inside of the office was very cozy, painted two-tone, an indeterminate green and a quite pleasant beige where the green was peeling off.

There was what looked like linoleum on the floor except where it had worn through, which was in the narrow path between the desk and the window. You could have played ticktacktoe on the pane.

A wonderful place, I thought, clearly not for show, and no distractions. A neat pile on top of the desk; my journal, portable, scripts, and brown shoes. I lighted a cigarette, was about to unpack, and then stopped.

On the desk were several picture books on Turkey, a Parker 51 pen, and a ceramic ash tray.

But back to the business at hand.

When I returned to Office One that first morning I set to work on what turned out to be a twenty-six-page outline of a new script.

I tried to incorporate the changes C.B.S.—meaning Aubrey—wanted, and from the beginning that made as much sense as a Ouija board.

In this area I have to confess that in all the months I kept thinking, Well, yes, this is what these vice-presidents and such *say* Aubrey wants, but if Aubrey and I could just get together I'm sure . . .

I came across a document—how and when is a secret I'll carry to my grave—written by one of the participants in the C.B.S. meeting that took place while I was being a small but complete triumph in Iowa.

Guess who dreamed up the *friendly lynch mob?*

> Not Daring, not Dorso,
>   Not Dunder, not Blitzen.
> Not Cooper, not Stromberg,
>   Not Prancer or Vixen.

In the document James Thomas Aubrey, Jr., Princeton 1941 *cum laude,* is quoted as saying, ". . . I think what we need is a lynch mob attitude, and maybe Cal stops the town from running Laird off his place."

In the final go-round I was trying to please James Thomas, Skippy, Rosenberg, vice-presidents in television till you can't rest, and me.

That morning in North Hollywood I thought I could do it. Maybe they were right. Maybe I was out of my head.

Norman Kahn, who always seemed to be suffering from a head cold, dropped into Office One from time to time to repeat that my being there had given everybody a feeling of great security.

Judy, a girl of enormous good nature, brought me lunch. She is a Californian who had spent some time in New York City, liked it for a while, then not liked it, and decided to come back home.

"That was the first time in my life I knew when to leave the party," said Judy.

"You're lucky to have learned that so early," I told her. "I'm not sure I know yet."

Toward the end of the afternoon Cooper dropped by to bless me and to say that he and I were flying back to New York on Friday to confer with Rosenberg.

I greeted this news with silence, and then said, "Jack, this is the script we go with, isn't it?"

"This is the one we go with," said Cooper.

I continued working on the outline of the new script on Thursday, and that night Evan called from St. Louis. The trip was going well, and he expected to be in Los Angeles on Monday.

"I probably won't be here," I said. "Cooper and I are flying back to New York Friday night. We have to confer with Rosenberg."

"But there are two of you and only one of him," said Evan, "and since the round-trip fare, first class, is in the neighborhood of $400, wouldn't it be cheaper and make more sense if he . . ."

"Look," I reminded him, "you have not yet taken Professor Dorso's graduate seminar on pilots and piloting. As he has mentioned a few dozen times, 'When a nation goes to war it doesn't start balancing its budget.'

"And anyway, we're economizing in other areas. Dorothy Fisher came into my office about four this afternoon and asked if I'd mind sharing Cooper's suite at the Pierre. I said I wouldn't, although I do, and inquired the reason. Dorothy said, 'To cut down on expenses.' I think they're stealing my ballpoint pens, too.

"But the real reason we're going to New York is that Stuart hasn't finished directing his *Defenders*—that's *not* the show that opens up with a great big bloodshot eye—and . . ."

"Merle," Evan interrupted, "do I keep heading west or do I turn around and go back to New York?"

On the Friday night flight back to New York Cooper was in an autobiographical mood.

"Julie [John] Garfield once said a very important thing to me. It was at a benefit in Chicago, and Garfield said, 'Your trouble is you're not sure if you have any talent. You ought to go to New York, get on the stage, and find out.' So I did, and that's when I was in *Magnolia Alley* and *Remains to Be Seen*. It was some of the best advice I ever got."

"Dora said that if I played my cards right, when I was Governor Bradford in *The First Thanksgiving* . . ."

"Hold your thought, Merle."

A motherly hostess gave Cooper and me some more macadamia nuts and another martini.

"Thank you, dear," said Cooper. "Of course, when I was supposed to play Ensign Pulver in the Broadway company of *Mister Roberts*, Josh Logan talked me out of it. He said, 'Go on the road, have a new opening every week, with new press notices' . . . Wonderful advice."

"And when I played *Träumerei* on my little violin . . ." I said.

"Hold your thought, Merle. . . . I've had to work for everything I ever got. From the time I was three years old. Nobody ever gave me anything in my whole life. . . . Now, Brando, I'll never know why I'm nervous when I'm around him. . . ."

"And then I wrote . . . 'Life is a bridge, and we walk upon it.' . . ."

Halfway to New York I asked him to read the article I'd written about the Iowa reunion. I happened to have a carbon copy with me.

When he finished reading it he said, "You've got a lot of funny lines here, Merle," and he added, "You're a very trusting man. It could get you into a lot of trouble someday."

Cooper, Stuart Rosenberg, and I met on Saturday morning in the moneysaving thirty-fourth-floor suite of the Pierre Hotel. Stuart glanced at the first page of the outline, which was still incomplete.

"It's about time we stopped writing crap like this," he said, pointing to the opening scene.

"But Suzy Parker hasn't read it yet," I wanted to say, but I did say, "What would you suggest?"

Stuart riffled through the pages.

"I've got it. The play should open with what you've got at the end of the first act. Opening shot, a giant slide fills the screen, like a big—and on it are thousands and thousands of those little . . ."

"Nematodes."

"Nematodes. Thousands and thousands. Just one big giant slide. *That's* the way you'll grab your audience."

"That's a beautiful idea, Stuart," said Cooper. "Merle, there's a typewriter and paper, and order yourself a sandwich, anything you want. Stuart and I are going out to have lunch and discuss budget. And God bless you."

After they left I wrote, "FADE IN on a screen filled with thousands and thousands of nematodes, all with bloodshot eyes."

By the next afternoon—Sunday—I had finished the twenty-six-page outline.

This time Stuart read it to the end and said, "Now I think we're getting some place. The ideas that Jack and I have suggested have made what was originally a . . ."

Cooper said—well, *you* know what he said.

I said, "Are we all agreed that this is the way we go?"

"Dorso hates the whole idea," said Cooper, "but I told him this morning, 'You can ask me to play something but I have to play it on my own violin. This is the way, or no way.'"

Rosenberg said, "This is the script I'm going to direct. Everybody will recognize that this is better than the earlier one and, as a matter of fact, Jim sees so many scripts he won't remember the one he approved."

Blabbermouth said, "If they won't do it our way, I'll give them back their money and take my script, the characters, and the county agent notes and go back to Brewster. They can start from scratch."

On Monday I wrote the first five pages of the actual script. Cooper shut the door between our rooms, but every time I stopped typing to light a cigarette or drink some coffee, he would stick his head in the door and say, "I just wanted to be sure you're still here and writing."

"Jack, how could I get out with this ball and chain around my neck?"

"I've made an official submission of your outline to William Morris," said Cooper. "And by the way, I've got your phone shut off. I don't want anybody or anything to interrupt your creative flow."

From time to time that Monday morning there was a knock on the door leading to the hallway, and when I opened it a startled man—there must have been a baker's half dozen—would say, "I'm from the William Morris office, and I'm here for the conference."

"I guess it's in the next room," I'd say.

None of the men looked as if he knew much about shorthand, but they all had Jerry-type haircuts.

Occasionally there was the sound of a telephone in Cooper's room, and always the insistent sound of argument and unjoyous laughter.

Then for a long time there was silence.

At a little before one in the afternoon Cooper opened the door; his room was deserted, and he looked pale.

"It's going very well, Jack," I said. "I've finished the first two scenes."

Cooper had not heard me.

"There's a three o'clock American flight to Los Angeles from Idlewild," he said. "I've got you a reservation on it."

"You're kidding."

"I've cut off all your calls, but Norman Glenn [then a Vice-President in Charge of Production and Sales at United Artists] has been trying to get in touch with you; he's called a dozen times."

"*Newsweek* has been trying to get in touch with me, too," I said. "They want to take my picture, but so far I haven't been able to . . ."

"If you talk to Norman Glenn, he'll want you to talk to Bob Aurthur," said Cooper.

"I know Bob's in bad health and heading for a nervous breakdown," I said, "but . . ."

"Norman and Bob will try to talk you out of writing the beautiful script that Stuart and you and I *want* you to write," said Cooper. "I want you to take the three o'clock flight, and I've already ordered the limousine. It'll be here in fifteen minutes. I'll help you pack."

"But I thought you and I were going to take the seven-thirty flight tonight."

"There isn't time for that now," said Cooper, going into the closet in his room.

He picked up my brown bag, threw it on his bed, opened it, and put in the pair of brown shoes.

"Don't worry about a thing," he said. "Just go to California. I'll handle the whole thing."

"Jack, what was the William Morris meeting about?"

"I've called for a boy to take your luggage," said Cooper.

"Well," I said, "my creative flow was flowing, but . . ."

"You'll write even better in California. And in California you won't be bothered with calls from Norman Glenn and Bob, who is headed for a nervous breakdown."

There was a knock on the door. It was a grandfatherly bellman.

"I've come for your bags, Mr. Cooper," he said.

"It's Mr. Miller who's leaving," said Cooper.

"I've only got one bag," I said, "and one brown suit, a pair of brown shoes and this typewriter and the eighteen millionth draft of . . ."

I went into the other room and put the incomplete script in the top of the typewriter case. The bellman helped me.

The telephone rang.

"I told her not to ring unless it was an emergency," said Cooper, picking up the phone.

"Who is it, dear?" Cooper said to the telephone.

"It's Norman Glenn again," Cooper said to me, putting his hand over the receiver.

I slammed shut the typewriter case, bending the carriage and an index finger.

"Merle," said Cooper, "the limousine will be here any minute," then into the telephone, "No, dear, Mr. Miller has already left for California. No, I don't know where he'll be in California."

The bellman looked at the brown shoes and the brown suit in which there were several brown cigarette burns. Then he looked at me; that's the last time I'll ever be a guest at the Pierre.

"I know it doesn't seem like much," I said, running into the bathroom, grabbing my toilet kit and jamming an inauspicious toothbrush into it.

"No, I cannot talk to Mr. Dorso at this time, dear," Cooper was saying to the operator. "I'm out to lunch. And now will you please hold all calls, dear. . . . Merle, the limousine is here. . . ."

The bell grandfather closed the brown bag, and I looked wildly around the wildly disordered suite. Cooper had held off the maid as well as the telephone calls.

"Well," I said, "if I've left anything . . ."

"I'll bring it, old buddy," said Cooper.

"The elevator's waiting, Mr. Miller," said the bellman.

"Don't worry about a thing," said Cooper, "I'll protect your beautiful script."

He shook my hand; the telephone rang.

"That's probably Norman Glenn," he said, "or else Bob Aurthur; Bob is going to wind up in a hospital. . . . Merle, if you're going to make the three o'clock flight . . . I made the reservation in my name; they'll give you the A treatment."

"I was going to cash a check, but since I've . . ."

"Here's thirty dollars," said Cooper, thrusting some bills into my hand. "That ought to take care of the tips on the trip."

"I'll pay you back."

"Ah, it's not money. It goes on the expense account."

"The elevator, Mr. Miller," said the bellman.

I said, "Jack, they're going to try to talk you out of doing the script that you and Stuart and I want to do, and you're mixed up with a lot of very good poker players . . ."

"I can play poker, too," said Cooper.

"Can I do the room now, Mr. Cooper?" asked the maid, who was the bellman's grandmother.

"Yes, dear, you can do the room now," said Cooper. "And, Merle, God bless you and have a good flight."

"You show people certainly lead exciting lives," said the bellman.

As I got into the elevator I heard Cooper say, "Yes, dear. . . . No, dear, Mr. Miller has left town. He didn't say where. . . . Yes, dear, I'll speak to Mr. Rosenberg. . . . Hi, Stuart, old buddy. . . ."

I had Cooper's seat on the plane, the window seat on the right as you enter.

The treatment I got was lordly and, because I like to hold up my end of these charades, I got drunk.

I've got news for you tipplers who travel first class, and this alone is worth the price of the book. Legally you can have only two drinks of the hard stuff on a plane, but you can have all the wine you want. I dimly recall draining the wing tanks.

When I floated into the throne room at the Sportsman's Lodge, Evan, who had arrived a few hours earlier, was there with a friend of his, Winkie Harris.

"I didn't expect you tonight, Merle," said Evan.

He introduced us and mentioned that Winkie, in addition

to being a dear friend, was a relative of Robert Sarnoff, president of a rival network, N.B.C.

"Ish thish woman a pie?" I demanded.

"I'm as American as they come," said Winkie.

And then I believe I told them the whole story.

When I finished Winkie said, "For a television writer you certainly have a vivid imagination."

Evan said, "You've convinced me of one thing. Always travel American Airlines."

The next morning I received a night letter from Cooper saying that he did know how to play poker; it was signed, "Love, Jack."

He got back to California that afternoon, and though he didn't come to the office, he telephoned.

"How's it going?"

"I'll finish the first act this afternoon."

"God bless you, Merle."

"What happened after I left yesterday?"

"A lot of meetings, with Dorso, the Morris office . . ."

"And what happened?"

"I told them either they shoot the script you are writing now or else. They did a lot of kicking and screaming, but they came around. . . . I'm not a bad poker player when the chips are down."

"Should I forge ahead then?"

"Forge ahead and take care of yourself because I don't know what in the world we'd do if you got run over by a car or something."

And so I forged ahead.

Norman Kahn frequently dropped by to comment on how much more secure he felt since my return.

A man named Jack Sontag, who had been hired as unit manager, looked in to ask after the state of my health.

I said I was in good health.

"I certainly hope so," said Sontag. "The way you've been working I don't see how you do it, and I hope you're happy with this office because if you aren't . . . because if there's anything more important than keeping our writer happy, I can't think what it would be."

Dorothy Fisher brought me coffee and said, "The way things are going it's crazy. If it keeps up like this, I'm going to have a nervous breakdown."

"There's a regular epidemic of it back in New York," I said.

Wednesday, Thursday, and Friday Evan and I worked at the Sportsman's Lodge. We spent at least eighteen hours a day on two typewriters, and when we had finished read aloud and revised what had been written.

The script had to be finished by Saturday when Rosenberg was arriving.

On Sunday, he and Cooper and the production crew were flying to Las Cruces to check the locations.

I thought I was going, too, but Cooper said, "Merle, you'll be too tired. We're going to need you fresh and rested for the week we begin shooting."

Shooting was to start the Monday after the following weekend, November 11.

"So take care of yourself," Cooper said. "I don't know what we'd do if . . ."

I felt a slight niggle in the instinct area, which turned out to be about as underdeveloped an area as you'll find anywhere, but Evan, who has the optimism of early Candide, said, "Cooper just doesn't want you to wear yourself out."

Thursday night Cooper called. He had just read the new first act.

"Merle, this is the best yet. I can't tell you how thrilled I am. Stuart will be here on Saturday, and I know he'll be just as thrilled as I am."

"I guess it was a good idea I did leave New York."

"The best thing in the world," said Cooper. "Have Bob Aurthur or Norman Glenn tried to get in touch with you?"

I said not as far as I knew.

"A month from now Bob is going to be in the hospital," said Cooper. "He's a very sick man."

Friday morning at around eleven Norman Glenn did get in touch with me.

He had given up trying at the Pierre and had called Harold Franklin at William Morris.

Harold had told him, "Merle's been catching trout at the Sportsman's Lodge since Monday."

Norman said, "Merle, how are you? Have you caught one yet?"

"I'm fine. Dozens. They've got some of the best trout fishing in the world right under my window."

"My only purpose in calling you is to ask you to call Bob Aurthur," said Norman. "He's back from Florida. Will you call him?"

I said that I would.

"I've got just one question," said Norman. "Have you been working on the changes that C.B.S. wants or on what we might call the *Enemy of the People* script?"

"Norman," I said, feeling my nose grow with each lie, "I've been sitting by the trout stream since I got here Monday night."

Norman said, "Call Bob Aurthur. That's all I ask."

"Are you all right?" asked Bob.

"Well, I've lost a little weight. I'm what you might call your average, run-of-the-mill ninety-eight-pound weakling, but otherwise . . ."

"Norman says you've been catching trout, and at first I thought okay, but then I tried to put myself in your place, and since I'm just as big a schlemiel as you are, I realized what you're doing. You're writing a new script."

"It really isn't a new . . ."

"Merle, it's ten days before shooting, and the C.B.S. changes still haven't been made, and I won't do them. My obligation to this project ended the day Jim Aubrey gave his okay to the script I cut. That's it. Period."

"Why don't you come out here? We could sit by the pool, catch some trout . . . and in a couple hours . . ."

"No," said Bob. "In the first place I've got to take Jonathan [his son] to Annapolis on Saturday, and in the second place I'm involved with a lot of other projects, including *Mark Dolphin*, which goes into production next week. . . . Come back to New York."

"I can't."

"Look, I'm your friend, and I want you to know that incredible things are going on that you don't know anything about. I think you ought to come back and protect your interests. Your contract is signed, isn't it?"

"I haven't got a contract yet; it's only been five months, and . . ."

"It's not believable," said Bob. "No one would believe it. You shouldn't be allowed out. . . . You are the most born loser I have ever known; you've got the self-protective instinct of a . . . lemming. Come back to New York. Otherwise you're going to end up in the worst trouble of your life."

"I can't do that. I've flown across the country three times in the last ten days and I'm exhausted, and I've promised Jack that . . ."

Bob sighed. "I guess maybe they're right."

"What's that supposed to mean?"

"I'll tell you when you get back, but right now I'll tell you that even if what you're writing is the best script in the history of television, it still hasn't got a chance. *Not a chance.*"

I called Cooper at the studio and told him what Bob had said, and that he wouldn't make the changes C.B.S. wanted.

"Let them hire one of their hack writers back East to do that," said Cooper. "You keep right on working here. . . ."

"Bob says the new script doesn't have a chance."

"You shouldn't have talked to Bob. He's called here a half a dozen times, and I refuse to talk to him. . . . Bring in the last act to Dorothy in the morning and call me tomorrow afternoon at four-thirty. Stuart and I are going to see Stanwyck, and then after dinner tomorrow night we'll get together on the new script. . . ."

I gave Dorothy the final pages Saturday morning. The script was sixty-six pages long, very nearly the right shooting length.

At four-thirty I called Cooper's house. The line was busy.

I called again at five; the line was busy.

When I called at five-thirty Cooper answered, "Merle, old buddy. I just walked into the house and picked up the phone and it's you. . . . Stuart and I had a wonderful talk with Stanwyck, and Stuart and I are going to Las Cruces in the morning, and Stuart was just saying, 'The way Merle has been working Merle needs a conference with us like a hole in the head.' Now why don't you go out and get drunk? And you're going to Malibu tomorrow—so tell Evan to drive carefully on the freeways because those Sunday drivers are crazy and armed with machine guns."

"Have you read the script?"

"All but the last act, and it's beautiful."

"Has Stuart read it?"

There was the briefest pause, and then Cooper said, "He hasn't had a chance yet, but . . ."

"Rosenberg hates the new script," I said to Evan. "And now I think Cooper's scared again."

"I didn't tell you," said Evan, "but Winkie's done some checking around, and she says there's so much intrigue involved with this project . . . Well, she says you'd just better play it cool. . . ."

"Idle gossip from a rival network," I said.

"Winkie and I are having dinner together," said Evan. "Why don't you come along?"

I declined, had dinner in the junior suite, and by seven that night was asleep.

The next afternoon Evan and I drove to Malibu, along the precipitous Mulholland Drive and through the spectacular canyons to the home of Bob and Edie Soderberg.

It is a beautiful house, but more than that it is a peaceful house, simply furnished and filled with the sound of the ocean.

I told Bob's wife, Edie, the wisest woman I know and also the nicest, that I was suffering from certain painful bruises of the interior.

"I don't know what's happening, I don't know who's to blame, and I don't know what to do."

Edie said, "Merle, what you have to do is just stand there and let it hurt."

Monday at nine I was having a haircut in the Sportsman's Lodge barbershop when I heard myself being paged. It was Norman Kahn.

We commented on the weather, which was threatening, and he inquired after my health; I asked about his cold.

Then Norman said, "Jack and Stuart just got back from Las Cruces, and they're going to be tied up in conferences all morning, and I'm sorry, but there doesn't seem to be any need for you to come into the office at all today."

"Norman, if you're telling me that I can have the day off, you don't have to apologize for that."

"I know," said Norman, "but take care of yourself, and have a good day."

The barber finished the haircut, and I went across the street and bought a clean shirt. I had a lunch date with Mike Zimring, who handles my affairs at William Morris West.

Then I joined Evan in the coffee shop and told him about the call from Norman Kahn.

"Am I being paranoid?" I asked. "I mean it seems to me that something is afoot."

"Maybe Winkie is right," said Evan, "but first things first. The car needs an oil job."

While we were at the garage I called the Cooper office to see if any of the mail Dennis MacMenamin had promised to forward from Brewster had arrived. He was giving the house its twelfth coat of paint; he said it needed that many to protect the wood from termites. He works by the termite.

"There's lots of mail," said Dorothy, "but where have you been? Mr. Cooper has been trying to get in touch with you for the last two hours. It's urgent."

"What is?"

"I don't know," said Dorothy, "but there've been a lot of telephone calls going back and forth between here and New York. Could you come in right away?"

There was just enough time to drop by Cooper's office before my lunch date with Mike.

That was the day I asked for the key to what I supposed was still my office.

As you know, I found that I had been stripped of my epaulettes.

A shortish man of about thirty-five with a crew-cut face was talking to Cooper's secretary, Judy. He was as pale as an East Coast vice-president.

Judy said that he was Everett Chambers, the new producer. I shook his hand and wished him luck.

Dorothy Fisher came out of Cooper's office; she looked even more harried than the morning in June when she had misplaced her contact lenses.

She smiled and said, "I'm sorry about your office and I want you to know I had nothing to do with it."

"I know that, Dorothy."

Cooper was just behind her; he, too, was pale, and he looked as if he'd lost a lot of sleep.

"I understand you're upset about your office, old buddy."

"Don't worry about it, Jack. The way things have been going that's just par for the course."

He led me into his office, which is large and has a refrigerator. He asked if I'd like a Coke or a beer.

I declined both.

He seated himself on an enormous couch to the right of the A.M.A. citation saying that *Hennesey* had done more for medicine than leeches.

I sat on a nearby leather chair and said, "I just met Mr. Chambers."

"Yes, C.B.S. insisted on a producer," said Cooper. "They don't seem to think that actors can do anything but act."

I held my thought.

"We've lost," said Cooper. "The fight to do the script we all wanted to do. Over the weekend there were calls and telegrams and conferences with lawyers, and we've *got* to go the C.B.S. way. I'm an actor. I have responsibilities and a family, and a reputation to think of, and if I blow this one . . ."

Then he punched his palm several times the way they do in the movies to simulate love, anger, grief, joy, frustration.

He went on, "At this point it isn't true that C.B.S. won't remember the script that Dorso submitted. In fact, as I understand it, now Jim Aubrey thinks *he* wrote it."

"In that case," I said, "it's a good thing he's got the job he has because he'd never make it as a writer."

"And so we've lost," said Cooper.

"Jack, are you sure it was this weekend we lost? And not *last* Monday?"

Cooper punched his palms several times the way they do in the movies to simulate love, anger, joy, frustration, grief.

"What do you mean by that?"

"I've been thinking a lot about what happened," I said, "and I was wondering if maybe it wasn't all over when you got me out of the Pierre. Maybe we'd lost already and you didn't want me to know. I don't know why. Maybe you didn't want to hurt my feelings. . . ."

"Merle," said Cooper, "that is absolutely not true. Why, even yesterday in Las Cruces Stuart was saying, 'How can we choose locations? We don't even know . . .'"

"Okay," I said.

"You do believe me, don't you?"

"I believe you."

"And the worst part is now I guess you're going to have to go back to New York. Bob Aurthur's conscience won't allow him to make the minor changes. . . . Where was Bob Aurthur's conscience when . . . ?"

"I'll go back to New York," I said. "Tomorrow."

"But that would be a waste of a whole working day. Now there's a three o'clock American flight."

"I can't do that, Jack," I said, and I thought, It's the same scene. A week has passed; we're on a different coast, but it's the Pierre scene all over again. They want me to get out of town.

"Let's see what other flights there are," said Cooper, rising and walking to the outer office.

There was another flight at five.

"The five o'clock then," said Cooper. "The limousine will pick you up at the Sportsman's Lodge at three-fifteen. And there'll be a limousine to meet you at Idlewild."

"What time does the plane get in?"

"Early," said Cooper.

"Twelve forty-five A.M., New York time," said Dorothy.

"Early," said Cooper. "You'll get to the hotel by two, have plenty of time for a good night's sleep, and be at U.A. bright and early tomorrow morning."

I looked at him and saw that he believed it all, every word.

"Where do you want to stay?" asked Dorothy. "The Gorham?"

"Who's paying for it?"

"U.A.," said Cooper. "Have them send the bill direct to U.A."

"I'll stay at the St. Regis," I said.

"Have a good flight, Mr. Miller," said Dorothy, meaning it.

"And take care of yourself," said Judy, meaning it.

I shook Norman Kahn's hand, and he said, "I wish I was going to New York with you because the way I feel now I could use a little of New York."

At the door Cooper shook my hand and said, "Merle, I don't know what we'd have done without you. Have a good trip. Call me every day. I'll be busy, but *wherever* I am, when *you* call I'll always be available, and God bless you, and what I think you ought to do after you finish the work in New York is go to Brewster, get yourself some rest, and I'll see you in Las Cruces a week from today."

"I'll see you," I said.

Evan drove me to Beverly Hills. I told him what had happened, and he said that he would stay in Los Angeles and confer with me by phone if necessary until the cuts in New York were made. Then he would drive to Las Cruces and meet me at the El Paso airport the following Sunday.

"Don't forget to bring the laundry and my brown shoes and my journal."

"By the way," said Evan. "You're having lunch with your agent. How much money have you got out of this so far?"

"Seventy-five hundred dollars," I said, "and then there's an additional $2500 coming when they start shooting next week."

"And how many rewrites?"

"I don't know how many, but I do know that if the Writer's Guild found out they'd drum me out of the union."

"I think you need more money," said Evan.

"Like how much?"

"Like $2500 more."

"I want $2500 more," I said to Mike Zimring, a calm man whose many virtues include the fact that he was born and raised in Waterloo, Iowa, and we remember the same depression.

"I'll tell Harold Franklin," said Mike. "I think you deserve it."

"You mean that's all there is to it?"

"This is a big project," said Mike.

Evan rode with me to the airport.

"I think you're caught right in the middle of a big power play," he said, "between U.A. and Cooper and C.B.S., and at this point for you it doesn't make any difference who wins."

"I'm not sure I care any more."

"But I've told you, you have to look at it," said Evan. "This is one of the biggest industries in the country, and it reaches more people and influences more people . . ."

"Anyway, I'll get them in New York to read the new script," I said.

"That's the important thing," said Evan. "This script is the best one. They're not stupid people. They've got to see it."

The student who has gone this far will not be surprised to learn that this was the night when there was no limousine waiting for me at Idlewild.

Not only that, after I demeaned and debased myself by riding to the St. Regis in a taxi, they put me in a broom closet next to the mop closet.

I got a good night's sleep, though, from four until about four-thirty, and then the garbage people started doing the things they do at that hour.

At nine Norman Glenn called, and before he could ask I volunteered that I was in excellent health, that I had had a wonderful trip, and that my hotel accommodations were unparalleled.

"Bob Aurthur isn't coming to the office today," said Norman. "He's sick, some kind of virus."

"What should I . . . ?"

"Take it easy. Just tell me what I can do to help entertain you today. Magazines, movie tickets, a show, anything you want."

"I'll probably sleep," I said, "but thank you."

I did sleep, for twenty minutes; then Dorso called. Could I come right over to the office?

I said that I could, and just before I left the broom closet I called Harold. The extra $2500 was all set.

"How's everything else going?" asked Harold.

"To tell you would take a book."

"Well, why don't you . . . ?"

"I'm going to," I said.

I took the new script with me to the U.A. offices.

Dorso, wearing his patriotic belt and with his jacket slung over his shoulders, blessed me for coming.

"Is Bob's virus psychosomatic or real?" I asked.

"Since my analysis I've learned that there really isn't any difference," said Dorso.

I took the new script out of my typewriter case and said, "Dick, I wonder if you'd do me a big favor . . ."

"Merle," he said, "there's no need for me to read a new script. There was never any question of using a new script. I told Jack that a week ago when you and he were in New York, and if you'd talked to Norman Glenn, Norman would have told you. And I told Stuart that. Stuart's problem is that he never understood your script. The kind of script he understands is where there's a man with his back against the wall."

"Stuart and I have never been what you'd call close," I said.

"Stuart is a man," said Dorso, "who could talk with enthusiasm and at great length about inventing the umbrella. . . . Now I think you ought to start making the minimal changes . . ."

I was put to work in the projection room, U.A.'s answer to North Hollywood's Building B, Room 29.

Before starting I said to Norman Glenn, "Do me a big favor? Read the California script."

Norman smiled—it is a good smile—and said he'd try.

"And if you could persuade Dorso . . ." I said.

Half an hour later Dorso came into the projection room.

"I've looked at the first few pages of the California script," he said, "and it will never work, and it will mean going back to C.B.S. to get new approval. . . . Now why don't you . . ."

Bob came into the airless projection room at nine-thirty the next morning.

I looked closely at him for signs of a nervous breakdown, but he seemed as calm as ever.

"What in Christ's name are you doing in here?" he screamed. "There's not a goddamn breath of air."

"I think that's the idea."

"Goddamn it to hell. Can't anybody around here ever do anything right?"

As Claude Traverse stopped by, Bob picked up my typewriter.

"Let's get Merle the hell out of this embalming room," he shouted.

Claude picked up the dissected manuscript, the scissors, and the pastepot, and I picked up my coat and the typewriter case.

For some time the three of us wandered up and down the halls, looking for an office.

"There is no place for writers in this whole damn building," Bob kept screaming.

"It's really all right," I said. "I don't mind, and besides, we are interrupting the secretaries and executives; they will never be able to make their calls to Istanbul, and the crocheting will fall off. . . ."

"Writers are what this goddamn operation is all about," shouted Bob.

Finally we discovered an office with a window and everything, and we were about to move in when a nervous man with the nose and demeanor of a bunny rabbit appeared.

"You can't go in *there*," he sniffed. "*That* office is for the accountants; the accountants are coming today."

"Jesus H. Christ," shouted Bob, "they've got offices for accountants but none for writers."

"If it weren't for the accountants, writers wouldn't get paid," said the man.

With a rapier thrust of epigrammatic wit I said, "If it weren't for writers, there'd be nothing to account."

At last we found another office. Bob closed the door, sat down, and gave me a cigarette.

"You don't look bad," he said, lighting one for himself.

"Should I?"

"Would it surprise you to learn that Stuart Rosenberg sat in my office last Friday and said that you were about to have a nervous breakdown?"

"At this point, nothing would surprise me."

"Would it further surprise you to learn that shortly after you left Cooper's office in California yesterday, Cooper called Dorso and said that you *were* having a nervous breakdown and said further that the script you wrote is totally unusable?

"And, Merle, Stuart kept saying that most of what you said that weekend at the Pierre came out gibberish, that you were on the edge. I said, 'Come off it, Merle's a writer.' And Stuart said, 'I've known a lot of writers and I've never seen one as close to the edge as Miller.'

"I said to Stuart, 'Look, in two days Merle turned in a twenty-six-page outline. I've read it, and while I don't agree with it, it's certainly not gibberish. Now who's crazy?' "

I said, "That was the outline the script was written from. The one that Stuart and Jack . . ."

Bob said, "I said to Stuart, 'Are you prepared to direct the script Aubrey bought?' Stuart said he was, and I said, "Then do you mean to say that you and Jack have had Merle in a hotel room in California for a week writing a script that neither of you had any intention of filming?' Stuart said that he guessed that was about the size of it, and I said, 'In all the years in this business that's the cruelest thing I've ever heard.' And Stuart said, 'I can't deny it.' "

I managed to say, "But why?"

"Who knows?" said Bob. "Maybe they thought you could pull off a miracle in California, write a script everybody would love, but as I told you on the phone, even if you had . . . Merle, this has got nothing to do with a good script or a bad script; it never did have. It has to do with pleasing one man, Jim Aubrey."

Bob looked at me, and then he rose, touched my shoulder, and left.

An hour or so later Bob returned. "It's incredible, *incredible*. Cooper just called Dorso again to repeat that you were having or about to have a nervous breakdown. When he got off the phone Dorso said to me, 'Merle looked all right to me. Is he all right? I wouldn't want to be responsible for a man having a heart attack.' "

I said, "You tell Dorso that you and I will have the minimal changes that C.B.S. wants by tomorrow noon. . . . And by the way, would you like the latest flash on *your* nervous breakdown?"

The changes were ready by noon the next day, and a little later I stopped by Bob's office. Jane Wetherell, Norman Glenn, and Joe Jacobs were there. Jacobs was chewing on his pipe.

Bob said, "See how near a state of collapse Merle is? Merle, tell them about the weekend you were a captive at the Pierre."

I did, giving my best performance since Governor Bradford. I played all the parts, Cooper, Rosenberg, the nameless men from William Morris, and the grandfatherly bellman. If I'd happened to have my little violin . . .

"After that," said Bob, "they smuggled him to California to write a script that they're now calling a therapeutic script. Cooper says, 'I guess it was just something that Merle had to get out of his system.'"

I looked at Jacobs, who the day before had approved the extra $2500.

"Pretty expensive therapy, isn't it, Joe?" I said.

"You could get years of analysis for that," he said.

A few minutes later I went downstairs to buy a copy of *Newsweek. A Day in Late September* had been published during the therapeutic week in California. I hadn't seen a single review but had been told there was a good one in the magazine.

There was, too; no photograph, but the words were fine, including a sentence comparing the philosophy of the novel to that of Camus . . . a sentence written by a contemporary whom I could not fault. . . .

I showed the review to the news dealer, the elevator man, and to Bob, and while Bob and I were discussing its sensitive perception, Dorso came in, carrying the revised script.

"I don't need to read *Newsweek* to know that Merle is a great writer," he said.

He pointed to the script.

"This is the one we go with. It's wonderful. . . . Now we're all getting on the phone at six o'clock our time, three o'clock California time. Stuart, Jack, Bob, Merle . . ."

I caught Bob's eye.

"Merle's catching a four-thirty train to Brewster," said Bob.

As I was about to leave the U.A. offices in New York, I heard Dorso's secretary say to Dorothy Fisher in North Hollywood, "Fade In: The vigorous outdoor face of Everet Calhoun, county agent." I decide not to wait for the other 64½ pages.

I spent the weekend in solitude.

The script Bob and I had pasted together?

There is nothing whatever to say about it; it was, or so I had been told, what one man wanted. Well, now he had it. It said in the contract I had signed but *they* hadn't that I was to be in Las Cruces, New Mexico, during the filming, and there I would be.

I called Dorothy Fisher on Saturday afternoon to tell her I was arriving in Las Cruces Sunday night and that I would not be staying at the Mission Inn with the others but at a motel John White had recommended.

Dorothy, whose voice sounded farther away than Southern California, said, "It's a little hectic around here."

That evening, Evan, en route to Las Cruces, called from Yuma, Arizona.

"There is no such place as Yuma," I said.

"You're so right," said Evan, "but I've got your brown shoes, the files, your best-selling journal . . . By the way, how's the novel doing?"

"Not as well as the journal. I'll see you at the airport in El Paso Sunday night at nine."

Sunday morning there was a telegram from Dorothy Fisher saying that the filming wasn't to begin until the following Wednesday, November 13, and suggesting that I not leave New York until I had heard from Cooper late Monday afternoon.

I called Bob.

"Look, if there's one thing that was made abundantly clear last week it's that Dorso is the boss. Right?"

"Right," said Bob.

"Does Dorso expect me to be in Las Cruces on Monday?"

"He does."

I then read Bob the telegram.

"Go to Las Cruces," said Bob. "I'll be on the set with *Mark Dolphin,* but call me. Every day. Without fail."

I sent a telegram to Dorothy Fisher:

FEEL IT ADVISABLE TO STICK TO ORIGINAL AGENDA CAN BE REACHED AT THE PALMS MOTEL IN LAS CRUCES ANY TIME MONDAY   MERLE

I wasn't quite able to stick to the original agenda.

When I arrived at the American Airlines ticket counter ten minutes before the flight to El Paso, the ticket I had been told would be waiting for me—well, of course.

Nobody knew anything about the ticket, and there was no space on the plane.

After accepting a personal check, an assortment of recriminations, and a tot of blood, the airlines booked me on a flight for the next morning.

I spent an extremely restful night in a papier-mâché motel secured at the seams by flour paste; it was built near the end of Idlewild's principal runway.

The next day was bright and sunny, and the flight was smooth, and as is my wont, I washed down the scrambled eggs with more than enough champagne.

As the plane approached El Paso I could see that the sky was once more crowded with cumulus clouds. It had been just five months since Cooper and I first flew there.

"Don't ask me what happened in New York last night," I said to Evan, handing him my raincoat, camera, shoulder bag, scripts, typewriter, overdue library books, and the folio of paper napkins on which I was making notes for the new novel.

"What happened?" asked Evan.

"Have you ever had the champagne breakfast American puts out?" I replied, suppressing a burp.

"Did you get them to read the California script?"

"No. They insisted on Aubrey's way."

"Should I ask how it is?"

I moved my head in a way I'd picked up from Larry White. Then I said, "Dorso says it's better than Camus's *The Plague*. On the other hand, Cooper says the script you and I worked on in California is unusable, that it's something I had to get out of my system, and that I'm headed for a nervous breakdown."

"Maybe you and Bob Aurthur could share a room in the same institution and cut down on expenses the way you and Cooper . . ."

"Rosenberg says that most of what I say comes out gibberish, which is, I gather, what he thinks of what I write, but other than that . . ."

We drove past the building where Harold Franklin, who grew up in El Paso, went to high school; not a single plaque.

Shortly thereafter we were in the open country, and the colors were as vivid and compelling as I had remembered. The yucca was no longer in bloom, but the cotton was, and we passed railroad sidings where there were huge bales of it.

As we got closer to Las Cruces the black-purple Organ Mountains once more dominated in the background, and there was, as before, snow on the peaks of several. Closer by were the now familiar lunarlike rock formations.

There was the same billboard outside of town, "40,000 Friendly People Welcome You to Las Cruces, the Home of New Mexico State University."

"Any signs of the invasion from Hollywood?" I asked.

"The only thing I noticed was a big marquee outside the Mission Inn Motel," said Evan. "It says:

Welcome Jackie Cooper,
Barbara Stanwyck,
Buffet Dinner $1.50.

We checked in at the Palms and then drove to the university campus to see John White. He was as friendly as before and took us on a tour of the photocopying room, the art department, and various offices. The rooms were windowless, air-conditioned, well lighted, and without personality. John said, "They say the no-windows saves money on the air conditioning."

On the bulletin board outside John's office was a glossy photograph of Cooper in levis and an open-neck cowboy shirt. The face was that of an engaging, ingenuous actor.

"Look what I found," said John, showing us a fat picture book of Cooper in *Peck's Bad Boy* and a Broadway playbill of some twenty years later, Cooper in Lindsay and Crouse's play, *Remains to Be Seen.*

"I'm going to try to get Jackie to autograph these for my kids."

John introduced us to various colleagues, one of them a graduate student in agriculture from Pakistan.

"We're pretty excited about you coming down here and doing the filming for the county agent series," said John. "Everyone in the Extension Service feels this is going to be something unique in the history of television."

I looked at John's open, eager face and said, "How's Leonard Appleton?"

"Fine," John said. "And there's a rumor around town that Don Chappell, who's in Hollywood right now with Cooper, may ask for a two-year leave of absence so's he can be technical advisor of the series. Know anything about it?"

I said I didn't.

On the way to Mesilla, where we were to meet Betty Bowen to talk about the autograph party, John said, "I guess making this movie is just about the most important thing that's happened around here since the White Sands Missile Range. Everybody's excited. All the women are wearing those tight toreador pants and my wife says there's been a run on the beauty parlors. Is it going to be a good show, Merle?"

"What's that?" I asked, pointing to a preposterous bird high-tailing it down the edge of the highway.

"Oh, that's a road runner," said John. "The Mexicans call it a *paisano*. It's the state bird."

In June the plaza in Mesilla had been crowded and all the benches had been filled. Now it was deserted; the bandstand looked run down, the paint was faded and chipped. The branches of the elm trees were barren, the benches rusty, and every so often, as if on signal, tumbleweed rolled through the rutted streets.

The Mesilla Design and Book Center was unchanged, however, and so was Betty Bowen, who owns and manages it.

She had read *A Day in Late September* and said she liked it.

"It's about people," she said, "*and* it's in English."

We discussed the autograph party, and Betty said, "Saturday or Sunday would be the best time. On Sunday people have more time to browse and buy."

I pictured cowboys in dusty boots and leathery faces coming in to buy what Orville Prescott in the New York *Times* that morning had called a "novel of sardonic wit and savage humor." That was before he said he didn't like it much.

"Saturday makes more sense," I said. "The filming will be finished by noon. Everyone will be gone by Sunday."

"When is Jackie Cooper arriving?" asked Betty.

"I think on Wednesday."

"Will he come to the autographing party?"

"We'll have to see," I said.

"You know Howard Duff is planning to use my back room," said Betty.

"Howard Duff?"

"Yes. Now he's married to Ida Lupino."

Betty led us to the room. It was long, handsome, and comfortable with a huge stone fireplace on one wall, a high-beamed ceiling, and a tile floor.

Betty said, "I know his wife's second husband very well, Collier Young, the writer. Do you think they're happy? I've got the only telephone in town so I guess there'll be plenty of excitement around here this week."

"Something I want you guys to see," said John as he drove us back to Las Cruces. "Jackie was looking for a place that could be his office in your show, and he looked all over town, and just when he was about to give up, by accident he came across the library building."

We pulled up in front of an attractive one-story building that had a lawn and neat plantings of semitropical foliage. It had all the outward signs of adobe architecture—*vigas* (the protruding roof timbers) and *zaguáns* (roofed-over open passageways). John, however, said, that the building was made of steel coated with stucco.

"The town fathers just had this place painted that beige color," said John. "Jackie said it would photograph better that way."

The new paint job was handsome enough until you got to the back. That had not been painted and was the original gray-white color, like an unwashed neck.

"I guess they're not going to film the back," said John, "but it doesn't matter. As soon as the filming's over the town's going to paint the whole building back to the original color. . . . You know, I heard Jackie say to Mr. Sontag— that's the production manager—that they could reproduce the front of this building in Hollywood for $9000."

A little girl with an armful of books came out of the library and saw us.

"When's Jackie Cooper coming?" she asked.

"I think Wednesday," I said.

"One more place I want you guys to see before we quit for the night," said John, "the oldest hotel in town, been here almost a hundred years, and you might be able to use it for a location sometime."

In the two-story lobby of the Amado Hotel was a huge stuffed white bear, steer horns, Hopi Indian dolls, some exquisite examples of Spanish silver, and a registry that Pat Garrett had signed.

Most of the rooms opened off the central corridor and painted on each door was a girl's name: Rosita, Esmeralda, Inigo.

I asked why, hoping for the juiciest.

The manager, a slight man with the manner of a scholar, said, "The woman who used to own the hotel named the rooms because she'd been told that was an old English custom. One room's named for Rosita, the chambermaid; Esmeralda was the manager's granddaughter, and Inigo was a horse."

On the way back to the Palms Motel Evan and I passed the Mission Inn. The marquee now said:

Welcome Jackie Cooper,
& Barbara Stanwyck,
Howard Duff.

"I guess Duff is playing Stanwyck's husband," said Evan.

"You couldn't prove it by me."

At one point Mike Dann had announced to the press that Dana Andrews was playing the part, and when I had been in North Hollywood the last time Cooper told me that Art Carney's agent said that Carney was busting to play it.

"I hope the buffet is still a dollar and a half," said Evan.

"I've got a feeling we'd better keep watching that sign. It may be the only way we'll know what's going on."

At the motel I said to Evan, "There will have been no calls, but I shall check at the desk to see if there have been any calls."

"Remember this is Armistice Day."

There had been no calls.

That night there was a Dixie Land Jamboree in the bar. A physicist from the university played the sax; a chemist was at the piano, and there was a student on the drums.

"How come on Monday night?" Evan asked Charlie Kennedy, the manager.

"Monday used to be a quiet night," said Charlie. "So we hired them to try their luck."

The experiment was a success; by ten o'clock the bar was jammed. The music was exuberant, mostly on key, and great fun.

A sloe-eyed girl whose hair was pulled back into a severe pigtail eyed me hopefully, then said, "You're with Jackie Cooper, aren't you?"

"More or less."

"How do I get to be an extra?"

"Honey, if I knew that, do you think I'd be wasting my time writing?"

Art, the pool boy, stopped by in the middle of a twist.

"I heard in town that when they start to make this picture it's going to cost $1000 a minute. That so?"

"More like $7000 a minute," I said.

"Boy, just let me work one minute a year," said Art, turning to give us the benefit of his left profile. "I guess you have to know an awful lot to be an actor."

"To the contrary, Art," I said, "to the contrary."

Art twisted off. I said to Evan, "I want to go back home to Brewster."

"If you leave now you'll be in violation of your contract."

"What contract?"

"Look, these guys are pros. You don't have to like them,

but they're professionals, and once they get here, you and Cooper and Rosenberg will get together—you have to, there's no alternative—and it'll be like you and Bob Aurthur and Frankenheimer when you were in Tucson with *The American.*"

"Not in a million years. Different situation, different guys. . . . Cooper's the same guy I liked last summer, but now he's scared. They're all scared. They're scared, and people who are scared do awful things to each other."

"They're *pros,*" said Candide.

We spent most of Tuesday by the pool. I had brought along *What to Name the Baby* and finally decided—she'd had a dozen names already—what I'd call the female protagonist of the new novel, "Allison. Of sacred flame."

Evan read the script that had been revised in New York the week before, and when he looked up, he said, "Well, as Bob Aurthur told you, you've got a lot more chances to say what you want to say."

The Hawaiian waiter—the day before he had asked if I was Henry Cooper, which I took to be an ingenious amalgamation of Hennesey and Jackie Cooper—brought me a telegram. It said:

CONTRACT SIGNED BY ALL PARTIES. BE STRONG AND OF GOOD COURAGE. HAROLD FRANKLIN

"That's a good omen," said Evan, "and I've looked. This is a good week for you Taurus people."

Fifteen minutes later there was a telephone call from Bob Kotlowitz, the editor of *Show* I'd worked with on the Iowa reunion piece. The magazine had decided for sure that it wanted an article on the filming of *Calhoun.*

"We could use some pictures," said Kotlowitz, "and I hope it's going to be funny."

"It'll be funny," I said.

That evening we had drinks with Cecil Herrill, an associate of John White's at New Mexico State University.

"I surely do hope you guys understand the philosophy behind a county agent," said Cecil. "You know Congress is looking critically at all Extension Services and, naturally, we're all concerned about how television will affect us."

I said that the philosophy of a county agent and his job were the reasons I'd decided to write the pilot.

"This is a good area for the series to take place," said Cecil, "because in a lot of ways this is the melting pot, much more than New York. Anglos, Mexicans, and Indians intermarry here, and nobody thinks a thing about it. . . . We find that people from the East at White Sands are much more prejudiced than we are here in Las Cruces. . . . I certainly hope you guys get in some of our real feeling. I've never seen anything like that on television."

Cecil rose to go. "I've got to go to a conference for a new batch of Peace Corps kids we're training at the university. The last crew went to Guatemala.

"By the way," he said, "I've got a daughter who wants to be an actress. How do I stop her?"

After a fourth vodka-tonic, I decided, oh, what the hell, be friendly. So I picked up the phone and called Jack Sontag, who was staying at the Mission Inn.

"I guess you know," I said, "I'm here at the Palms. But since we're all going to be working together, don't you think maybe I ought to come over to the Mission?"

Sontag, who seemed to be in a hurry, said, "We're running out of room here, so if you're comfortable . . ."

"There's been a lot of antagonism up to now but since we begin to shoot tomorrow and have to work together . . ."

"Jackie and Stanwyck and the others are getting here at eleven tomorrow morning," said Sontag. "Jackie will be in Room 29."

"What did he say about moving to the Mission?" asked Evan.

"As has been true down through the ages, there is no room at the inn."

Following another vodka-tonic or so, I said, "Not enough people know what a modest, benign human being I really am. A sort of St. Francis of show biz."

"In that case, why wait until tomorrow to talk to Cooper?" said Evan. "Why not call him now? He's probably been so busy . . . He'd appreciate a call from you."

And so, having a reputation to uphold, I once more picked up the phone. It was a little after six California time; so I called Cooper at his house. Barbara answered.

Barbara said, "Hello, Merle. How are you feeling? How's your health?"

"Fine. How's Jack?"

"Today he looked beautiful. He'll be home in about fifteen minutes and I'll have him call you first thing."

"Thank you for saying I'm a sweet man."

"But you are a sweet man, darling, and a thoughtful man, and Jack will be home any minute now, and I know he'll want to talk to you, and I'll have him call you first thing, and I hope you'll take care of yourself, darling."

"You, too."

"God bless you, sweetie. . . ."

When I went into breakfast the next morning, a young waiter was saying to Evan, "Will you bring Barbara Stanwyck here to the Palms? Bring her on Friday."

"Why Friday?" asked Evan.

"I work on Friday," said the waiter, walking on.

Evan, without looking up at me, said, "Maybe Cooper never got home."

By ten fifty-five that morning I had drunk more coffee than Balzac—he put away sixty cups a day—and had written almost an entire chapter of the novel I had postponed in June.

It was stream-of-consciousness writing in the best Joycean tradition, "Now is the time for all good men . . ."

At ten fifty-six a four-engine plane that looked as if had been shot down in *Hell's Angels* circled Las Cruces, then landed.

Fifteen minutes later motorcycles with sirens screaming led a motorcade past the motel.

"I wonder who that could be?" I said, slipping another paper napkin into the machine and typing, ". . . to come to the aid of their party."

"He'll be calling you any minute now," said Evan.

Five hours passed. Over the loudspeaker a Mr. Thornberry was called to the phone three times, a Mr. Maxwell twice.

At four the loudspeaker announced that there was a call for Mr. Miller.

I picked up the phone with moist and trembling hands.

"Hello, Jack," I said.

A half-remembered voice said, "This is Everett Chambers. How are you, Mr. Miller? How are the accommodations? How is the food?"

"The room is fine, the food is fine, and I'm fine, but I'm not so sure of the outside world."

Mr. Chambers made a laughing sound, and then for quite some time cleared his throat.

"Well," he said, "Mr. Cooper has asked me to call you and tell you that your script has been rewritten."

When I could speak I asked the inevitable question, "By whom?"

"I honestly don't know," said Mr. Chambers.

I said, "Mr. Cooper asked *you* to call *me* to tell *me* that *my* script has been rewritten?"

"I know he ought to do it himself, but in my position unpleasant tasks like this fall to me. In television things like this happen all the time."

"Nothing like this has ever happened to me."

"I know about sensitive creative people," said Mr. Chambers, "and I know what a shock this must be for you. What I'm trying to do is prevent any anger you may feel from getting in the way of Mr. Cooper's and Mr. Rosenberg's rapport with the actors."

"In other words, I'm barred from the set."

"Of course not, but you know how hectic . . ."

I said, "In the first place, I have nothing to say to Mr. Cooper, and from here on in anything I have to say to anybody associated with this project will be said through my emissaries to whom I pay a great deal of money to perform various unsavory tasks. And through my union."

"If it's any comfort to you, this is coming as an equal surprise to United Artists and to C.B.S., who are being notified at the same time."

"That's a great comfort, Mr. Chambers. Thank you."

For a very long time I just stood by the telephone.

Then I called Bob Aurthur, who was on the *Kibbee Hates Fitch* set in New York.

"I don't believe it," said Bob, and, after a moment, he said, "I believe it. Dorso got a telegram from Cooper on Saturday saying that the script that was phoned to Dorothy Fisher was no good and, like the script you wrote in California, absolutely unusable. Dorso called and asked him what in Christ's name was wrong, and Cooper said he and Rosenberg wanted to make Zac Laird angry with Cal in the first scene, and they wanted to have Abby already divorced when the play opened. Dorso was very relieved, and he said, 'To write that in will take about eight minutes and since Merle is going to be in Las Cruces, what's the problem?' Cooper said, 'I guess there isn't any.'

"But *this* . . . it's the first I've heard of it, and I'm sure Dorso's never heard of it. Do you have any idea what Cooper's and Rosenberg's script is about?"

"I'm only guessing, but I bet it opens with a big, bloodshot something or other filling the screen, and while it's not exactly copied from *An Enemy of the People* . . ."

"I'll get in touch with Dorso and call you right back," said Bob.

My next call was to Harold Franklin, and he said, "I'll make sure that you're fully protected. In the meantime, don't leave town because if you do that will give them a perfect excuse to do you out of your royalty. . . . I'll get in touch with Lou Weiss, who handles the U.A. account for us, and I'll call you back. But in the meantime don't leave town."

Bob Aurthur called back, "Dick Dorso says he knew nothing about the new script, and so far as I know he didn't, but I think you should get out of town. I think this is demeaning and debasing for you."

"Harold Franklin says I should stay until I'm officially released."

"Call Dick Dorso and he'll officially release you."

Dorso said, "I have a representative in Las Cruces named Howard Gottfried [Vice-President and Production Supervisor]. He'll call you either later tonight or first thing in the morning and tell you you can come home. . . . And, Merle, I think this is very humiliating for a writer of your stature."

"When do you suppose they got the new writer?" Evan asked. "Or writers. It could be several."

"Maybe when we were in California, maybe after. Maybe when Cooper called about that rummage sale they were having he'd already shopped around and got himself and Rosenberg some marked-down scribes."

Gottfried, who was staying at the Mission Inn, perhaps a fifteen-minute drive from the Palms, telephoned a few minutes later.

"I've just talked to Dick Dorso in New York," he said, "and now I'm officially releasing you and telling you you can go home."

"Thank you, Mr. Gottfried."

"I think it is just terrible that a person of national renown and a man of letters is treated this way. . . . I'm sure you'll have something to say about all this."

"I have a feeling I will."

"I suppose you'll call a press conference."

"Maybe several."

"I think you should," said Mr. Gottfried. "It needs to be said. And I heard you're going back to New York by car, and that's good because it will give you time to think over what you want to say and how you'll want to say it."

"Don't worry, Mr. Gottfried, I'll have no trouble saying it."

I didn't go to bed at all, and when the phone rang at seven-fifteen the next morning, I was taking a shower.

Gottfried was calling from the Mission Inn, still a fifteen-minute drive from the Palms.

"Mr. Miller, what are your plans for leaving town?"

"Goddamn it, I'll leave town when I'm goddamn good and ready."

"But you don't understand," said Gottfried. "I don't want you to leave town. Something has happened."

"What?"

"Confidentially, I've read the first act of what they're planning to shoot, I'm going to call New York right away. I'll call you back in an hour."

The hour and the day went, no call from Gottfried.

Early in the afternoon Art stopped by the pool where Evan and I were eating lunch al fresco.

"They've started the picture over in Mesilla," he said. "A friend of mine got an autograph from Barbara Stanwyck."

"If we drove out to Mesilla," said Evan, "we could park the car a little ways away, and nobody would notice us, and we could at least find out what the new script is about."

At one-twenty Harold Franklin called. "There's a big policy meeting at U.A. Rockets are being fired back and forth from New York to Las Cruces. They've asked if you'd mind sitting tight until you heard from Gottfried."

"Harold, I'm sitting right in the middle of no man's land, and, believe me, I'm sitting tight."

"I understand that C.B.S. has heard about this, and it looks like the biggest war in the history of television. . . . But in the end *your* script . . ."

"*It's not my script; it's James Thomas Aubrey's script.*"

"Merle, don't muddy the waters. I understand that U.A. is telling Cooper that if he tries to shoot his script, he will have to pay the entire cost of the filming and of the project up to now."

At two o'clock John White called. "They started filming in the square this morning, but now they've stopped. There are a couple hundred people around, fifty or so extras, and they've just left them standing there, and they're all sort of wondering . . . Is Jackie with you?"

"No, John, Jackie is not with me."

The afternoon edition of the El Paso paper quoted Sontag as saying that the shooting had been suspended for "technical reasons" but would be resumed the next morning.

That evening Evan and I drove to Mesilla. A statue of Benjamin Calhoun, Cal's grandfather, stood in the plaza. It was made of plaster of paris and had apparently been flown in from Hollywood. I read the inscription I had written for the base. That had not been changed:

"For what is the purpose of a man's life if not to make the world a better place?"

While we were having drinks at the Billy the Kid bar we started talking to the hostess, a pretty girl named Rosemary, who was dressed in a few tasteful feathers fore and aft.

She said she was from New York and it turned out she was a good friend of two friends of mine, Marc Brandel, the novelist, who is a client of Harold Franklin's, and Richard

Gehman, the magazine writer, who used to be a William
Morris client, and who lives not far from the glass house.

Rosemary launched into an enthusiastic discussion of one
of my novels, *A Gay and Melancholy Sound*.

"It wasn't that Joshua [the protaganist] didn't feel things,"
she said. "It was because he felt too much. . . . But why
are *you* writing for television?"

"Well, you see, Reggie Rose came out of *The Defenders*
with an equity of $2,000,000, and that isn't even a *big* show.
. . . But what in God's name are *you* doing in Mesilla, Rosemary?"

"I like it here," said Rosemary. "I like the people. They've
got a social conscience."

The waiter at La Posta, which serves excellent Mexican
food, was a blond, over-eager young man named Frank
Davis, a student at the university. He guessed at once that
Evan and I had something to do with *Calhoun*.

"You're from the East," he said. "I can tell from the accent.
I married a New Jersey girl."

As he served the *enchiladas* Frank said, "I understand
you guys are having script problems?"

"Who told you that?" asked Evan.

"My mother."

"Your mother?"

"She's an extra," said Frank, "and she has a way of finding
out things."

"Do you suppose she could find out what the script is
about and who wrote it?" I asked.

Frank said he'd ask her to try.

Bob called early the next morning.

"They're not using the new script," he said, "and, Merle, I
think there's one thing you ought to understand. Cooper was
brought up in the old tradition of Hollywood where they
used to have as many as six or seven, sometimes more writers

on a script, and so he didn't think anything about it when . . ."

"That's a reason, not an excuse," I said.

Bob said, "Just be sure old Jack doesn't call and old Stuart and you find yourself wanting to get back in that warm circle again. Good luck, and call me."

Betty Bowen called ten minutes later.

"Merle, what about the autographing party? Unless I get an interview in the paper by noon today there won't be *any* publicity."

"Are they shooting in the square?"

"They started at seven this morning, but you should have heard the goings-on yesterday. I've told you, I've got the only telephone in town, and they were in and out of the store like crazy. . . . There were five, maybe six calls from New York, and they were all shouting and such language, 'Come on out to Mesilla, then, get an injunction, close the show, kill the project.' . . . And when Jackie Cooper got off the phone he said to me, 'It isn't always this mad.' Merle, is it?"

"I'll be out for the interview in about an hour."

"Barbara Stanwyck is real sweet; she's made a lot of friends. Do you think Jackie will be at the autographing party?"

"No, Betty."

A few minutes before leaving for Mesilla I received yesterday's call from Mr. Gottfried.

"I'm terribly sorry I didn't get back to you yesterday, but it was a somewhat hectic day. There were many disagreements. No, I don't mean disagreements. I mean fights. Not that there was any physical violence. It was mostly a matter of who said what to whom and what promises had been broken. . . . Your name wasn't even mentioned, though, Mr. Miller."

I said that that was a great comfort to me.

"And you can leave town any time now."

"Mr. Gottfried," I said, "I may never leave town, and I'll be out in Mesilla in ten minutes."

"Congratulations on their shooting your script," said Gottfried.

Evan and I were driving the white convertible, and the top was down. Our arrival in Mesilla did not go unnoticed.

The town was very different from the one we had seen on Monday. Sheriff's cars blocked all the roads, and the square had been roped off. Crowds of people were pressed together, and hundreds of school children watched from the side streets. School had been dismissed for the day.

An outdoor art exhibit had been set up in the plaza; the bandstand was freshly scrubbed; the benches had been painted, and several property men were taping leaves on the branches of the elm trees. Dense bluish smoke curled up from the floodlights as the lighting crews trained spots on the scene being filmed.

Cooper, wearing tan dungarees, a blue denim shirt, and a Stetson, was standing near a new Studebaker pickup that John White later told us had been muddied and dented for the occasion. It wasn't at all dusty, though.

Miss Stanwyck, looking very much the movie star, stood a little away; she had on beige frontier pants, high, supple leather boots, a beige blouse, and had an orange neckerchief knotted around her throat. Her face was framed by her silver hair.

Howard Duff was sitting on a camp chair, wearing a blue business suit and looking fatigued.

Barbara Luna, a beautiful Spanish-American actress who had been cast as the assistant home agent, sat nearby. In the script Miss Luna's job was to teach girls how to keep house, garden, raise livestock, and perform other chores around the barnyard.

Miss Luna was wearing a tight red dress, dark glasses, and high-heeled shoes.

"Maybe the dress gives her confidence," said Evan.

Rosenberg, who was holding an enormous megaphone, yelled, "Cut. Take ten."

The extras, all in their Sunday best, relaxed and asked several of the stars for autographs. Miss Stanwyck was the most favored.

I said to Evan, "Are you coming into the bookstore?"

"Since this seems to be the closest we'll ever get to the shooting I want to watch."

I was interviewed by Louise Nussbaum, society editor of the Las Cruces *Sun-News*.

While I was talking to Louise, Cooper crossed the square and spent a long time examining a Model T parked in front of the bookstore. He would look at a feature of the car, then into the bookstore. I pretended to be elaborately unaware of him.

Evan later said that Cooper stayed by the Model T a little while longer, then walked slowly across the square, looking back once or twice.

After that, he mounted a chestnut horse that was tethered on the other side and with a final glance in the direction of the bookstore rode off into the sunset.

It was then a little after ten in the morning.

After the interview I joined Evan.

John White, loaded down with flashbulbs and cameras, came up to where we were standing.

"Betty says there were a lot of hysterical phone calls yesterday," said John, "and I hear the people in New York don't want a line changed, not a word. Is that because of art?"

"Of course," I said.

After a while Evan and I started away, Evan a little ahead.

I am very nearsighted and, in addition, on my second pair of bifocals, and when I saw a small dark man come toward me with his hand outstretched, I placed a smile on my face and put out my hand.

"Hello, Merle, how are you?"

Then I recognized Stuart Rosenberg and lowered my hand.

"No, I don't think I want to shake your hand, Stuart," I said.

Rosenberg's hand remained suspended for a while, and then he said, "All right, Merle, I guess that's up to you."

The filming was completed outside the library building in Las Cruces on Saturday morning.

The cameras were rolling, and Miss Stanwyck was saying something to Mr. Duff.

I edged my way to the front of the awed crowd.

Now Duff was speaking to Stanwyck.

One of my spirited quatrains? I couldn't be sure.

I looked down at a five-year-old Spanish-American girl leaning against my thigh.

"Now I understand how Beethoven felt when he was conducting his Ninth," I said.

"No understand," she said, edging away.

That afternoon the asthmatic plane circled Las Cruces once or twice, then headed west.

The autograph party took place as scheduled, in what had been Howard Duff's room.

Betty said, "I asked Jackie if he'd mind autographing a few books, and he said, 'For old Merle, why, of course I will. . . . And you tell the others I said they should, too.' "

Cooper, Miss Stanwyck, and Miss Luna had signed maybe a dozen books. During the course of the afternoon I must have autographed at least fifty more. Betty sold perhaps half a dozen.

"We just didn't have time to get enough publicity," she said. "I draw all the way from Santa Fe on these parties, but there just wasn't enough publicity."

"Otherwise business must have been wonderful this week," I said.

"It was a terrible week, all the streets cut off. People who come to see something like *that* don't buy books."

Later Evan and I wandered through the once more barren and deserted square. The art exhibit was gone; the statue of Benjamin Calhoun was gone, and so were the leaves the property men had taped on the elm trees. A gusty wind once more tossed tumbleweed through the rutted streets.

"What do you think will happen next?" I said into the wind.

"They will finish the film," Evan said. "It will be sold; the *Calhoun* series will be the biggest thing since *The Beverly Hillbillies;* it will run longer and make more money than *I Love Lucy,* and next year when to tumultuous applause you are called forward to receive your Emmy you will suddenly find yourself all choked up the way all those writers always are, and you will say, 'I don't really deserve . . . If it weren't for the producer—the director—and the star . . .' "

Evan and I spent the rest of November and December, assembling what turned out to be more than 350 pages of notes on the saga of Dick Daring.

On December 28, I had lunch with Bob Aurthur and he said, "Jim Aubrey has seen a rough cut of *Calhoun*, and he loves it; it looks as if it's locked. So multiply your royalty by at least twenty-five, which means you'll be richer by $25,000 this year alone, and you won't have to . . ."

"It isn't quite $25,000," I whispered, "and don't let this get around, but when Harold Franklin got back from Greece and the contract was finally drawn, well, the fact is, everybody at C.B.S. and U.A. and William Morris, which are all big corporations, felt that since I didn't invent the idea of the county agent series and didn't come to *them* with it, but they, that is, *you*, came to *me* with the idea, and since the other expenses were already so high, and since in a project like this we all have to put our shoulders to the wheel and our noses to the grindstone, well, my royalty is only going to be $500 a week, but that's all right with me."

"I do not believe it," said Bob. "It's absolutely incredible. . . . Look, *my* royalty as creative consultant is $750, and *you're* the writer. . . . You are the most born . . ."

I said, "When you're finished talking about money, let's talk about art. Once Aubrey saw the script on film, he fell in love with it, right?"

"That's what I'm told," said Bob. "They've penciled it in Monday nights, ten to eleven, which is prime time. . . ."

"When will I be allowed to see it?"

"Never. You and I will never be allowed to see it. When it goes on the air, they will come and lock us up and put us in a room with no television set. And they will continue to do this even during the reruns. Mark my words, we will never be allowed to see *Calhoun*.

"By the way, there's a new scene. When Aubrey saw the first rough cut, he looked at Barbara Luna, who looks very Spanish-American, and said, 'Is *that* the love interest?' "

"Maybe Miss Luna made him feel guilty."

". . . And so Cooper had somebody write a whole new— no, Merle, I don't know who—a whole new scene involving that girl at the art colony that you wrote about in the notes."

"Daphne Rinehart."

"There's an American name for you; yes, Daphne Rinehart, and in that part they cast a girl who's physically the exact opposite of Barbara Luna. Diana Hyland, who's fair, blue-eyed, and blonde. I'm told she charged them $3500 for one day's work."

"That's *American* all right."

"Shooting that one scene must have cost at least $15,000, maybe $20,000," said Bob, "probably more. . . . No, I *don't* know who wrote it, Merle. . . . It was sort of a *Hennesey*-type scene. Takes place the night they burn the Laird orange grove. Cooper goes to Hyland and tells her he's got to break their date, and she tells him that she had no intention of keeping the date anyway, something like that. Then he proceeds to tell her the entire plot up to that point."

"It sounds like a dandy addition to the script, and I'm sure that since I had nothing to do with it, everything went off without a hitch."

"Not exactly," said Bob. "Cooper had the scene written by one of his writers, but when he brought it to New York, Stuart Rosenberg read it and didn't like it, and then Cooper decided he didn't like it, and there was quite a bit of screaming and carrying on, but finally they shot it."

I said, "Then Aubrey saw it and loved it, and some Monday night next fall, between ten and eleven, all of America except for you and me will be privileged . . ."

"Not exactly," said Bob. "When Aubrey saw the scene *he'd* suggested, *he* didn't like it, and so they threw it out, and now once again, Barbara Luna . . . Anyway, start multiplying your $500 royalty by at least twenty-five. . . ."

A few days later Dorso called me in Brewster; he, too, told me about the new scene and the fact that it had been thrown out.

"Isn't this all getting rather expensive?" I asked.

"Look, Merle, as I may have told you, when a country goes to war it doesn't start thinking about balancing its budget, it thinks only about winning. . . . An additional $50,000, an additional $100,000 even. After this much money has been spent, you just can't *stop* spending."

"Who's the war against?"

"It isn't *against* anybody. Now we are fighting to win, to sell the pilot, and we *will* sell it."

"Are you sure?"

"I'm as sure as I've ever been sure of anything in my life. . . . By the way, I understand you're thinking of writing a book about all this. . . ."

I said that I was.

"There's just one thing," said Dorso. "Don't paint me lily-white because there was a time when I wasn't acting in your best interests, a time when I wasn't your friend."

"When was that?"

"That afternoon when you and Bob were talking about the review of your book, and I said I already knew you were a great writer, well, at that point I had already agreed with Cooper that he could hire another writer to put some *Hennesey*-type jokes in your script, and I wanted you to know that so that when you write your book . . ."

"You needn't worry, Dick. By the way, am I ever going to be allowed to see the film?"

"Of course. Any time it's convenient. We expect an answer print in New York sometime next week, and when it gets here, of course you can see it. I *want* you to see it."

"Is it any good?"

"It's very good. The script you went to Las Cruces with was seventy-five to eighty per cent right. It should have been polished, all the things you do on the set when you see that a scene is awkward or a line of dialogue doesn't work. But I think the pilot is very good. I think it could have been the best pilot to date if it had been done with any enthusiasm. . . . You *must* see it."

During most of January the telephone in the glass house never stopped ringing.

Bob had talked to David Susskind, who had said that he heard that *Calhoun* was locked; Dick Dorso had been told by Mike Dann that they were starting to ink it in, Monday nights, ten to eleven. C.B.S. was testing *Calhoun,* and a cross section of bootblacks had said that they liked Calhoun because he stood up for the little fellow, and a sampling of cub scouts thought Barbara Stanwyck was . . . And Norman Glenn heard that . . . And Jerry the Barber had told . . . And Nat Lefkowitz had seen the film and thought that not since Lillian Gish in *Orphans of the Storm* had there been a performance to equal that of . . . And at lunch at the Oak Room at the Plaza Harold Franklin was told by Harold Stern that the enthusiasm at the network was so high that . . .

On January 31, 1964, I called Bob Aurthur and screamed, "What happened?"

"What do you mean, what happened?"

"Harold Franklin just called and said that the C.B.S. schedule for next fall has been released, and Monday nights between ten and eleven there's something called *The Lawmaker,* and there isn't a mention of *Calhoun* anywhere. . . ."

"Merle," said Bob, "the C.B.S. schedule is in a wild state of flux. Nobody knows what's going to happen or what they're going to do. This year the networks were all of a sudden in a mad race to announce their schedules. So all three of them came out at the exact same time. You can trace it back to a statement that Aubrey made last year. He said he was going to have the entire programming for C.B.S. locked in by January 15. He delayed it one week, and then another, and finally, with the quote, intention to lock in, unquote, this wild confusion came about and everybody panicked. The other networks felt that they *had* to announce their schedules at the same time."

"Sounds perfectly normal to me."

"No, this is a different kind of insanity. One of the things I know will happen is a real reshuffling. I know for one thing that *Tarzan* is already out of the schedule. If it was going to be set in Africa, the network would have had a large racial protest on its hands. . . . And, anyway, there's panic on the street [Madison Avenue]. Benton and Bowles and Young and Rubicam, they're all saying, 'We don't want to sponsor the programs you're offering.' I'm sure there'll be considerable reshuffling. But C.B.S. is delighted with *Calhoun.* Everybody says that Aubrey loves it. One of the reasons that it's not on the schedule is that they haven't seen a finished print yet. It'll be in New York Tuesday or Wednesday. . . ."

"Half a million homes," Bob said at lunch on February 3, "half a million homes."

"What's that supposed to mean?"

"They're making a lot of tests with *Calhoun* at C.B.S., chimney sweeps, Indian scouts, blacksmiths. They want to find out what John Q. Publick thinks of it, and the other day one of the testers said to Dorso, 'You could have picked up half a million homes.' "

"That's a lot of homes. How?"

"The tester—I assume he's at least a Ph.D.—said, 'You

could have picked up half a million homes if the county agent had just had a dog.' "

After a moment of enraged silence I said, "It was *you* who said there were too many Lairds, and as a result of *your* suggestion I was forced to kill off the Laird dog, Jebediah, and now it turns out . . ."

That afternoon before entering the airless projection room at United Artists Television to see *Calhoun,* I had a talk with Dick Dorso.

Toward the end of it I said to him, laughing, "I understand they think Calhoun should have had a dog."

"That's right," said Dorso, "and when I heard it I could have killed myself. Why hadn't *I* thought of that?"

I looked at him and saw that he was serious.

"I've been sitting in on a lot of these tests," said Dorso, "and for the first time I'm really beginning to understand what a mass audience means. . . . You write a book and it has a sale of thirty thousand, and it's a best seller, and a movie, even a highly successful . . ."

"God bless you, Dick," I said.

Most of the actors in the pilot of *Calhoun* were excellent. Cooper was likable and convincing; so, although she looked a little glamorous for a home agent, was Barbara Stanwyck; so, despite the hair-do and the dress, was Barbara Luna, who was also very beautiful.

There was not, however, any indication of who a county agent was or what he did, and Miss Stanwyck's sole function as a home agent was to hand Calhoun a few tools in the opening scene.

Nothing in the film could possibly have made anyone feel guilty—unless, by chance, he had had something to do with what was on the screen.

There was also nothing to move, enlighten, arouse, enlarge, or entertain anyone.

I later learned that the *Calhoun* project had already been dead and buried on February 3; it had drawn its last breath on Monday, January 27.

All three of the pilots that U.A. had made for C.B.S. had died that day. (The other two were *Mark Dolphin* and *Kibbee Hates Fitch.*)

The combined cost of the three films had been close to $1,250,000, but that's not real money. Under an agreeable arrangement with the Director of Internal Revenue most of it is written off under the general heading of *corporate development.*

Of the three projects *Calhoun* came closest to being scheduled, but the hysteria and hostility aroused by the creation and filming of the single fifty-two-minute pilot made it a dubious long-term undertaking.

Later, James T. Aubrey, Jr.—"I see a man in a dusty pickup in the Southwest"—said that he had never liked the county agent idea much anyway.

"As to the other persons who have made any considerable figure in this history, as some may desire to know a little more concerning them, we will proceed in as few words as possible to satisfy their curiosity."

John White is still agricultural editor and head of the Department of Information at New Mexico State University; Leonard Appleton is still county agent of Luna County; Don Chappell is still county agent of Doña Ana County. Grover Xavier McSherry is still specializing in cotton, cattle, and children; Arthur Alvillar, Sr., still makes a good living for his family at the ranch near Las Cruces, and next year Raul Alvillar has every intention of winning first prize in the National Tractor Driving Contest at the 4-H Club Congress.

Dick Dorso has resigned as Executive Vice-President in Charge of Programming for United Artists Television. He moved from the sixteenth floor to the eighteenth floor at 555 Madison Avenue to become vice-president and partner in Ashley-Steiner, which, translated, means he is once more an agent. Among his clients is Talent Associates-Paramount Ltd., meaning David Susskind and Daniel Melnick.

Norman Glenn, who had been Vice-President in Charge of Programming, moved one office to the left to replace Dorso as E.V.P. in C. of P. for U.A. TV.

Howard Gottfried moved to Beverly Hills and was appointed Administrative V.P. in C. of P. for U.A. TV.

Hunt Stromberg, Jr. has become West Coast Vice-President in Charge of Programming at C.B.S.

Michael Dann remains as East Coast, etc., and still makes a great many public pronouncements.

Larry White remains as Director of Program Development at C.B.S.

Harold Franklin, in addition to continuing his good services at William Morris, also sits in on the weekly program meeting at U.A. TV in New York.

Stuart Rosenberg was nominated for an Emmy for his blacklist show on *The Defenders* and, according to *Variety,* may join Screen Gems as a producer-director if contract negotiations can be finalized with the Senior Vice-President of Screen Gems.

Jackie Cooper, the onetime child star, has become Senior Vice-President in Charge of Production and West Coast Operations for Screen Gems [S.V.P. in C. of P. and W.C.O. for S.G.], the television producing company owned by Columbia Pictures.

Robert Alan Aurthur is now writing a screen play at Talent Associates-Paramount Ltd.

James T. Aubrey, Jr., continues as President of C.B.S. Television. In late January he exercised his stock option and now owns 27,000 shares of C.B.S., which has a market value of $1,250,000.

His network is expected to make a profit of about $100,-000,000 next year.

As for our hero, he never did find out who wrote the script that was never filmed.

This volume was completed on April 15, 1964.

I took a long rest and the next day went back to work on the novel that had been interrupted the previous June.

That afternoon the telephone rang.

Evan was in the gracious living area of the glass house, making some last-minute changes in *Only You, Dick Daring!*

I had asked not to be disturbed under any circumstances.

"Hello, Harold," I heard Evan say. "No, he's not. He's out walking in the woods . . ."

I picked up the phone in the study. "Hi, Harold."

"Merle, I know how you feel about a television series, but when I heard about this one, I said, 'There's only one writer in America . . . and this is going to be a multimillion-dollar . . . Are you still there?'"

"Still here."

"At *least* $1,000,000. World War II is very big right now. . . . There are four G.I.s, maybe in the Pacific, maybe the E.T.O. . . . Maybe—well, *where* they are, that would be strictly up to you as the writer, but you write so well about the war, and . . ."

"No, Harold."